THE LEADERSHIP IMPERATIVE

The
LEADERSHIP

What Innovative Business Leaders Are Doing Today

Robert Heller

IMPERATIVE

to Create the Successful Companies of Tomorrow

TRUMAN TALLEY BOOKS/DUTTON/NEW YORK

TRUMAN TALLEY BOOKS/DUTTON

Published by the Penguin Group
Penguin Books USA Inc., 375 Hudson Street, New York, New York 10014, U.S.A.
Penguin Books Ltd, 27 Wrights Lane, London W8 5TZ, England
Penguin Books Australia Ltd, Ringwood, Victoria, Australia
Penguin Books Canada Ltd, 10 Alcorn Avenue, Toronto, Ontario, Canada M4V 3B2
Penguin Books (N.Z.) Ltd, 182–190 Wairau Road, Auckland 10, New Zealand

Penguin Books Ltd, Registered Offices:
Harmondsworth, Middlesex, England

First published by Truman Talley Books/Dutton,
an imprint of Dutton Signet,
a division of Penguin Books USA Inc.

First Printing, March, 1995
10 9 8 7 6 5 4 3 2 1

LIBRARY OF CONGRESS CATALOGING-IN-PUBLICATION DATA:

Heller, Robert.
    The leadership imperative : what innovative business leaders are doing today to create the successful companies of tomorrow / Robert Heller.
        p.   cm.
    Includes bibliographical references and index.
    ISBN 0-525-93900-8
    1. Industrial management—United States. 2. Organizational change—United States—Management. 3. Corporate reorganizations—United States. 4. Total quality management—United States. 5. Leadership. I. Title.
    HD70.U5H433   1995
    658.4—dc20   94-34861
                                                                                    CIP

Printed in the United States of America
Set in Times New Roman and Helvetica Condensed

Designed by Steven N. Stathakis

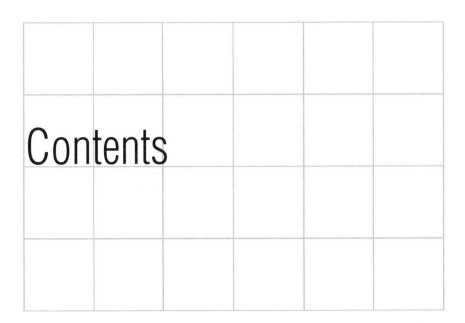

Contents

1738

93182

THREE: THE ROAD TO REINVENTION: HOW TO CHANGE CULTURES

FOUR: BREAKING AWAY—AND OUT: HOW TO DIVIDE AND CONQUER

SIX: THE SHARPER EDGE: HOW TO STAY COMPETITIVE

SEVEN: THE SHOCK OF THE NEW: HOW TO RENEW CONSTANTLY

EIGHT: DECLARATIONS OF INDEPENDENCE: HOW TO FIX YOUR FATE

NINE: TRIUMPHS OF TEAMWORK: HOW TO MOBILIZE GROUPS

TEN: THE TRUE QUALITY: HOW TO MANAGE MUCH BETTER

Introduction: Reinventing Management

New managers and new methods are reforming and transforming American business to win the new century's management wars. They will win, not only by virtue of their applied strengths, but by default. Those managements that stick with the ways in which they have always managed will be history.

This isn't Cassandra-like soothsaying. It's a description of what has actually happened to companies which were once wonders of the business world. What do Caterpillar Tractor, Digital Equipment, Fluor, and IBM have in common? All suffered calamitous setbacks in the eighties, and all were among the heroes of the stupendously best-selling *In Search of Excellence.*

Very few of the stars praised by Tom Peters and Robert H. Waterman, Jr., shine in today's business firmament. Today new names are leading companies in new ways, obeying the imperatives of an environment that has changed dramatically since the early eighties. Compaq and Eckhard Pfeiffer, Intel and Andy Grove, and Bill Gates and Microsoft have risen on the tide, not only of new technology, but of the new management ideas. The two streams flow together. Fast change can't be managed by old methods.

In old-line companies, too, the leadership imperative has been recognized. Jack Welch at General Electric, Roberto C. Goizueta at Coca-Cola, Robert Allen at AT&T, Charles F. Knight at Emerson Electric, and Robert Eaton at Chrysler are among those CEOs who have recognized what Peter Drucker has named "the new realities." These leaders are determined not to follow in the footsteps of those who took great companies and led them into the ranks of the once-great.

In his new book, *The Frontiers of Excellence,* Bob Waterman tackles the obvious question raised by the high dropout rate of the original *Excellence* heroes. He calls the question "irritating and tough." It lies at the heart of the leadership imperative: "Why do some great companies, like IBM, stumble badly while others, like Procter & Gamble, remain vibrant?" Alas, that very sentence lands him in the same difficulty.

In his account, P&G is presented as the heroic pioneer of an approach which truly is central to the new management: "the self-managed team concept." P&G's strategic success, Waterman argues, has much to do with its "relentless drive to make self-direction a management reality." On this reading, P&G's strength springs not merely from its fabled marketing, but from "the raw ability to out-innovate the competition," both with new products and through "cost advantages" won by "the enormous productivity gains of self-directed work." Its system "gives people everywhere the control they need to feel and be their personal best."

What a contrast with the following firm: "the ultimate hierarchy—to be unkind, an inwardly pointed pyramid of anal-retentive order-takers loathed by competitors and retail customers alike." But the two companies are identical. The latter (and later) description of P&G appeared in *Fortune* in March 1994. In this portrait, P&G's success had rested on over-charging for its products: high internal costs and falling market shares, said *Fortune,* had now forced P&G to redesign "the way it develops, manufactures, distributes, prices, markets and sells products," turning the company "upside down."

You could claim that this "teardown and rebuild of nearly every activity that contributes to high costs" is evidence of vibrancy. But it hardly supports Waterman's encomium. His own explanation for the Feet of Clay Syndrome (which plagues all authors who select corporate paragons) is that great companies "lose their edge": the moral being, "Learn from the best while they're good and move on." The truth, though, is that IBM was already deeply flawed when *In Search of Excellence* was written: and P&G's root-and-branch problems, too, didn't spring up overnight.

In reality, the camera can lie. Outsiders focus on what they want to see and miss the larger picture. But it's equally easy for insiders to ignore the obvious. Many managers have failed to see that largeness itself, the last bastion of the big, has ceased to offer either competitive advantage or even simple protection. The competitive disadvantage of large scale has been obvious for decades. For most of that time, mass slowed down the giants, and gave openings to the new and nimble. Yet the leviathans remained rich and powerful.

Today, static managements are obsolescent, weak, and failing. In the next few years, they will be obsolete—and failed. Renewal and nimbleness have become paramount necessities for the large and established, just as staying new and agile is imperative for the younger business. But managers are in luck. New technologies commonly arrive, like components in modern manufacturing, just in time. And the new technologies of management are saving the day.

Without the telephone, organizations couldn't have spread to the multiple locations that markets were demanding. The computer came just in time to stop paperwork from clogging up the world. The jet arrived when otherwise the international spread of commerce would have stumbled to a halt. Other powerful examples abound. Now, new tactical and strategic technologies are available, just in time to give management the new essentials: information, speed, control, and excellent outcomes.

Some of this technology is truly technical, including that of the seismic revolution in information and communications. But management technology is dominated by the use of the human computer: by the application of thought—not solo, but teamed with other brains. The hard technology of product and process provides the tools, which far surpass those available to previous generations. The soft technology of managing people—including, and especially, your-self—applies the hard tools in order to make miracles.

I have identified ten key strategies around which the new revo-lutionaries are reinventing management. The old reactionaries are still in the majority, and it is a large majority at that. Their numerical supremacy won't last long, however, because their ascendancy in all other respects is rapidly draining away. The new understanding is proving decisive in these ten intertwined arenas:

- How to devolve authority—without losing control
- How to achieve radical change—in the entire corporate system, not just in its parts
- How to change cultures—in timely and lasting fashion
- How to divide and conquer—winning the rewards of smallness while staying or growing large
- How to turn "organization" from incubus to stimulus—by new approaches to central direction
- How to stay competitive—in a world where the old, sure ways of winning no longer work
- How to achieve constant renewal—stopping success from sowing the seeds of decay
- How to mobilize people's own motivation—the only kind there truly is
- How to make teamworking work—the new skill to which there's no alternative
- How to achieve total quality—by managing much better

On each of these ten critical leadership strategies, examples of success abound to enlighten and encourage. Many are in these pages, along with the opposite: examples of CEOs who have climbed the highest summits without showing the courage or common sense to alter profoundly—or even dismantle—the apparatus which estab-lishes their own importance (and self-importance). Corporate life cre-ates cozy chairs in which cosseted CEOs try to manage the unmanageable by remote control. It can't work: which makes it far from surprising (to everybody but the CEOs) if their companies don't work either.

All those inoperative corporations, though, had been created or recreated by highly successful businessmen. These corporate fathers had managed their offspring over decades, through all the vicissitudes of growth, transition, and challenge. The business genes of these entrepreneurs are still vigorous, widespread, and effective. To reinvent management, those genes need only be allied with the new knowledge about what makes people and organizations work effectively and enjoyably.

Both knowledge and the entrepreneurial urge must also be adapted to changed and changing social, political, economic, and technological climates. With all that done—and it's a great test—management can be reinvented to build success that not only matches but outdoes the past. This book tells how reinvented managers at all levels, in companies of all sizes, have become true leaders. By finding the right answers to those ten searching issues, they and their organizations are throwing off the past to build better futures.

Prologue: The Fall of a Colossus

"The fact that we're losing market share makes me goddam mad. . . . Everyone is too comfortable when the business is in crisis. . . ." Within hours, the anger of John F. Akers, the fifth chairman of International Business Machines since the first Thomas Watson, had sped around the company—and then around the world. Akers meant his broadside to be private, confined to a few senior managers. Like many of this chief executive's good intentions, it miscarried.

The incident is an epitome of the fate of IBM, the quintessential American corporation of the mid–twentieth century. The distance the company has fallen, dropping like Icarus out of the sky, can be measured by what Frank Cary, who tapped Akers for advancement, had said a few years before. Asked about the chances of IBM sustaining its success, Cary had rated them as "100 percent." In 1991, the year of Akers's attack, the company lost $7.75 million a day; in 1992, $13.4 million; in 1993, $22.1 million.

Even the way in which Akers's words burst upon the world explains much of what happened in the interval between Cary's 100 percent and those enormous losses. A well-meaning executive, impressed by the boss, had wanted his own staff to share the message. He distributed the memo via electronic mail, forgetting that the system is worldwide and instantaneous.

The metaphor is unmistakable. A world market that the great corporations once tied up like a Christmas parcel has burst wide open. The wonder of electronic mail is only one part of a technology that has burgeoned, and is burgeoning, at breakneck pace. The speed of change has outstripped the capacity of oldstyle corporate leadership to respond and its ability to control. Inadvertently, John R. Opel, speaking as outgoing chairman, put his finger on the problem: "In IBM the transition from one CEO to another recalls the adage that the more things change, the more they are the same." But in the late twentieth century, things are changing more than ever, and they will never be the same again. Insistence on what Opel praised, a "common culture, rooted in . . . unchanging beliefs," is fine for unchanging times: but not for an age of turbulence.

Akers, the new man pitched—all unsuspecting—into the maelstrom, had enjoyed a typical fast-track career, American-style: Akers had spent "five years running two different groups, two years now as president, and I have been involved in all parts of the business." Typically enough, nothing in this all-parts experience had tested the ability to command a major corporation, not for a short spell, but a whole decade. The career pattern epitomized the centripetal nature of management in the traditional American corporation. As all power gravitates inwards, its exercise falls to those most adept within the hub.

The economic pressures, however, have crowded in on America's corporate leaders from the outside, with many harsh financial results. But hard economic facts are only the skeleton of the crisis of a corporation. The flesh is human. Great organizations develop rich and deep cultures, lifestyles which are sanctified by success and consecrated by conceit. The attack by Akers on his own company—the shot heard round the world—was aimed at those human targets: and inevitably, it was aimed at himself.

The smoke signals rose almost from the moment this square-jawed IBMer took charge. Down in the ranks, and in the marketplace, insiders and customers had been telling tales of woe for years before the outburst. The tirade to his managers indicated that Akers was in a mood to accept the criticisms. But could he cure the disease? Recent history at many large companies says otherwise. The chief comes out with ringing declarations of intent; reorganizations and redundancies are eventually ordained; inadequate outcomes appear—all a couple of years too late.

IBM was not among the giants (ten picked out of dozens) praised by Harvard professor John P. Kotter for achieving effective long-term cultural change in the eighties. General Electric, led by Jack Welch, was among the praised. But GE, unlike IBM or General Motors, is a conglomerate without a core; so Welch could (and did) move in and out of businesses at will. IBM could (and did, with typewriters) sell the odd peripheral activity: but the bulk of the assets can't be shed.

The assets are inalienable, and not amenable to easy treatment, either. As Keith H. Hammonds remarked in *Business Week,* "The restructuring, the cost-cutting, the new message can be effective for starters, but it takes follow-through to make sure they're more than skin-deep." So what was the answer for IBM? The magazine turned to six sources of wisdom and got some very strange replies. A former non-executive director thought unhelpfully that, since the company had the "horsepower" and the "science," you only needed "to get right in there and rattle the cage."

The boss of Nucor, a relatively small steelmaker much loved by devotees of open management, wanted Akers to "nag" managers into cost-effectiveness by one-on-one or small meetings: great for lesser Nucor, but a non-starter for giant IBM. Irving S. Shapiro thought that IBM should emulate Du Pont, the company he once chaired, which "took a generation" after its nylon triumph to learn the competitive frame of mind. But IBM doesn't have a generation, or even a decade, to spare when its industry is in a state of chronic technological convulsion.

Furthermore, Du Pont isn't much of a role model. Once preeminent, the Wilmington company is now just one of the chemical boys, beset with giant problems of its own. In March 1992, the *Wall Street Journal* noted that to crack these problems, Du Pont needed "to restructure a bloated bureaucracy." The group's chief executive since 1989 seemed to echo those sentiments: "Du Pont needs a top-to-bottom overhaul," said Edgar S. Woolard, Jr.

IBM's malaise of the nineties was thus not peculiar to itself, but symptomatic of an illness affecting many giant corporations in the United States—and in the West as a whole. The distinction, of course, is increasingly meaningless, as business goes global: none more so than IBM's. From Duluth to Frankfurt, Japan to the old Soviet Empire, Australia to Norway, IBM is still synonymous with "electronic data processing"—the arid name for the scintillating computer technology that's changing the world.

Unlike other industries, the information technology czars can expect everlasting growth in their business. True, the computer market has become cyclical. Today the "dream machine" is universal, and saturation points approach or have even appeared. But new markets have constantly been born as others have aged. The trouble for the corporate establishment is that new births challenge old superiorities, and that the managers inside are prone either to miss the changes in the environment, or to react ineptly.

But how could that happen to IBM? For long it was the Most Admired Corporation in America—selected year after year by its peers as leader for quality of management and for almost every other attribute of excellence. Either the peers were fooled, or this truly was the best-managed corporation. If the latter, IBM's downfall looks discouraging for American capitalism. If the best-run business, in the most modern industry, a competitor feared even by the Japanese, can fail, what of lesser champions? What of General Motors?

What, indeed. For 1991, GM reported losses twice as great as IBM's. The large American corporation as a species was patently, to use Akers's words, "in crisis" as the last decade of the twentieth century began. Eyes began to open, even in boardrooms where blindness had been rampant. The GM board had been unaccountably tolerant in the long, disastrous reign of Roger B. Smith; now it turned on Robert C. Stempel, its own poor choice as successor, and forced his resignation.

Other boards, for the first time in decades, began to question, not only the competence of CEOs, but their stupendous monetary rewards (heaped on them, of course, by those same boards). Excessive compensation, unmatched by any unusual or even everyday economic contribution from many CEOs, has played some part in the decline of big-time corporate performance. Like the bacterial infection which complicates a viral attack, the pay scandal has seriously undermined the patient's condition. But over-payment is a pernicious symptom rather than an underlying cause.

The disease can swamp even the strongest natural defenses. On a day in February 1992, the old IBM duly died. The world's most prodigious money machine reported an enormous, $2.8 billion loss. The brilliantly commercial, supposedly benevolent corporation whose jobs-for-life employees occupied an internal world controlled as effectively as its external markets—that's gone. That was the end of an old story. A new one can still be written.

Another IBM, with its splendid people, unbeatable customer base, myriad patents, brilliant laboratories, fine factories, great product lines, superb branding, and massive sales firepower, still exists. To exploit such assets with renewed success, however, a new corporate culture is needed—not just for IBM, but for American big businesses as a whole. They have a mountain to climb.

The best performers in U.S. capitalism have faced the least foreign competition in general, and the least Japanese competition in particular: food and drink companies, for instance, service businesses, and drug manufacturers. Many of their markets are highly competitive at home. But the competitors all play by the same rules, and their sheer size, up to now, has been protective.

In other industries, other major corporations have been tested to near-destruction. Peter Drucker saw their decline coming from a long way off. More recently, in early 1992, he said that "The *Fortune* 500 is over"—meaning, in the magazine's words, that big businesses must "slowly and painfully transform themselves into a new kind of creature." How slow? How painful? How new? The answers look important even in the context of a $5 trillion economy. The *Fortune* 500 account for $2.2 trillion of sales (more than the gross domestic product of a united Germany) and employ twelve million people.

That, however, is four million fewer people than at the start of the eighties, and is one stark measure of absolute decline. Millions of the *Fortune* 500's employees and billions of dollars of their sales lie outside the United States, which makes the numbers worse, not better, since the bulk of the cutbacks have been at home. "With curious serendipity," wrote *Fortune,* "the start of the decade coincided with a new set of imperatives for American industry—to review the mistakes and excesses of the past, or to make fundamental changes and to gird for the fiercely competitive times ahead."

It could be argued that the cutbacks of the opening nineties, by lowering the cost base, set the stage for the rousing recovery in profits as economic recovery came. But that may be illusory, like the rebound in British corporate profits that was prematurely celebrated after the Thatcher recession of 1979–80. Later events proved that getting "leaner and fitter" à la Thatcher by closing plants and slashing workforces (essentially the *Fortune* 500's recipe) was not the fundamental change required to turn past failures into future successes.

That "new set of imperatives" for American industry, after all, was obvious throughout the eighties. If essential action was dodged earlier, what are the chances of basically the same managements (those guilty of "the mistakes and excesses" of the past) leading a true corporate revolution? The conventional view is that the right road runs towards breaking up the giants into smaller, focused units—the new method of combining the power of sheer size with the swiftness of the relatively small.

Once IBM briefly enjoyed such a business, when the PC people, tucked away in Boca Raton, Florida, presented their sponsor with a world-beating product in little more than a year. Eventually, the corpocracy closed in, and the usual tale of delays and deadbeat moves began. The corpocrats never took the true lesson of Boca Raton to heart, even though the moral—independence generating incandescent triumph—was trumpeted forth at the time by the group's publicity people.

Had the semidetached model been followed by creating other quasi-independent satellites, Akers might never have needed to curse his managers. The PC saga really did point the way to cure corporate elephantiasis. In theory, the remedy lies in internal breakup, breakout, or buyout. You reduce headquarters to a supervisory and long-term strategic role: you give full power to autonomous business teams which are free to create their own cultures and battle plans. Under this disposition, the head office doesn't preside over multilayered cakes. On the contrary, it might very well pressure the business bosses into laying off the layers themselves.

Akers was heading towards just such a reconstruction when he was abruptly replaced. His successor, Louis V. Gerstner, Jr., came from travel and financial services (American Express) via tobacco and food (RJR Nabisco). On the face of it, he was a triple threat to the past: an outsider to the company, an outsider to the industry, an importer of other outsiders. Nobody can rightly complain if IBM's herds of sacred cows are led to slaughter: but the first victims at IBM included radical plans to break up the business.

"Of the thousands of customers I've talked to," Gerstner told *Fortune,* "not one has argued that they want IBM to be broken up into little pieces." But why would the customers care, one way or the other? However, the issue goes beyond whether this particular turn-around man, in this particular corporation, was right to reject this particular plan (much favored by the conventional wisdom). It is whether, with any strategy, the giants can achieve transformation under men like those who presided while the great corporations were humbled.

New men and women, however, can build a new corporate society. What died on that February day in 1992 was an old society, which, while it worked, was one of the most successful in history. What will replace it? The following chapters track the answer to a momentous question.

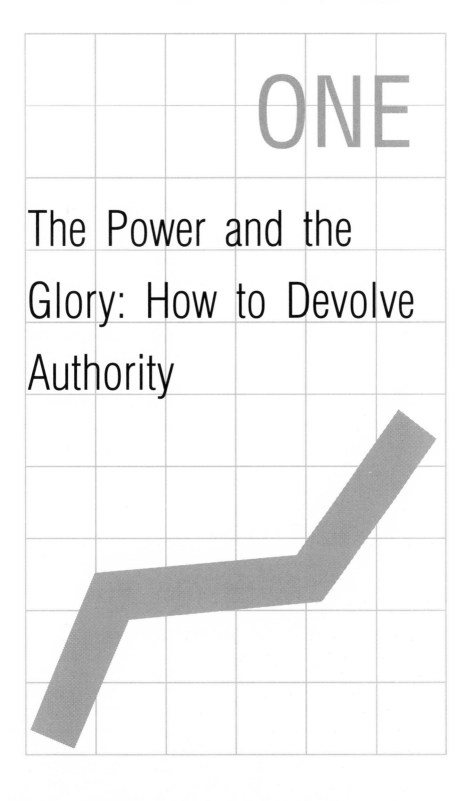

ONE

The Power and the Glory: How to Devolve Authority

The Abdication of Lee Iacocca

1

The Man on Horseback rides across history. In nation-states, great corporations, and small businesses alike, the people respond to the lure of leadership. Superb leaders resolve many difficulties for their subjects. They make all the decisions and take all responsibility. They make all the rules. They assume all ultimate power. And in the process, they become indispensable—because they have created a potential vacuum that, by definition, nobody else can fill.

The auto industry, in its maturity, still reflected the Horseback Syndrome that developed naturally in the pioneering days. Hired hands stepped into the riding boots of self-made giants like Henry Ford. Late-twentieth-century managers like Lee Iacocca learned one-man leadership in a Detroit which had a "dominant design" in everything, from engineering (engine at the front driving the rear wheels) to management (man at the front, driving everybody else).

As the human engine drove, all other cars in the fleet followed the same dominant design. Bigger fleas, the poem goes, have lesser fleas upon their backs to bite 'em. In the traditional hierarchy-bureaucracy (of which Detroit produced some supreme examples), the bigger fleas all bit the littler fleas. Each sought to create a sub-empire in which they, like the supreme ruler, could exploit, and be protected by, the myth of the indispensable man.

The dominant designs, in engineering and management alike, have crumpled before a Japanese team-centered onslaught that respected none of Detroit's rules. The intense pressures have forced irreversible change on all its companies—and the most responsive, strangely, has been Iacocca's Chrysler. Iacocca had more right to reign supreme than anybody; his proud horsemanship, after all, had saved the company from bankruptcy. Yet even before The Man got, somewhat reluctantly, off his horse, his company had gone further to make the boss dispensable than either Ford, his previous employer, or General Motors.

In late 1993, GM actually perpetuated the myth of the indispensable man in an extraordinary battle with another resident of Jurassic Park, Volkswagen. The great mystery about the Volkswagen espionage scandal isn't whether its red-hot production director stole secrets from his previous employer. Much odder was the conviction on the part of both GM and Volkswagen that their futures revolved around the services of José Ignacio López de Arriortúa.

Even if the Basque's record were as marvelous as his publicity suggested, that didn't solve the mystery. This is said to be the age of teamwork and collaboration. Both apply especially in the realm where López made his legendary reputation: purchasing, a key activity in which the Japanese have taught Detroit and the whole West far-reaching lessons.

True, López came complete with a team of dedicated followers: but their "warrior" name and style don't suggest the cooperative, mutually supportive way in which vendor and customer are now supposed to work. In this new world, price is relegated, at most, to equal ranking with quality and reliability. In contrast, the wonder-man's contribution to GM in Europe—which propelled him to new CEO John Smith's side in Detroit—has been admired almost entirely in terms of cutting prices (other people's, that is).

Both in America and at Volkswagen, moreover, López went for samurai-style confrontation rather than the gentler Zen approach to suppliers. Since the key to new-style global purchasing is collaboration, not coercion, what happened in the United States is no surprise.

When López launched full-tilt into his American program, ordering suppliers to cut costs and prices or lose GM's business, the result was resentment, and some costly impacts on GM as its affronted suppliers bit back.

In contrast, Chrysler asked for its suppliers' help in improving productivity and added value—and one result was a flood of suggestions (3,900 in all) that lopped an estimated $156 million off costs. Chrysler began making money again: not much money at first, but much better than a loss. The enlistment of the suppliers wasn't the only new initiative at Chrysler. The company also enlisted

- All five hundred of its top executives, assembled in a rural retreat for a no-holds-barred "Truth Week," which examined every aspect of the business
- A team of twenty-five young recruits, who spent a year at Honda's Ohio plant: after covering customer satisfaction, continual training, and the devolution of decision power to the shop floor, they submitted a report—which was acted on
- The divisional executives, who stripped away layers of bureaucrats and supervisors and stopped fighting turf wars
- The dealers, who gained from a $30 million investment in two-day training workshops
- The designers, who got a $1 billion technical center where synchronous teams work on new cars—with minimal management interference
- *The outgoing chairman, Lee Iacocca, who surrendered his right to review, revise, and reject designs*

That last point is emphasized because it strikes to the core of reinventing management. In his *Iacocca,* the hero has a bitter, eloquent passage describing how Henry Ford II, arriving after everybody else was satisfied with Iacocca's beloved Mustang, arbitrarily (and at great expense) insisted on more rear legroom. Detroit's *droit du seigneur,* whenever exercised (which was nearly always), confirmed where power really lay, and, even worse, directly contradicted the principles of effective, team-based management. The new dispensation at Chrysler is thus doubly significant, symbolically and managerially.

All six points form an object lesson, not just to GM, but all managers who want to manage more effectively. Chrysler's not out of the wood yet, and may never be. "We do run better scared," claims Iacocca. But his abdication—not the reluctant retirement that followed, but his surrender of CEO prerogative—may have been the boldest act of a brave career.

The payoff came for his successors, who at the end of September 1994 were resting on the comfort of a $6.6 billion cash cushion and could afford to double Chrysler's capital spending over 1992, to hit $4 billion, to boost their leading strength in the minivan market, and even, maybe, to placate large shareholder Kirk Kerkorian's large demands, fired off on Novermber 14, for more of the loot.

Managing by real teamwork is no longer an option. It's a necessity, and the team includes everybody, inside and outside the company, who contributes to its success. For real teams, there'll be nothing to fear, especially from competitors who are still stuck in the old ruts.

Sharing the
Responsibilities

2

Why have General Motors and other bureaucratic hierarchies taken so long to carry through crucial management change? The answer's simple. In situations which cry out for new methods of managing, the task of renewal lies in the hands of people who know only the old ways. As President Gorbachev found to his cost in the old USSR, old dogs are unwilling to learn new tricks. This doesn't mean that they can't. It does mean, however, that they won't—unless the whole environment is changed so radically that only new tricks will work.

How the embattled leaders of GM and IBM must envy the freedom of a greenfield company—like, say, the automobile industry's Japanese transplants in the United States and Europe. Nissan Motors in Sunderland can serve as good example. The northeast of England had never housed a car plant before, let alone one whose owners, being Japanese, took a wholly foreign approach to the dominant design of management. "Foreign" here doesn't mean nationality, but method. An all-British top management established a revolutionary environment in which new dogs happily learned new tricks.

David Wickens, one of the British directors, gives an inspirational account of his company's approach. The inspiration lies in the evidence that ordinary people can achieve extraordinary results: if, paradoxically, you treat them like ordinary people. The six essential steps sound very ordinary themselves:

1. Secure top-level commitment to change
2. Involve the appropriate people in diagnosing the needed changes in detail
3. Promote the need for change
4. Plan the change process
5. Develop the people
6. Maintain and reinforce the change process

Have any programs for any management remedy ever been put forward without demanding top-level commitment? Usually the demand is impractical: simply because top managers overwhelm themselves with so much operational detail that there isn't enough time to commit more than words to customer satisfaction, quality, service, world-class performance, or anything else. The way in which these CEOs choose to work forces senior executives into MBLS: management by lip service.

Lip service in turn (as GM found time and again in its efforts to reshape its destiny) guarantees the failure of good intentions. The logical solution is to change the way top managers work. If you delegate operational matters, concentrate on things that only top managers can do, and demonstrate change by example, MBLS can be replaced by effective action. You forget the concept of going "down" the organization. Mentally, there is no down: everybody is equal when it comes to achieving better performance.

By asking people for their opinions, and involving them in reaching solutions, you take a giant step forward in promoting change. But this isn't a matter of gung-ho morale-building: instead, systematic, planned progress is required. Wickens is enthusiastic (and so am I) about finding some quick, visible fixes: that is, obvious large improvements in limited but conspicuous areas—getting rid of reserved parking spaces, or starting a manufacturing cell to service a single important customer.

The crucial point is that corporate change is anything but a quick fix. Time, trouble, and the Bruce Principle (if at first you don't succeed, try, try again) are all required. But people's energy and commitment may wane unless they see that change brings benefits. Their work on getting those benefits will be the foundation of their personal development, which, of course, can never end, any more than change itself. The enemy of change is complacency: managers must be their own most severe critics—forever.

The smugness at GM, though, reached staggering proportions. A senior executive once announced that there was nothing wrong with the company. The only problem lay with the customers: they just didn't appreciate the excellence of its cars. The great value of making customer satisfaction a top corporate priority is that smugness shouldn't survive listening to customers—especially if service is involved: for achieving perfection of service is inherently impossible.

Even achieving acceptable levels of service productivity has defeated most managers. That's a major theme of Peter Drucker's essential book, *The Post-Capitalist Society.* He argues that, with service workers now in the majority, economic progress depends on raising their unacceptably low standards of productivity. That in turn must rest on new concepts and new approaches. In particular, managers of service workers must ask a new question: "What are the expected results from this work?"

To express that thought in other ways, how do you know if a shop assistant, bank clerk, or civil servant has performed well? What are the criteria? Equally important, how do service workers themselves know that they have succeeded? Unless there are targets, there can't be achievement. As Drucker points out, that isn't a problem with his other work group, "knowledge workers," who are self-motivated and whose satisfaction comes from the application of their expertise. But they can't succeed in isolation—inevitably, nearly all of them belong to a team.

It may well not be a fixed team, or even a fixed kind of team. It will soon be a truism to say that management has moved from fixed, vertical hierarchies to fluid, horizontal teams. That isn't because the gurus, with a single voice, advocate the team approach (though that is perfectly true). It's the simple necessity imposed by complex tasks. You can't introduce modern "simultaneous" or "concurrent" product development, for example, unless you have teams cutting across functions. And if you can't achieve simultaneity, you will be beaten out of sight, and in the marketplace, by those who can.

But will the team be playing baseball, soccer, or tennis doubles? As Drucker says, the three variations are very different. Success won't come if you have the wrong team for the situation. The formations are as follows:

1. For repetitive tasks and familiar work, use the *baseball* organization. Every member of management has a fixed role and operates independently. This doesn't mean separately—the pitcher and the catcher cooperate closely, the fielders interact for double plays and other defensive measures, and baserunners and hitters work together on hit-and-run plays. But the team never operates with all members in unison.

2. For known tasks which require greater flexibility and responsiveness (like a new-product team), the *soccer* principle is perfect. Orchestras and surgical teams, too, move to the same tune: everybody has a fixed role, and there is a fixed procedure (the orchestral "score"): but no individual can perform without the others, and success depends on working in unison.

3. For tasks which require constant improvisation, and need to maximize individual contributions, *tennis doubles* have to be played. This is (or should be) top management at work: the partners complement each other's strengths and weaknesses, and work as individuals to achieve a combined effect. This isn't an orchestra, but a jazz combo.

Drucker charts the development of American management, starting from the baseball mode, in which the chief executive works through subordinates with fixed functional or line responsibilities that are seldom exercised in combination. That's the corpocracy in action. Today, though, the better top managements are playing jazz, with a genuine team in which the CEO is primus inter pares—first among equals. The team ranges freely within the agreed overall theme; but it never knows exactly what the final outcome will be.

The jazzmen depend heavily, however, on their colleagues: the soccer or orchestral players. Beneath the corporate summit, all functional management is now shifting into the soccer, orchestral, or operating theater mode, in which specialized skills need to be combined, and sometimes supplemented. That's in order to deal with situations where experience is essential, but where adaptations to circumstances, and even experiments, are constantly required.

This definition obviously applies to developing new products. But it applies with equal force to new processes. There's a crucial difference here between East and West. Another American thinker, Lester B. Thurow, points out that American firms spend two-thirds of their R&D money on product and a third on processes. The Japanese are exactly the other way around. As General Electric discovered when it examined firms whose productivity exceeded its own, process holds the key—the *how* rather than the *what* of what you do.

The key process is that of management itself, which leads back to Wickens and the Nissan factory. The prime job of management at Sunderland is to facilitate. The thirty-six managers who look after four thousand employees don't operate in a multilayered hierarchy but as motivators who don't direct people, but "empower" them. That isn't, incidentally, a term that Drucker much cares for—he says that empowerment is as much a term of power and rank as the old ones it's supposed to replace.

Instead, he prefers to talk about "responsibility" and "contribution." But Nissan really does have the right idea: for instance, job titles aren't hierarchical, but generic: engineer, senior engineer, supervisor, administrative assistant, controller, and so forth. I'd go further, preferring titles that are simply descriptive of the work done: chief marketer, head manufacturer, information manager. That's not a new principle: newspapers and magazines have used it for many decades.

You know exactly what the foreign editor, news editor, or fashion editor do from their titles. Their work, too, is much like playing jazz: the final product is all one thing to the customer, but results from many players making their own individual contributions by using their special skills, with ultimate reference to the leader of the band. That cuts down management numbers, while simultaneously increasing interplay; and that's the path which all organizations will be forced to follow.

That unison paradoxically means, first, more division of labor.

Drucker gives the example of nurses (and you could add policemen) whose productivity improves dramatically when their clerical duties are handed over to clerks. In one British case, too, substantial advances were won when the specialist knowledge of the nurses was exploited to improve the running of the hospital. The nurses knew far more about the faults, and how to correct them, than anybody else: but nobody had ever asked them before.

The obvious and wonderful merits of team management can, however, be over-praised. In real life—and that includes the Japanese factory transplants—team-based organizations run visibly better: but they don't run perfectly, or to everybody's satisfaction. Even knowledge workers, Drucker's new creative class, are capable of laziness and inefficiency. Managers can offload much of their function on others; they can't offload their responsibility for making things happen.

A fundamental issue is the treatment of failure. What is the correct reaction to poor performance? The traditional Western response is to treat incompetence as a disciplinary offense: one infringement gets a warning, repetition brings punishment—perhaps dismissal. If you leave failures in place, runs the argument, you undermine the efforts and motivation of others. Conversely, summary execution encourages by bad example.

On this philosophy, only a blithering idiot would adopt the following policy:

> If we don't understand why a manager consistently underperforms, we promote him. In 74% of cases, performance improves immediately.

Far from being an idiot, the speaker was Minoru Makihara, the chairman of Mitsubishi. Akio Morita, chairman of Sony, went further:

> When I find an employee who turns out to be wrong for a job, I feel it is my fault, because I made the decision to hire him. Generally, I would invest in additional training, education, or a change of duty. As a result, he will usually turn out to be an asset in the long run.

The theme common to both chairmen is that managerial ability is not an innate constant. How well managers perform is determined, to an overwhelming extent, by their environment and the tasks and support which they are given. Every corporate turnaround elicits far superior performance from people who previously contributed to failure. Nearly every management buyout likewise sees discarded managers of discarded businesses bettering not only their own pasts, but often the performance of those who cast them out.

By the same token, every manager has dismissed, or seen dismissed, failed colleagues who have thereafter succeeded brilliantly elsewhere. In my own experience, I was told, on taking over responsibility for a business, that one of my first tasks would be to fire the top man. Two successive superiors had found him incompetent and mutinous. Since the level of quality in his operation had become insupportably bad, removal seemed logical—but I thought it worthwhile to ask the target to explain his underperformance.

Out poured a long and largely justified list of major and minor complaints about how he had been mismanaged by his direct bosses. The wrongs were swiftly and easily righted, morale and quality shot up, and the manager—no longer treated like a dog given a bad name—proceeded to show one rare talent: the ability to pick excellent people. The many such stories prove the wisdom of the Mitsubishi-Sony approach: if you regard underperformance as your fault, not theirs, you are far more likely to turn bad managers into good—and far more likely to create and lead a great team.

Does team-based management unhorse The Man in all organizations at all times? The crude answer is that sometimes only the fire of a charismatic leader can cut through: to shake up the system, seismic shocks are necessary. In turnarounds, this argument is usually decisive. Nobody appoints a committee man to rescue a company in crisis. But turnarounds—and their leaders—are notoriously prone to either lapse or relapse, simply because the saviors have improved the performance without fundamentally improving the system.

Turnarounds have similarities to projects (like the aforementioned new-model programs), since in both cases the leaders start with a relatively free hand and a clear, deadlined mission. One key difference is that, once the target has been achieved, the project leader usually moves on. Leave the leader in place, like the late Don

Estridge, brilliant father of the IBM PC, and the result may well be a gigantic flop like PC Jr.

Project leadership and building an organization are not the same thing, even though both require skill at handling teamwork. The great organizers, however, know how to turn functional and cross-functional teamwork—including the crucial areas like purchasing—into a way of life, avoiding waste and achieving synergies (internally and with external suppliers) through flexible and adaptive systems.

If José Ignacio López de Arriortúa had been such an organizer, GM wouldn't have needed The Man so desperately: his system would have worked fine without him. GM's undoubted success in Europe while López was beating down the suppliers can't be attributed solely to one man, anyhow. Purchasing, while critical, is only part of the pattern. The overall picture is that GM in Europe reaped the fruits of an earlier, costly, farsighted, and comprehensive strategy. It attacked and reformed a mixed bag of cars, whose variable standards of design, engineering, competitive appeal, and build had been a license to lose money.

"Comprehensive" is the key word. The rage for "business process reengineering" has thrown up numerous cases of spectacular results—just as striking as those which, somewhat problematically, López claimed early in 1993 for what were very short-lived assaults on Volkswagen's production processes. But many of these splendid, shining examples (as at both GM and Volkswagen) come from companies whose overall results are unimpressive.

Place a radically improved engine in a beaten-up old heap, and you still have a rotten car. The bureaucratic, compartmentalized world of Detroit provides endless opportunities to demonstrate this principle at the expense of the firm. Big German business, whose supposedly heroic stature once matched the later Japanese reputation, can be even worse. As late as mid-1993, Volkswagen hadn't yet embraced the concept of the product champion: the single, responsible leader who is given sole charge of developing a new model from start to finish.

Anything that smacks of the *Führerprinzip,* the strong leader principle, isn't easily acceptable in Germany, whose two-tier board system explicitly treats the chief executive as a first among equals. Even though, in practice, some bosses are much more equal than others, that only adds to the López mystery. Not only did Volkswagen attach enormous importance to recruiting the supplier-squeezing genius, but it gave the Spaniard untrammeled power to work his will.

Relying on one man, however brilliant, eventually runs into trouble: that is, unless the talents of everybody else in the organization are mobilized and released in new ways that will outlive the peerless leader. Often, the latter seems as indispensable as did López to his two corporate suitors. But any system that hinges on one irreplaceable person is plainly and deeply defective. It's far more important to reinvent the system than to hire The Man. Spread responsibility and you raise results.

The Comeback
of Compaq

3

What does a personal computer have in common with a packet of soap powder? Not that long ago, the answer seemed to be nothing. The high-tech growth stars like Compaq rested securely on their high technology and their premium prices. In 1991, though, Compaq's years of relentless success hit the wall. Sales fell by a sixth, and profits dwindled 71 percent. Pierced by the low-price competition of the clones, Compaq's bubble had burst—and the wound could have been fatal.

The high-tech fall had low-tech affinities. Listen to top executives from Unilever or Procter & Gamble, rivals in suds, and you'll hear the same litany: the relentless rise of retailer, competitor, and customer power is causing new and acute pricing dilemmas. Among the world's top brands, the battle is on, as much for survival as success. Under pressure (just like Compaq and other branded PC suppliers), many market leaders have had to slash prices. What that spells for lesser brands (and their managers) is even more painful: many have succumbed.

According to one adman, "This is about deciding which are the mega-brands and which are the also-rans." Another expert is more apocalyptic: in the supermarkets, any product below number one and number two in the brand-sales pecking order "will get squeezed off the shelf. It's doomsday." For investors, the writing has appeared on more than the wall. In mere months after Marlboro Wednesday, in April 1993, when the leader sliced 40 cents off a cigarette pack, $47.5 billion vanished from the market value of America's two dozen brand leaders.

Yet there's a large and obvious paradox. Nearly all markets—for industrial and consumer products alike, for computers as for cookies—are fragmenting as customers seek more and more variety. How do you reconcile that fact with supermarket shelves restricted to two mega-brands and one "private label," the supermarket's own brand? There's no simple answer, but managers must find one if they want to satisfy, let alone delight, the paying customers.

Markets have moved from being relatively stable, and mostly manageable, to volatility and turmoil. Top brands and top companies can no longer rest comfortably on mass advertising, unchanging business formulas, everlasting rules, and unassailable market shares. This doesn't mean that managers can throw branding to the winds. On the contrary, the more vigorous the battle for share, the more valuable the possession of names and reputations that can last for decades—longer even than the products themselves.

For brands to work wonders today, however, managers must be far more innovative and resourceful in all they do—from product planning and speed to market to selling and the marketing mix. For a start, that mix must be different. The Big Brand era relied heavily on television. But TV costs have soared even as the audience monopoly has weakened. In 1965, brands waxed fat on sixty-second commercials: now, nearly half of all American commercials last a brief fifteen seconds.

Many old brands, having fallen below the affordable TV level, have been axed. Indeed, brand execution has become an epidemic only less virulent than the previous proliferation (with seven toothpastes, for example, becoming thirty-one within a decade). But managers mustn't forget those variety-craving customers. New, smaller brands are surging into the gaps (or niches) left by big-brand marketers. Unless the latter can match newcomers in marketing inventiveness, their charges will die.

It will be suicide, not murder. Far more brands perish as victims of mismanagement than are killed. The received view, though, is that assassins are at work. Stores' private labels are taking great bites from the branded market, and nobody knows how deep the bites will go: but 25 percent or more is possible. Often, in another form of suicide, the manufacturer making the own-brand is a brand owner. You can only sympathize with the managers concerned: it looks like a no-win situation.

If you don't supply own-brand goods, some other supplier will. Whether you do or not, retailer power, reinforced by private label, will drive down your margins. The spreading strength of private label must have eroded the ability of brand owners to command premium prices. Premium pricing, however, has never been the true basis of the brand. Its real power lies in creating a customer franchise, in nurturing faith in the magic name over many years of customer satisfaction.

That foundation can never crumble, given effective management. Thus, in recent years, Coca-Cola, the granddaddy of all brands, has multiplied its market value tenfold—despite the New Coke fiasco. The successful customer revolt against that misguided change in the famous recipe shows that the franchise was even stronger than the firm. One expert argues that brands will live on for owners who (like Coke) can "demonstrate the superiority of the brand and manage to build a direct relationship with the consumers."

That statement, while glimpsing the obvious, confronts managers with a billion-dollar question: how? One answer is to be inventive, not only in marketing, but in invention itself. *Fortune* looked at thirty "big labels" to divine which brands were "thriving, troubled, or under fire." In case after case, the thrivers are thrusters, earning accolades like "launches one new product a day" (Rubbermaid), "new models multiply" (Swatch), "low prices and constant innovation are key" (Frito-Lay), or "a continuous stream of new products."

That last reference was to Compaq. Note the emphasis on innovation: note, too, that far from pricing at a premium, Compaq has been exerting price leadership downwards, not upwards: gaining huge market penetration without weakening the brand—indeed, while *adding* new, lower-priced lines. In the new market climate, the big brand-name company hopes to use larger volumes and higher efficiency to boost profits. That's why Procter & Gamble has explicitly adopted a "value pricing" strategy, abandoning the game of promotional roller-coasting (money off one week, prices up the next) for consistent low prices.

For the competent, the rewards of branding remain profound—and so do the risks of the unbranded. There's one enormously profitable product line, for instance, with 80 percent of the world market, most of whose users haven't been aware of its existence. But its maker has begun advertising heavily to build the brand. The company is Intel, which badly needed to make PC buyers (including Compaq's) brand-conscious before rival chipmakers stormed the microprocessor market.

Without its notably effective "Intel Inside" campaign, the company might well find itself on the outside looking in. And that proves the point: when the going gets tough, the tough get branding. More, they change their own mental branding. Blunderbuss marketing has become a substitute for thought, a barrier to rethinking, to finding new ways of creating the loyal customers who are so hard to win, so easy to lose. Blunderbuss management, relying on old weapons and ways, is another self-erected obstacle. Its removal can have magical effects.

After a single quarter of losses, the rethought Compaq moved steadily forward, proliferating those new products, until the steady progress became a surge, doubling sales to $7.2 billion, rising 253 percent above net income at the trough to reach new peaks in 1993, and trebling global market share in personal computers to become number one in 1994. Those 1993 profit levels were left far behind in 1994 as well: nine months' net income doubled on sales increased by half.

That was the reward for dropping the blunderbuss and departing from the conventions: not only those slavishly followed by the industry but also the internal shibboleths that—far more than the competition—cripple a company's ability to compete.

Breaking the
Rule—and the Rules

4

There's one overriding management lesson to be learned from Sam Walton—one of many that can be taken from that salty entrepreneur. Starting in 1962, and building Wal-Mart into the world's largest retailer well before he died in 1992, he based his relentless rise on nine rules for managers. The rules mostly concern fellow employees (Walton called them "associates" or "partners"). He advised that you should share, communicate, and celebrate success with your partners, and motivate, appreciate, and listen to them.

The retailing sage also stressed commitment, control of expenses, and exceeding customers' expectations. All good, solid, wrongly ignored stuff, but hardly revolutionary. The revolutionary rule is the tenth: "Break all the rules." There's no more valuable prescription for a period in which events aren't obeying the rules—a development which is deeply disturbing for managers.

That's because all companies, and much managerial thinking, are governed by rules, some written and some unwritten. All companies also have pervasive myths, spoken or unspoken, about themselves. Both the rules and the beliefs may be founded in deep error, and may contribute to worse. If you break the rules—looking at the company, say, from an aggressive competitor's viewpoint—the truth can shock the myths to destruction.

The astonishing tale of Compaq's comeback from near-disaster is a convincing demonstration of this principle. In October 1991, two undercover men from the Houston company toured the Comdex computer trade show in Las Vegas. They had a secret mission: to discover what it would cost to assemble a PC from the components on display. Posing as a pair of entrepreneurial clone-makers (the competitors who were undermining Compaq's economics), they obtained low enough quotations on enough components to cobble together two amazingly cheap prototypes back in their motel.

"In some cases," reported the *Wall Street Journal,* "they were able to get price quotes . . . even lower than giant Compaq." That's another general rule blown away. In fragmented and competitive businesses, the economic advantages that can be won, even by an IBM, through placing large orders are much less significant: certainly nothing like great enough to offset vastly higher costs for overheads, advertising, and bureaucratic delays.

The extent to which internal rules build unnecessary delay into the system justifies what's known as "time-based competition," in which every process is analyzed, taken apart, and reassembled to eliminate excess time. At Compaq, for instance, the lead-time for producing a badly needed, low-priced PC had been put by management at six quarters. That doesn't sound long, but the time was actually *halved* after the Comdex undercover operation.

It wasn't only an undercover caper so far as the suppliers were concerned. It was also unknown to the chief executive of the company, Rod Canion. In an astonishing example of breaking the rules, brilliantly reported by the *Journal's* Michael Allen, chairman Ben Rosen had gone behind his CEO's back—and plunged in the knife while there. Canion was fired, during a fourteen-hour board meeting, held almost immediately after the Comdex episode, although his possible ouster must already have been in Rosen's mind.

The episode makes Walton's point dramatically. In unconventional times and situations, conventional behavior doesn't stand a chance: you must dare to be different. Rosen, one of America's leading venture capitalists, has strong views on the role of the board: "I

think the owners of the company should be represented by the directors. That has ceased to happen at a lot of companies where management dominates the board." The corollary is that, occasionally, the
directors must dominate the management.

Canion and his co-founders owed Rosen plenty. At the very start
he had steered them away from their initial product idea and towards
the portable computer that launched their rocket. Every company
needs somebody with a wider vision, who can see the forest as well
as the trees—somebody who is acutely sensitive to trends. Rosen's
long experience with the tumultuous ups and downs of high technology helped convince him that the rules of the PC business had fundamentally altered.

It was a sea-change. The low-cost clones had led the computer
market into a commodity phase in which "a box is a box is a box."
But even in a young growth star, you can easily build a proud, rule-
bound tradition—too proud to accept that a Compaq is only a box.
Rosen's undercover agents, a marketing manager half his chairman's
age and an engineer, had confirmed a truth that went right against
the rules of the Compaq culture, but which it dared not ignore.

Like IBM, though in far less time, Compaq had developed an
all-embracing internal view that governed its external actions to a potentially fatal degree. Internal rules and corporate myths stem from
what Peter M. Senge of MIT calls a "mental model." In that model
Compaq's managers, from CEO Rod Canion downwards, saw their
company as the high-quality, high-end champion that was the preferred choice of people who were serious about their personal
computing needs.

So the management couldn't and didn't see the company's collapse into loss as a failure of the system. The system needed tighten-
ing up by reorganization, layoffs, and other cost-cutting—but radical
changes in the rules of an engineering-led culture weren't necessary.
The chairman's swift intervention changed all that. In writing about
his cat, drowned in a murderous attempt on a goldfish bowl, the poet
Gray noted that "one false step is ne'er retrieved": by the same token, one radical rule-break must lead to others.

With CEO Canion gone, the low-end line was entrusted to an
"independent business unit," or IBU. It was placed outside the
Compaq mainstream (and quite a distance from related company ac-

tivities) as a deliberate means of dodging the product development system. This, Canion's pride and joy, had become unduly conservative and rule-bound—in only an eight-year history. The irreligious low-end team, working under the code name Ruby, was allowed to make its own rules and break Compaq's.

Dedication to top quality has its virtues, but also its vices. Note that this wasn't quality as in Total Quality Management: quality had meant the highest specification, irrespective of need or even technology—the packing cases, for instance, "could survive a fall down the Himalayas" and were priced accordingly. On more sophisticated items, according to the *Wall Street Journal,* "it sometimes seemed that over-engineering had become a religion."

All companies breed shibboleths, unchallenged articles of faith, as well as rules. For instance, the purchasing department placed price seventh in a list of strict priorities. That was faithful to the rules of total quality: no less a list of commandments than the famous fourteen points of W. Edwards Deming admonishes companies not to award business on the basis of price alone. But you can't maintain that pure commitment in a market where price-cutters have changed the rules.

Richard Swingle, the product development man who headed the Ruby project, went direct to suppliers—and hammered them on prices. The suppliers squeezed out included Compaq's own lines: when Taiwanese circuit boards came in 30 percent cheaper, Compaq lost the job. The Texas plant could likewise have lost building the entire computer to offshore suppliers. But an intriguing and prophetic intervention occurred at a briefing of plant workers.

Doug Johns, the new head of the PC division, was explaining the reasoning behind going offshore when one "crusty old" employee (remember, the company was only born in the 1980s) stood up and told him Compaq workers should be allowed to bid for the work. "With all due respect," said the veteran, "you're kind of new at this, *and you don't know what we can do.*"

Johns took the point. Further investigation showed that Compaq could cut its manufacturing costs down to competitive levels, but not by sticking to the same rules of manufacture. Thus, the Ruby engineers found from their global explorations that you could simplify board manufacture. That done, the computer could be produced on a single line. That done, computers came off at one a minute—an eighth of the previous time.

Break the rules, change the habits, and the savings a supposedly efficient organization can find are staggering. Compaq saved $6 a box on packing cases (from an $11 price) by accepting a lower specification, and saved $10 a unit (down to $1) on chassis tooling by using one size for a number of different models. The big issue was whether a low-priced range should bear the Compaq label; the appearance of the first version ("wave-like front and turquoise buttons"), like its name of Echelon, shunned any Compaq connection.

That much anarchy was too much for Eckhard Pfeiffer, the new German chief executive. He held back $20 million of parts orders while he pondered the issue over the Christmas holidays. His decision was governed by the need to sell low-cost solutions to large corporate customers; they, he reasoned, still wanted a Compaq, so the Ruby team started, the day after Christmas, rushing through a Compaq-like redesign.

The team has since been reabsorbed into the rest of the company, but so have its no-rules rules on cost-cutting and development time. According to one executive, "The IBU changed the way this company did business forever." The tremendous success of the new ProLinea line turned the change into a triumph and, in this particular ferocious market, that had by no means been certain. But the logic of Compaq's response, under chairman Ben Rosen's goading, can't be faulted, including its readiness to break the rules on another matter—cannibalization.

The threat of losing high-priced, high-profit business by introducing lower-priced products has deterred innumerable managers from making down-market moves. But in today's conditions, Swingle, who got promoted to head all of Compaq's new product development, is surely right: "Either you eat your own children or somebody else does."

In important measure, the story recalls the team that famously launched IBM's PC from Boca Raton in Florida. It was the prototype of the "independent business unit," set free of every corporate shibboleth in order to mount a crash program. But while the PC operation was eventually absorbed back into IBM, its lessons were not.

The way the company did business didn't change, partly because rules like non-cannibalization remained sacred.

Note the nature of the three reported interventions in the Compaq saga: one by the chairman, without whose push Compaq wouldn't have undergone this rebirth; one by the new CEO, who used his prerogative to ensure that a make-or-break project didn't break the overall corporate posture; one by a "crusty old worker," who spoke out and was listened to. Two of the three interventions, moreover, were "behind the back" moves.

Rosen wouldn't have undermined the former chief executive had he been confident that Canion would respond to the initiative, in the same sensible, swift way that the PC boss responded to the crusty fellow. Being able to say what you mean and be heard—meaningfully heard—is basic to breaking the rules. It must apply at all levels.

As the book *Sam Walton: Made in America* advises, "Listen to everyone in your company. And figure out ways to get them talking." Part of Walton's reasoning was that only those in contact with the customer really know what's going on—like whether the company's high prices are adversely affecting sales. Customer comments to that effect, relayed by a thirty-year-old marketing manager (who became one of that pair which did the undercover work at Comdex), actually set Rosen off on his Compaq crusade.

Another Walton argument is that "to push responsibility down in your organization, and to force good ideas to bubble up within it, you MUST listen to what your associates are trying to tell you." Listening, though, doesn't just mean hearing—it means acting on what you hear, if it makes sense. The manager (like Pfeiffer on the design issue) has the right and duty to challenge the challengers. But they should only be overridden by fiat (as then) where you can't, by experiment, test what is right: whether the old rules still stand, or whether their abolition is required—Sam Walton's anti-rule rule.

In new-technology companies, though, the opportunities for fatal ossification come especially thick and fast. After all, Compaq's plunge from star to fallen idol took only a couple of quarters. But the same process, though on a longer time scale, is overtaking companies of much lower technology. It's driven by two forces: the quickening rate of change in customer-driven markets, and the widening of competition as truly global markets develop. As in computers, proprietary positions have become highly vulnerable.

Both brands and imperiums have lost power and dignity. The rules have changed accordingly. Even where most of the rules stand, they may not be enough. For example, you can draw eight principles for all managers from the basics which are, or should be, familiar to all modern production managers. The eight are

1. Constantly improve non-financial performance measures
2. Analyze and simplify all processes
3. Launch many quick-fix, fast-payoff projects simultaneously
4. Commit fully to a very few long-term, big-improvement programs.
5. Always include quality in the latter
6. Concentrate improvement projects where the payoffs are biggest
7. Have high targets, reasonable expectations
8. Trust, train, and educate—all the time

But there's a ninth rule, one that I gleaned from Shin Taguchi, son of the famous Japanese inventor of the Taguchi Method. In presenting this highly technical way of engineering quality into the earliest (and—see the sixth point above—most cost-effective) processes, Taguchi reserves capital letters for a very non-technical instruction: "We need to THINK HARD." What managers need to think hard about is the rules, the way things have always been done. Some things don't need doing at all. All others can be done better—some within the rules, but more and more Walton's Tenth is the rule that counts. Break all the rules.

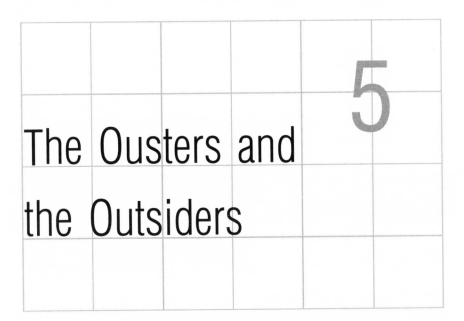

The Ousters and the Outsiders

5

You have to feel sorry for Kay Whitmore, the ousted CEO of Eastman Kodak. True, in the decade before his enforced departure the group's earnings per share only edged up by a miserable 1.1 percent per year. But that was actually the eighteenth best performance among the fifty largest groups in the United States, many of which lost money in 1992. Furthermore, Kodak's glacial growth rate *doubled* the performance of Motorola over the same period: and Motorola's CEO, George Fisher, was the man imported, with $5 million for starters and a $22.3 million stock package, to revive Kodak's fortunes.

True, Kodak (unlike Motorola) had lost ground against Japanese competition and made a disastrous merger (with Sterling Drug) unrelated to its own business. But so had many other companies whose reigning monarchs stayed in place. No doubt, Whitmore might have done likewise; the board that ousted him, after all, had shown no impatience with the snail's pace of Kodak's reforms. The CEO was only forced out when mounting pressure was exerted by investors, who have less patience and more rigor.

The similar, prolonged benefits of the doubt given to James Robinson at American Express, John Akers at IBM, and Robert Stempel at General Motors are no surprise, either. Boards have historically been unwilling to dethrone CEOs: they are even less eager when, as at IBM and Kodak, no successor is in sight. Nobody on any board can relish the prospect of conducting a public search, in the full glare of the media, until they finally anoint a Louis V. Gerstner or a Fisher.

Left to themselves, the IBM directors might even have stuck with Akers until his mandatory retirement, two years on, at the age of sixty. As at Kodak, external pressure removed this option. Groundswells of opinion played a part in all the ousters. The opinion formers were merely expressing the obvious: the incumbents had failed. For instance, in the week after Stempel's boardroom discomfiture at General Motors, *Business Week* noted that the restructuring and refocusing of IBM under Akers hadn't "done much for investors." Their investment had fallen in value by 9.2 percent annually between 1987 and 1991.

"Sounds like GM," said *Business Week*. "No wonder it's on California Public Employees' Retirement System's list of poor performers. Still, 'Akers has the board's full support,' says a spokesman. Most observers agree. But he's on a red-hot seat." The heat intensified for nine more months before becoming unbearable. In all these cases, the heat has to be shared by the board: IBM's had "fully supported" Akers through all the false dawns. The IBM directors even backed the absurd last fling of Akers's regime, when two senior retirees were brought back to bolster the CEO's indefensible position.

A glance at this board's composition in the 1991 annual report readily explains its shenanigans. It was almost a parody, rather than a paradigm, of the boardroom system that has helped lower the flags of many large U.S. corporations in the past decade. The board was far too large for an effective committee (eighteen members); it was headed by a chairman who was also chief executive; it was stuffed with retirees (a third of the number, including former chairman John Opel); and it was short on relevant business experience.

Eight members were drawn from other industries: none of their companies manufactured or marketed in manners remotely analogous to IBM's processes and needs. Of these eight, three came from health care and two from chemicals—which would have given a visitor from Mars a very odd idea of the company's business. Two were media and entertainment executives. The last was Stephen D. Bechtel, Jr., of the plant construction business that bears his family name. The balance included four representatives from academe and two lawyers.

Whatever their qualifications, most held little ownership stake. One Florida correspondent wrote to a magazine editor that he could "rest assured that shareholder discontent with company performance will never affect the majority of IBM's board. Ten of its seventeen members own less than 1,500 shares each. Collectively it is not in their interest to challenge the lackluster performance of CEO John Akers, an action that might jeopardize the maintenance of their $55,000-per-year retainers."

Even in the mid-nineties, the IBM situation is replicated across the board—or across the boards—in most large companies. Because of uncertainty and denial, they dither and dillydally before changing the CEO: they're being asked to risk replacing the devil they know to fix a crisis which they don't want to recognize. If crisis looms, though, today's pressures for change are plainly heavier, but only because the effects of mediocre management, or worse, are felt so fast in the stock price.

When companies run into serious problems that have worsened over many years of inadequate therapy, the case for turning outside to save the patient looks especially powerful. The board at last appears assertive and active (its members, of course, have usually been supine and passive for years). The external choice marks a clean break with the soiled past. It also fires a shot across the bows of entrenched management wedded to the old ways. The outsider, moreover, has a license to kill, and, unlike any insider, a relevant track record, usually from a previous turnaround.

Gerstner was picked by IBM (for a sign-on cost of $4.9 million and a $10.8 million stock package) because of his work in hoisting RJR Nabisco's head above its oceans of debt. Bereft, RJR Nabisco then turned to Charles M. Harper because of his brilliance in transforming ConAgra, a dull food processor, into a fast-moving consumer-goods force. Choosing proven horses for appropriate courses is sound policy. But the illogic is obvious. The turnaround kings had to start somewhere.

Before their breakthroughs, the outsider heroes were like everybody else: supporting players, faces in the executive crowd. Who, outside financial services and American Express, had ever heard of Gerstner before Kravis, Kohlberg and Roberts, desperate to protect its investment in the biggest-ever buyout, picked him for RJR Nabisco? For that matter, who outside Motorola and electronics knew of Fisher before chairman Robert W. Galvin spotted and promoted his talents?

Inside every company that turns outside there's similar latent talent of a high, maybe the highest order: even when the corporation has apparently failed. That was patently true at both IBM and Kodak. Why does the internal talent get held down under the water—instead of being allowed to swim powerfully towards ambitious corporate objectives? It's the most important question in management. Answer it correctly, and you have the answer to almost everything else.

Denying the Deniers

6

The spate of axed chief executives, and their replacement by outsiders, began to look like a major trend in the early nineties. Indeed, *Business Week* argued that "CEOs with the outside edge [are] in, as never before." But then the flood abated—but not because sitting CEOs had been galvanized into better performance by the sight of their axed peers. Simply, Wall Street started booming. When that happens, investors sleep easy, and so do heads that wear the executive crown.

In truth, the crowned had little reason to worry, even before the market took off. Summit instability was always more apparent than real. For every boss who bit the dust, hundreds journeyed on towards safe retirement—rightly or wrongly. For every company that hunts an outside head, scores of boards promote insiders: possibly a time-server taking his turn, maybe a man who, like an ideal new product, will surpass his predecessors by being both different and better.

The male noun and pronoun may be politically incorrect, but they're factually accurate. Out of one thousand top American CEOs surveyed by *Business Week* in late 1993, just three were women. That

0.3 percent shows no change from past surveys. As for the other characteristics of the top occupants—average age 56, length of tenure 8.5 years, 21 years averaged with the beloved company, most likely to have been fledged in finance or accounting—they also have altered little.

Companies put great store in this stability at the top. IBM's John Akers noted before his own ouster that "many American companies seem to have a tenure for the CEO of only four to five years. That's not the way IBM has historically approached the challenge," with only six leaders in seventy-eight years. In fact, Akers's weak arithmetic grossly exaggerated the stability. Tom Watson, Sr., and his natural successor, Junior, ruled the company for fifty-seven of those seventy-eight years. After that, five CEOs averaged five and a half years apiece, three years *less* than the actual U.S. corporate average.

The external replacement of Akers and other corporate chieftains involved a double malfunction of the typical comfortable, durable system. First, it failed to evolve the right top management and to direct that management towards achieving the right results. Second, the absence of internal heirs showed failure to develop the company's most valuable human resources. The dual failure is highlighted by a simple question: Would any company deliberately adopt a policy of always appointing its chief executives from outside?

Obviously not: the unmistakable signal sent to able insiders would be counterproductive, and the chances of developing a coherent long-term strategy and culture would wither away. The outside appointment is not a plan, but an accident. Too many companies, alas, are accidents waiting to happen—a description that surely applied to Kodak, GM, IBM, and others.

What prolonged their agonies was denial—defined by one consultant as "an unconscious coping mechanism to block out and not deal with major change that may have some pain associated with it." The CEO, naturally, denied to himself and others that his own failings were causing the problems. The board not only accepted the denials, but went one stage further—denying to itself and the outside world that its support for the CEO was mistaken.

Denial is much more comfortable psychologically than facing hard facts. A study led by Professor Jeffry Nutter of the University of Georgia provides resounding evidence on this point: all but 5 percent of forty-six major companies, each with sales of over a billion dollars, blamed losses made in the 1980s at least in part on "poor economic conditions." *Fortune* reports, however, that "only 13% said that bad management or mistakes may have had anything to do with it, and invariably these forthright types were new executive teams pinning the tail on their ousted predecessors."

In many years in journalism I found the same. New managements are perfectly prepared to confess to the dreadful failures of their forerunners. Managers who are still in place after presiding over the setbacks are only slightly more likely than politicians to admit their mistakes. It took the new man, Gerstner, to confess publicly in March 1994 to IBM's sins of sluggishness, internal and external, that had been evident to outsiders for at least a decade.

It isn't surprising, perhaps, that these massive, long-term failings were missed by a board whose business experience was either negligible or confined to other big battalions. But what about the managers further down? Many lower executives in the troubled companies certainly knew how grave and grievous the problems were. At GM, for instance, David C. Munro was the auto giant's chief economic forecaster for ten years. When he left, the company had already halved in size since his arrival—and he wasn't sure "what will be left when the company enters the next millennium."

Munro diagnosed two main ailments: "elephantine mass" and insularity. "GM doesn't have a very good history of pulling in information and ideas from others," he says, "and at the top it has a history of resisting change from outside. There are an awful lot of people in that bureaucracy who only know what others are thinking down the hall." The same painful observations were being made at many other corporations. It isn't just a question of resisting change from outside, though: resistance to change proposed from *inside* can be even more deadly.

Consider the following case: The CEO of a major bank composes a mission statement for the company. It is to be "the best retail bank" in the nation by 1997. Asked how they will know they are the best, executives down the line say they haven't the slightest idea. The CEO hasn't attached any measures or targets to his ambitions: and the management cadre has played no part in the formation of the mission. What are the chances of said mission being successful? Significantly less than even.

Consider also this case: A large financial services company sets up informal, separate sessions at which the top management and the stratum immediately below look at the composition and purpose of the board and the executive committee. The lower managers point out that the two bodies have five members in common, yet persist in the fiction that they are entirely separate. The juniors propose reforms that will greatly improve the effectiveness of both bodies and of the departments beneath them. What are the chances of the proposals being adopted?

The answer to that question—almost zero—is strongly suggested by another aspect of the same company. It had recently celebrated its 150th year of existence, and was proud of its past. Yet nobody had given any thought to the next 150 days. No business plan existed, even for the current year. A committee had once been formed to draw up a five-year corporate plan: in presenting the document, the committee argued for a small planning department to monitor the plan's implementation. The department was rejected, and the plan was never enacted.

The true-life stories may sound bizarre, but the situation they portray is common. Time and again, talking to managers at all levels, I'm struck by their competence, knowledge of the business and its key people, and understanding of what modern, effective management requires—even if they've spent all their lives in one narrow industry and have very little knowledge of thought and action beyond its frontiers. Yet their cynicism is equally striking: they don't believe that what needs to be done will be done.

They are usually all too right. Top managers allow huge gaps to open up between their perception of their own management excellence and the reality. Take the CEO of the bank mentioned above. He had gathered the importance of aiming for the highest achievable goals, but hadn't understood that the goals were useless to his subordinates unless defined in measurable and appropriate terms. Four key questions arise:

1. Are we measuring the right things?
2. Are the measurements accurate?

3. Are we taking action to improve performance on those measures?

4. Are we using the measures to reinforce the behaviors we want—from everybody, including top management itself?

Self-evidently, all those questions must be answered in the affirmative. Yet that dangerous gap between perception and reality means that often they don't get asked—even by managers who know perfectly well that they should be. That omission is one luxury which genuine Total Quality Management doesn't allow. For instance, SGS-THOMSON's top managers (emulating the vast majority of Nutter's sample) could have declined all blame for the losses incurred when the semiconductor cycle turned sharply downwards in 1990.

"Poor economic conditions" undoubtedly existed. But these managers, indoctrinated in the TQM gospel, dug down below the easy explanation to ask why excessive numbers had been hired just in time for the downturn. Better quality of management wouldn't have prevented the decline, but would have ameliorated its impact. The company duly set about achieving that quality. Cutting costs and firing people were still required—but the negative was combined with a positive, bottom-to-top change in the targets which the organization set out to achieve and the ways in which it sought to achieve them.

The phrase "bottom-to-top" is crucial. The Nutter study noted that in its billion-dollar-plus subjects, although average employment had fallen by about 5 percent, there was "no evidence of abnormally high levels of forced turnover in top managers." Coupled with abnormally high salaries for the latter, this creates another dangerous perception-reality gap: between how top management perceives itself and how it is perceived by its internal customers—the rest of the staff. You can extrapolate some telltale signs of this gap from *Fortune*'s exploration of companies in denial. The telltales are

1. A higher energy level after meetings than beforehand: Do people talk about what wasn't said rather than what was?

2. Managers who pass down top-level messages while stating that they don't agree

3. Aversion to taking risks, external or internal

4. Political jockeying for the favor of superiors
5. Failure (see above) to seek out and live by meaningful measures of performance
6. Excessive top management interference in operations

   The sixth point often leads to the sudden adoption of fashionable techniques, like TQM. As one academic puts it, managers who "deny the need for change" instead "adopt an efficiency focus, pounding the same thing over and over rather than asking, 'Are we doing the right thing?'" That guarantees failure, for true TQM, like true reengineering, demands radical reshaping of the organization as a sine qua non.

   Managements in denial may therefore be stressing the need to become "competitive" and "world-class" while simultaneously standing in the way of achieving ends that are not only highly desirable, but mandatory. Down the post-war decades these managements have created organizations at once far too large and much too introverted. All the surgery and medicaments of the eighties and early nineties, the years of corporate crisis, were supposed to cure both conditions: to turn thinking and actions outwards and to bring down excess size.

   The therapies, though, have had terrible, counterproductive side-effects among the managerial ranks. There's a crucial trade-off between the gains of a reorganization and the losses in morale and security. In companies in upheaval, people of all generations will tend to see better opportunities outside—better than those in a company undergoing continuous shake-ups against a background of deep uncertainty about its future and therefore their own. They are very unlikely to join another company of the same mold.

   The brightest and best of the younger generations won't want to stay put, either. Like their better elders, they will gravitate towards other employment. The brain drain virtually guarantees that the corporate accidents and the problems of bureaucracy, "elephantine mass," and insularity will recur. Those characteristics are inimical to the new environment—one in which, as C. K. Prahalad of the University of Michigan tells his audiences, opportunity management is as important as operations management, companies that fall behind stay behind, and customers demand, not only to be satisfied, but to be surprised.

If you want the internal talent to respond to this challenge (and if it doesn't, the corporation is doomed), the recipe is obvious. Indeed, it's the one which the relatively junior executives in that 150-year-old financial services company worked out for themselves—in a ninety-minute workshop, at that. Divorce the board from the corpocracy, separate the senior management from the operations, and devolve authority down the line to self-managed teams headed by effective leaders.

The resulting effectiveness will be shown by characteristics which reverse the signs of denial. Meetings will have defined objectives and will always result in agreed action commitments. Top managers won't settle strategies and policies until they are supported by a fully informed consensus among the teams and their leaders. Balanced risk-taking is expected, encouraged and, if successful, rewarded. Internal politics are suppressed by insistence on promotion on merit and by instant, generous recognition of achievement at all levels.

That demands living by meaningful measures of performance and targets to which all managers subscribe. Most important of all, top management recognizes that its own job is to add value, and that the board's function is to ensure that this happens—not through mergers and acquisitions, but through building the businesses and the talents within them. As Prahalad says, "A firm's capacity for organic growth is the ultimate test of top management's value added." That's the acid test, all right—and managers in denial not only fail that test: they are incapable of providing excellence in leadership or anything else.

TWO

The System Pushes Back: How to Alter Everything

The Job Cuts of
the Giants

General Electric under Jack Welch has been hailed as a legendary example of how to use massive reductions in operations and employment (where savage cuts won Welch the nickname "Neutron Jack") to boost efficiency and profitability. One GE business making small motors perfectly exemplified the strategy. It shed 5,300 jobs (42 percent of the total) in a decade, closed two out of a dozen plants, saved $25 million through pay cuts, and plowed $200 million into new equipment and products.

What about the other side of the equation? The efficiency and profitability won by the cutbacks? They didn't exist. The strategy was a disaster: "Productivity went to hell," said a GE man. Low morale and poor cooperation, both engendered by the cutbacks in jobs and pay, had more than offset the savings in a way that helps explain a strange fact about Welch's GE: its relatively slow growth in earnings per share over the 1981–91 decade.

The number was 5.3 percent per annum. Given Welch's high managerial reputation, that's a poor performance (161st out of the *Fortune* 500) in return for the severance of 120,000 jobs. Were too

many of those jobs lost from businesses which, under better management, might have generated rapid organic returns? The numbers for
other downsizing companies suggest that this is the hard truth. At
least GE made profits: often, losses in jobs and losses in big bucks
go hand in hand.

In an article on America's grievous loss of well-paid jobs, *Fortune* published a listing, taken from among the five hundred largest
U.S. companies in manufacturing and services respectively, of the
biggest job creators—and cutters—of the 1981–91 decade. The ten
greatest cutters (with job shrinkage ranging from 138,900 to 44,235)
were Mobil, GE, USX, Union Carbide, Exxon, Ford, Armco, Bethle-
hem Steel, Navistar, and Du Pont. Half of them had financial deficits
in 1991.

Two others, Mobil and Armco, had *negative* growth in earnings
per share over the decade. GE's modest 5.3 percent was easily the
highest of the three positive performances. Move on to the mid-
nineties, and the story's no different. Consultants Wyatt & Company
looked at 450 major companies that downsized in 1991 and 1992.
Two-fifths of the shrinkers didn't even succeed in cutting their costs.
Less than half improved their profits. Two-thirds of those aiming for
higher productivity were disappointed—just like the managers of
GE's small-motor business.

GE's figures look even dimmer when compared to the ten "biggest gainers" in employment. Their job gains were by no means
small, ranging from 36,341 people for Baxter International (scientific
equipment) to no less than 218,000 for PepsiCo. Seven of the ten
showed annual gains in earnings per share that started above GE (at
6.6 percent for Baxter) and ran up to 49.9 percent for Tyson Foods.
General Mills, Boeing, and PepsiCo all *doubled* GE's financial
growth rate: it was *tripled* by Philip Morris (17 percent) and
ConAgra.

A similar tale is told in services. In virtually all cases, service
is provided by people, and the more the service company grows and
prospers, the more men and women it must hire. The biggest gains,
260,000 jobs in 1985–91, were duly recorded by Wal-Mart, whose
growth in earnings per share was equally phenomenal at 31.4 percent
annually.

The obvious question is which came first, the chicken or the egg, the bad business or the big layoffs? The predominance of cars and steel in the list of losers, and of food and drink among the winners, might suggest that irresistible market forces drove unemployment down in the former cases, and up in the latter. Job gains are also exaggerated by acquisitions (Philip Morris) and job losses by divestments (GE).

Against that, PepsiCo achieved stunning gains (218,000 jobs) largely by organic growth, while the U.S. car and steel companies notoriously sharpened their beds of nails by across-the-board failure to compete effectively with Japanese rivals. The excess jobs were not the cause of under-performance: the latter created the excess jobs. And eliminating these by no means guarantees that a new trend of dynamic long-term performance will develop.

Attack labor costs when sales are growing, and the results will be dynamic. But if sales stagnate and market share drops, the last state of the business will be as bad as the first—if not worse. Managements have laid off workers instead of tackling the true systemic and strategic causes. What they create isn't new growth—it's new problems.

After the painful demonstration of that truth at GE's small-motors business, the local management had the sense to reverse engines. Instead of concentrating on the cost of labor, the company completely changed its deployment. Workers in small teams were empowered to organize their own work with modern methods: "We now see," said one of the reformed managers, "that the productivity available is really extraordinary."

Here, internal revolt, in the form of sub-normal productivity, conveyed a message that management was fortunately able to hear. In most cases, plants, products, and jobs are condemned to death by top management. There's no appeal, and often no good reason. As consultant Geary A. Rummler told *Fortune,* layoffs are "an easy way out" for "rationalizing" CEOs, who are usually reducing excess labor that they have personally created.

"Rationalizing" means closing plants: "downsizing" means closing jobs. Rationalizing, downsizing managers are often today's heroes. They shouldn't be. The truly rational course is to develop valuable plants, not shut them, and to increase valuable employment, not fire valuable people. As Rummler says, layoffs "are a major admission that senior management has really screwed up." Worse still, the screwing-up usually doesn't end with the layoffs.

Companies are systems: linked parts and functions which intimately affect each other. So what happens if you disturb the system by a violent assault on one of its parts—pushing down labor costs by job-cuts, say—without reforming the system as a whole? MIT's Peter Senge (see Part Five, Chapter 4) has the answer in a marvelous, pregnant phrase: "However hard you push, the harder the system pushes back." It sure does.

There's no gainsaying what Gary Hamel and C. K. Prahalad wrote in their influential fall 1994 book, *Competing for the Future:* Companies should concentrate on "raising the numerator in productivity (revenue and net profits) rather than from reducing the denominator (investment and headcount)." They note that "an inefficient firm that downsizes, without improving its capacity for resource leverage, will find that productivity improves—for a while." Sooner or later, though, the price will be paid. "Technological leadership, brand loyalty, distribution reach, and customer service" are all at risk. And if they're lost, the screwup will be terminal.

Management's Leading Powers

2

There was once a wise old lawyer whose clients included several members of the most exclusive male clubs. Every now and then, one of the clients would call to say he wanted a divorce. The lawyer's answer was always the same: "Don't do it, dear boy. You'll only do it again."

That's roughly the advice which should have been heeded by many downsizing CEOs. Slashing employment and costs can become a bad habit. A survey conducted by the Kepner-Tregoe consultancy found that, even among companies counting their slashing a success, over a third intended to ax again within twelve months. The reason's simple, according to T. Quinn Spitzer, K-T's chief executive: "Most cost-cutting actions do not remove work, only the people who do it."

The work still has to be done, and the absence of the removed people may well increase real costs and reduce effectiveness. The result can be a depressing exercise in chasing your own tail: depressing not only in terms of workforce morale, but financially. In manufacturing, Eastman Kodak cut twelve thousand jobs: its return on equity collapsed by two-thirds, and its CEO lost his job. In services, American Express has seen its return on equity halve—and its CEO eased out, too—despite heavy job cuts (or because of them).

The issue isn't cutting costs, but *managing* them by linking the costs to an effective strategy. As the previous chapter showed, companies that shrink most are outperformed by those that expand. If a business is growing organically, raising sales and profits, employment will also rise (preferably at a slower rate). If it's cutting employment, capabilities are usually being reduced in reaction to ebbing profits and markets, and the cutbacks may diminish the very strengths on which future dynamism depends.

"Change management" has a powerful appeal to management in the nineties. But it doesn't just mean traditional restructuring, altering the form of the organization and the roles and number of the inhabitants. What really pays off is the deeper kind of change: reshaping the organization culture, not the organization chart, so that people's behavior will alter in ways that benefit the customers and hence the company.

You often find the same managements involved in both approaches at the same time. Thus, in 1994 one financial services company mounted its first-ever effort to change a culture with which everybody was generally dissatisfied. As the change seminars for senior management unfolded over four weeks, large managerial job cuts were announced in the regional organization, which would be followed, it was announced, by twice as many losses at head office. What was the relationship between the cultural exercise and the redundancies?

A negative effect was immediately obvious, since those who were going to lose head office jobs by year-end hadn't been identified. On a far larger scale, IBM has been guilty of the same mistake. The announced job losses damage morale as people see their colleagues, some of them friends, shown to the exit. The promise that further, unidentified losses will follow makes managers worry about being next. Insecurity is the greatest enemy of effectiveness, which promptly suffers. But there's an even more pernicious and more general error: *if the two forms of organizational change don't go hand-in-hand, neither will provide the full desired benefits.*

I've italicized that sentence to emphasize its extreme importance. The supporting evidence is overwhelming. In 1987 I published a book entitled *The State of Industry.* It was based on seventeen interviews with companies, mostly represented by their chief executives, which had ridden out of severe recession at the start of the decade. At the time, they were apparently riding high. Most had cut back on superfluous employees, facilities, and products: all had adopted outward-looking and competitive strategies.

In the seven intervening years, four of the companies have been taken over—two of them (including Jaguar) after awful results—while two (including ICI) have been split in two. Of the other eleven, only four survived the period without significant setback: the gases group BOC, drug manufacturer Glaxo, the ICL computer business, and Vauxhall Motors, the British subsidiary of General Motors. The failure ratio is about as bad as the notorious undoing of the hero companies in *In Search of Excellence.*

Cutbacks in employment, whether enforced by recession or technological change, should never be conducted in isolation. They must be combined with rethinking the entire business system, and all its sub-divisions, to establish new and more productive methods of working in all functions. That way, the slimmer labor force can build a better future. At Compaq, for excellent example, the double whammy of cost-cutting and rethinking produced a swift, nine-month turnaround, and, from 1991 to 1993, a doubling of sales and a tripling of world market share.

The ultimate test for leaner organizations is what they can do in the shape of organic creativity, utilizing all the talents within the organization by the application of genuine team management. That's unquestionably an increasing and highly effective mode—and a highly suggestive one. Why does the ultimate ad hoc operation, the crash program like that which gave Compaq the low-priced ProLinea line in nine months, so often work so well? So much better than the routine work of the organization on continuing processes?

It's because the principles and pressures are entirely different from those of conventional management. The crash program has *(a)* a clearly defined purpose and *(b)* a tight deadline that imposes *(c)* a strict order of priorities for *(d)* a dedicated, specially selected team that carries no passengers and *(e)* improvises as it goes along towards *(f)* an objective whose success or failure will be clearly known.

The contrast is acute in most companies, to judge by the common complaints in all six areas. Managers say that they have either no objectives or conflicting ones, fuzzy deadlines, lack clear priorities, that their colleagues are incompetent and over-promoted, that procedures are rigid and irrelevant, and that standards of success and failure are opaque. Reshuffles and firings won't resolve these difficulties, and neither will top-down dictation, unless it has full bottom-up support. Consider these key questions:

1. How fast do decisions get made and policies executed? Are the processes involved under constant review and continuous reform?
2. Are managers and others praised and rewarded for innovative ideas turned into successful action? Is innovation an organizational and individual priority?
3. Are the measurement and reward systems aligned to business objectives, and are the measures presented in a simple form that everybody can understand?
4. Does the assessment of managers include the productivity of their people—and the latter's upward assessment of their bosses?
5. Are there clear and ambitious goals for the business, and does everybody agree with the aims—and have clear and ambitious goals for themselves?
6. Can individuals make a real difference to outcomes, and are they encouraged to do so?
7. Are mistakes treated as opportunities for learning—and not as occasions for punishment?
8. Does everybody contribute to the strategic thinking of the organization?
9. Is the company deeply committed to outdoing the competition in all important and measurable ways, and does it insist on continuous improvement on all important measures (notably those affecting the customer)?

The bad aspect of too many organizations isn't that they can't honestly answer yes to all nine questions, but that the questions simply never get asked. That's especially tragic because implementing the change from no to yes is relatively simple and inexpensive under all nine headings: while the benefits of, say, cutting down the number of levels through which decisions must pass are obvious and immediate—and that last word, "immediate," is vital.

That's why my heart sank when in spring 1994 IBM chairman Lou Gerstner warned that recovery would only take place "over time" and not "overnight." Often, change programs are given very long time-horizons. It's essential, though, to achieve fast, overnight improvements that are measurable and recognized, not least because of the impact on morale, but also because nobody knows what will happen in three years' time. The future, remember, is a series of presents running in sequence.

The longer you delay in achieving evident transformation, the greater the danger of creating a widening gap between rhetoric and reality. The rhetoric-reality gap is twin to what Ben Rosen, the chairman of Compaq, calls a "differential": that is, a divergence between what management wants (or, still worse, says is happening) and results in the real world. If you find yourself explaining away the gaps, either belittling their importance or blaming them on circumstances beyond your control, you are treading into highly dangerous ground.

That way lie smugness, complacency, and arrogance, the deadly enemies of success. That's why recognizing the "differentials" and acting to remove them are so important. Rosen believes that this new habit is the strongest reason for hoping that Compaq will never again encounter the crisis, similar in some respects to IBM's, which drove it into loss. In other words, the present management must act like an incoming group, facing up to unsatisfactory outcomes, assuming that internal faults are to blame, and acting swiftly to eradicate them.

As a case study of what happens when self-delusion takes over, Porsche is the perfect (or imperfect) example. Management sat by and watched for ten years while sales of its sports cars, once world leaders, fell from over 50,000 a year to just 14,300 in 1993. The underlying failure was basic: over-reliance on the increasingly ancient 911 as new model development languished.

The new chief executive, Dr. Wendelin Wiedeking, certainly adopted organization change in the structural sense: a new board, reduction of the first six management layers to four, and reform of the world sales organization. In the process, a third of the managers were fired or redeployed. Yet none of this drastic action, with two thousand jobs lost overall, could be effective without deeper and wider change. The 911 now takes 30 percent fewer man-hours to make than in mid-1991: but eighty-five man-hours is still 70 percent higher than the rival Japanese norm.

Wisely, the Porsche management turned to Japan for help, using a team headed by a man who held the top engineering post at Toyota. Workers apparently responded extremely well after early doubts. But Porsche management was half-expecting a less cooperative attitude once the crisis was past. If that happens, it won't have listened properly to its own production director, who told the *Financial Times* that "we have to use the crisis to change things, not just saw off heads."

That sentence could only be improved in one respect. The company needs to change, not "things," but *everything*. Even continuous improvement, which Wiedeking wanted to implant permanently before the crisis momentum was lost, isn't enough by itself. Rather, you have to adopt the attitude expressed by Michael Bloomberg, whose Bloomberg Financial Markets has become the fastest-growing provider of financial information in Wall Street—breaking successfully into a market dominated by Reuters.

That dominance didn't worry Bloomberg a bit: "Whenever you see a business that's done the same thing for a long time, a new guy can come in and do it better. I guarantee it." The "new guy" mentality is precisely what I recommended above: but the newness must be shown by better behaviors as well as better business ideas. Companies setting out on long-range cultural change programs too often forget that attitudes are much harder to change than conduct. What difference would these Bloomberg ideas make to your outfit?

1. No private secretaries, not even for the boss
2. No private offices, and all partitions made of glass
3. No job titles, even on business cards
4. No entrance from the elevators to two of the three office floors—so that people are forced to mingle
5. No sales commissions, but instead bonus certificates that give employees a share in revenue growth that adds 25 to 100 percent to salary
6. No signing powers for non-payroll checks and contracts for anybody, save Michael Bloomberg

That last insistence ensures that the proprietor knows everything that's happening. There's more than a whiff of autocracy. But that has its uses—something which mustn't be overlooked in the wholly justified enthusiasm for participation and empowerment. As Rosen says, speaking of the impact of Eckhard Pfeiffer as Compaq's CEO, "It's been a learning experience for me" to see "the difference a single person can make to a large organization." Paradoxically, it's the ultimate test of democracy: can it produce strong leaders who can lead with the full consent and participation of the led?

That leadership will have to be of the kind Bloomberg advocates, in which top management recognizes that all ideas don't come from your "smart people." He says that his "main job is to keep us from developing a structure that will preclude a kid we just hired from walking through the door and saying, 'Why not try this?' " In that one sentence, you get the truth about organizational change in a nutshell. Getting the structure and the numbers right is the first step, and very important: but animating the structure to achieve the right actions by rightly motivated people is vital.

That's a central purpose of any organization, and any organizational change—to create so thriving and developing an organic activity that the organization can provide excellent, well-paid employment for all its people, and renew them continually with new blood. That's why GE's Welch has been attempting (see Part Five, Chapter 5) to harness energies right through the corporation, including the shop floor. That demands a painful act: the abdication of power. *Fortune* magazine once enumerated five kinds of power that top managers can exercise over their subordinates:

1. Rewarding, by word, pay, or promotion
2. Punishing, by word, discipline, demotion, or expulsion
3. Exercising authority—either specific (i.e., the power of "signing-off" on a decision) or tacit (if the boss doesn't like it, nothing happens; if he does, it does)
4. Deploying expertise—the greatest expert has the most powerful say in the area concerned
5. The reverence paid to a leader, for whatever reason, by others in the organization

The magazine thought that the last two powers had waxed as the first three—automatic, even autocratic powers—had waned. That waning must become increasingly apparent as horizontal, product, or project-based teams, as at GE, cut across both functional and national boundaries. Team groupings, carried to their logical conclusion, depower the center. Its remaining and fundamental role is to exercise and delegate a sixth power: the power to lead people in chosen and supported directions that will safeguard and enhance their futures.

That power involves the choice of both the ends and the means ("the way we do things around here") that will optimize contribution and generate satisfaction internally—and externally, where the customers live. As service quality experts stress, and as the correlation of new job creation with increases in profits suggests, the external and internal go hand in hand, just like the two forms of organizational change.

"Hollowing the corporation" (by hiving off all possible activities to outside contractors), "rationalizing" (by hiving off whole businesses), and "downsizing" or "right-sizing" (by hiving off employees) are all euphemisms. They add up to a total process known as "deconstruction." It can too easily turn to destruction. If so, the results are hollow indeed. But use the sixth power properly in the interests of all the people, by using all of the people, and you should never need euphemisms.

The Hollowness
of Sun

Nobody has taken the strategy of concentrating on "core competencies" further than Sun Microsystems. The workstations champ no
longer runs its own distribution, makes its own chips, services its
own machines, manufactures its own components. All it does is design chips, software, and workstations, which others make and Sun
markets. It has truly "hollowed out" the business—and it's by no
means alone.

The new trend is for corporations to minimize both assets and
overheads by playing a sophisticated game of pass-the-parcel: they
"out-source," not only central services (like information technology)
that can easily be purchased from others, but also much of their production. Some use the term "modular" to describe out-and-out out-
sourcers, companies like athletic shoe pioneer Nike; PC marketer
Dell (which for a while maintained a streak of 100 percent quarterly
increases in sales and profits); or Exabyte, which sells computer tape
drives, and has multiplied sales a hundredfold and employment twen-
tyfold, without building a single plant.

Against that background, it's easy to understand the strategic shift at Brooks Brothers, the U.S. menswear chain, in wholly ceasing manufacture. In 1988, the company was acquired by Britain's Marks and Spencer, which has been "modular" in this sense from its very beginning. None of the goods bearing the M&S chain's omnipresent St. Michael label are made in its factories; it has never had any. But the garments are designed, the cloth purchased, and the manufacturing methods laid down by the retailer. There's two-way traffic; M&S will accept improvements suggested by its suppliers. But the tune is called by the paying piper.

Private-label retailing, which all stores practice to a greater or lesser extent, isn't really out-sourcing, though. That term applies far more to electronics manufacturers, whose products, by their nature, are assemblies. Because of the complex, specialized technologies involved, nobody could hope to make every component themselves, which is the extreme form of "vertical integration." Rather, in computery you can, like Sun, be almost 100 percent "horizontal"— buying in virtually every manufacturing item, and most corporate services, from outside suppliers.

Like digital watches before them, personal computers have become a "Mickey Mouse" business: the labels and the advertising are different, but the contents of products purporting to come from different manufacturers are to all intents and purposes identical. The same trend applies in lesser degree to most businesses: the proportions of manufactured items bought in from outsiders have risen universally. And the tendency to disband in-house service departments in favor of outsiders is also widespread.

Does that equate with a powerful new management principle? In the supply of manufactured goods, few leaders have wholeheartedly followed the rising Sun. Of the ten most admired U.S. corporations in *Fortune*'s 1993 poll, only fashion house Liz Claiborne is "horizontal" in that, like Marks and Spencer, it has no factories: it goes one further by having no stores, either. But the rest of the top ten include Merck, Rubbermaid, 3M, Coca-Cola, Procter & Gamble, Levi Strauss, and Boeing, all of which are highly committed to products and production alike. The same would be true of any similar list in Europe or Japan.

True, the degree of vertical integration has dropped sharply. Even IBM, which once neither bought from outside makers nor sold to them, now has products bearing nothing of its own save the label. But the truly hollow companies are in a different, new game—and a hazardous one. The hazard lies in the fact that they can only preserve their strength and fabulous sales per employee (Sun's are $280,000, 49 percent better than IBM's) so long as they set the pace, either by value or technology.

By definition, though, the technological lead must pass (indeed, in PCs has already passed) to component and peripheral makers. Many have stronger franchises than the systems suppliers who are their hosts. For instance, Hewlett-Packard won 43 percent of the $5.4 billion U.S. market for printers. Its major rivals come from Japan, whose strategy is similar: to achieve, in vital technologies, key components and high-selling peripherals, the same dominance that swept American and other Western companies out of other industries that the latter had created and controlled.

Hollow companies offer no competition to this powerful strategy. The hollow company is dangerously close to being a private-label wholesaler: the danger being that one day the retailers will cut out the hollow middleman with their own private labels. In an age which has learned the vital importance of breaking down the boundaries between design, engineering, manufacturing, and marketing, the hollow corporation not only separates out key functions, but places many outside the firm.

Out-sourcing can, true, produce spectacular savings in overhead. For instance, the Swiss-Swedish electrical power group, ABB, reduced the 6,000 people once housed in two head offices to 150. Almost a third of the departed went into new service companies, set up quasi-independently to provide HQ functions on a contractual, profit-making basis. In this new world, the function of managers isn't only to manage their own people. They must manage relationships with suppliers—and with customers—to achieve the best outcomes for their own businesses. But that can only be done by maximizing the results won throughout the entire business system.

The Virtues of Virtuality

4

In 1993 Steelcase, the major U.S. furniture company, went ahead with plans to break into the fast-growing market for supplying home offices and small businesses. To crack this new nut, the company established a new venture, Turnstone, that would take its orders over the phone. The selling proposition was that the happy customers would get the furniture of their desire *within five days.* Virtually unbelievable, you may think: and virtual is the word.

The Turnstone offer isn't simply an example of highly efficient customer service. The efficiency is only a consequence of something that sounds much grander: the venture has been established as an example of *The Virtual Corporation.* That's the title of a book, co-authored by William H. Davidow and Michael S. Malone, that describes its subject thus: "To the outside observer, a virtual corporation will appear almost edgeless, the interface between company, supplier and customers permeable and continuously changing."

The definition may appear slightly edgeless, too, but not to Turnstone. Its task is to deliver real, virtual products, "produced instantaneously and customized in response to customer demand" with the intimate aid of partner-suppliers. The company thus doesn't stop at its own boundaries. Virtuality goes beyond the now familiar importance of regarding the ultimate customer as the starting point for the business system. Every supplier, it's now argued, and sometimes practiced, should be regarded as part of your company.

Even that doesn't broaden the concept enough. If you subscribe to the theory of "virtual corporations," you believe, to quote *Business Week,* "in a single entity with vast capabilities" that "will really be the result of numerous collaborations assembled only when they are needed." In this concept, the future of the business is determined, not simply by its own strengths ("key competencies," in the jargon), but by its shifting alliances with outside partners.

In a business that's run according to the precepts of virtuality, the company does far more than make brilliantly fast deliveries of customized orders. It takes in a whole raft of techniques and trends to change processes and practices, but not in isolation. You have to tackle the system in the round. And you need the full resources of the information revolution for that purpose. The virtual corporation is inevitably built around and sustained by its data processing systems, even unto its people management.

Would you, for example, be prepared to install "a computer system to track the daily objectives of every company employee"? In this way, T. J. Rodgers, who heads the aggressive Cypress Semiconductor, chosen by IBM to weaken Intel's microprocessor hold, can dispense with middle managers and personally review the progress of 1,500 employees against their ten or fifteen goals *every week*. It takes about four hours, he claims, and the employees need only thirty minutes to update their lists—no doubt reflecting the helpful phone calls which Rodgers makes to the laggards.

This example from Davidow and Malone is at the high end of the virtuality spectrum. The gains available at a lower, more technical level are by no means negligible. For example, what about a 25 percent rise in sales, and a 67 percent improvement in stockturn, leading to 25 percent more gross profit? These results for a jacket and slacks maker flowed from giving all members of the supply chain instant access to retail and wholesale data on sales, orders, and inventories. Response can thus be instant (or "quick," in the virtuality jargon) and instantly profitable.

There's also a carpet retailer whose costs fell by 13 percent after accepting a supplier's offer to meet orders daily—and, what's more, deliver direct to the customer. The retailer needed some considerable persuasion. That's generally the case, as the Swiss chemical giant Ciba found in trying to get a German intermediate supplier to collaborate on quality. The Swiss met with a flat "Nein," maintained over two years. Then the supplier capitulated, not to the force of reason, but to the fact that all its customers were making the same demand.

Lady Thatcher's famous nostrum, TINA (there is no alternative), had triumphed over inertia. The old ways are more than systems: they are states of mind. Very few managers find it natural or comfortable to rethink: that is, to challenge the intellectual (and emotional) bases of the way they operate, even though rethinking offers large, and often cheap, scope for improvement.

As with Ciba's German supplier, though, the day-to-day pressures of the management task are forcing companies into the radical modes—facilitated by their information technology systems—that Davidow and Malone identify as the essence of their virtual corporations. For every company, quickness of response is now of the essence: it should govern every process and the provision of every product and service. And it can't be won through the traditional adversarial relationship between supplier and manufacturer.

That tradition is "dead," says David Bundred, of Britain's Lucas Industries. He believes that "strategic sourcing, supplier relationships networking, and partnership relationships are the future." One by one, the planks of the old purchasing policies, marked by constant wars, with price as the casus belli, have been ripped out: because today, customers want the "variety, velocity, quality, and cost-competitiveness" that can only be provided through collaboration.

The new demands are revolutionizing not only external relationships, but internal ones. That's because "openness, equality, and partnership have to extend to functions within companies." In some cases, the internal and external partnerships are formed willy-nilly. As noted in the previous chapter, there are advanced products (PCs being an acute example) which contain nothing but bought-in components, and where alternative suppliers may simply not exist. In other cases, the competitive advantages of cooperation are simply too great to ignore.

The issue for managers is not whether they desert the Old Guard and join the revolution. Rather, it is whether they move forward by progressive steps, responding to the current and future pressures, or take a truly bold plunge into the future. Davidow and Malone naturally favor the brave course. All employees, they say, will have "to revise the way they deal with one another and with the outside world"—a tall order if ever there was one—for "the virtual corporation to appear here, now."

It's beginning to be seen. Companies are greatly shortening response times and achieving extraordinary, customer-led variations in what was once standard mass production. As managements adapt to the new necessities, using the same amazing tools of the information technology revolution, the very nature of management is changing. Just as the Ford-style assembly line has been outdated by developments like self-managed, flexible manufacturing cells, so hierarchical order-and-obey management has been overtaken by flexible, cellular working in changing, self-directed groups.

Virtual employees will be virtual self-managers, relying on information technology instead of middle management for the rapid transmission of messages back and forth. It's argued that the universal pressures are intensifying to an either-or degree: either companies adapt to the new imperatives of virtuality, or they will be overwhelmed. The challenge can't be met by simple downsizing. Such cutbacks, however swingeing, are self-defeating unless they march in step with adoption of the new processes.

Is the virtual corporation more than the apotheosis of Bundred's purchasing revolution? Davidow and Malone claim that virtual managers will do more: they will have the ability to master the information tools of today—and tomorrow. "Further increases in computer power enable us to predict the future, to predict behaviors, to perform simulations, and to take virtual walks through design." The dream is that manufacture, testing, and distribution of goods and services will be pulled together into a simultaneous, instantaneous whole.

The problem for most managers is to identify their own futures in this glorious vision. Obviously, a manufacturer who can (like Toyota today) produce a new car to detailed customer specification within seventy-two hours has a serious competitive advantage over one who takes seventy-two days. In high-tech electronics, too, state-of-the-art manufacture and the quickest responses are obligatory: otherwise, you're out of business.

The virtuality doctrine, however, argues that nobody is exempt. Sooner or later, the smartest competitor will learn to deliver a markedly better product or service cheaper and faster. Against such competition, laggards—costlier, slower, and deficient in quality—can't long survive. Indeed, that's why several American industries (a matter that greatly concerns Davidow) have slumped in face of Japanese competition.

"Believing in the post-industrial myth," he says, "we have let our manufacturing industries decline." Future economic power depends on spearheading the further stages of a manufacturing revolution which the Japanese have led. For their lead to continue, though, would be deeply anomalous, given that the fundamental technologies, still exploding along an exponential growth curve, are dominated by the United States.

American thinkers likewise dominate the theory of virtual management, in which the corporation "is going to employ its customers as co-producers in everything," and "to find itself increasingly customer-managed." In practice, Japanese companies were the first to form customer-supplier alliances: but leading Western companies are now going much further into integrating internal computer systems with external suppliers of information—right down to the individual customer.

While much of the virtuality thesis concentrates on the new technologies that make these advances possible, "simple organizational innovation will be as important to the virtual engineering process as all of the computer power we can bring to bear." The Japanese successes in world markets were largely won in the mind, not the laboratory. It's the willpower to take advantage of invention, innovation, and intelligence, and the understanding of the human role in exploiting change, that are crucial.

The facts of the virtuality case are self-evident and surely decisive. But decision-makers must surmount some uncomfortably high hurdles. Take the supplier-customer relationship, where collaborative intimacy is basic to virtuality. Exchange of sensitive information and the relegation of price in priority are wholly foreign to traditional, secretive, untrusting, and price-dominated ways of doing business.

Similarly, empowered workers who are able to make the decision to respond to customers are another requisite: the new working methods presuppose responsiveness and creative input at all levels. These conditions can never be achieved in a multilayered command hierarchy. Virtuality is advocating a socio-political revolution in inter-company and customer relationships and within the firm. As practical observers, though, Davidow and Malone see the difficulties and the time-lags—as does Bundred.

Speaking to a conference on purchasing, logistics, and supply, Bundred introduced a sour note of reality: "I have to say from personal experience that the old system is a long time dying, and the corpse has a habit of sitting up and hitting me." The purchasing people concerned can't be blamed entirely. They are prisoners of corporate systems that are geared to the earlier technology. Manufacturers once made unchanged products in enormous runs on inflexible production lines, buying in supplies only of basic materials and standard components. They generally made the more complex components in-house, often as a deliberate counterweight to external suppliers.

Whether in-house alternatives existed or not, companies liked to have several alternative sources, not only so that one could be played off against another, but to eliminate the risk of dependence. That still sounds entirely logical to most managers. Incorrect policies often do have the at-first-sight semblance of sense. Yet real supplier partnerships are slowly being constructed, despite the odds against them, and relationships of trust are likely to develop externally, as they will between managers and others inside the organization.

That should happen out of sheer necessity, as managers make the transition to lean, adaptive, information-based organizations. But will they? Davidow and Malone worry about the "unwillingness of management to surrender its control." However, political and economic revolutions create their own dynamism. The forces the authors vividly identify are hard at work within organizations which, in all outward respects, appear to contradict their thesis.

Look, for example, at the compulsions on car makers, no matter how hidebound they may be in other ways. Today they are forced to depend utterly on single sub-assemblies produced by a sole supplier who may well have conceived the design, and whose quality and reliability are crucial to the model's success. In company after company, industry after industry, the practical necessity of velocity, value, quality, and cost-competitiveness is forcing de facto partnerships of the kind that virtuality demands.

The breakdown of hierarchy and emergence of project-based teamwork are likewise being urged on by events. Ask any assembly of managers if they have recently been involved in project groups, and half are likely to say yes. On the shop floor, too, virtuality's responsive, self-managed teamwork is appearing, not because the theory attracts managers, but because irresistible practical improvements in costs, flexibility, and productivity are available. Competitive necessity, too, is forcing all managers and processes towards full, computerized participation in the knowledge-based reinvention of management.

Is there an alternative to that reinvention? Obviously, the pace of change varies greatly from industry to industry and from company to company. In the slower-moving areas, managers can go peacefully about their old business, confident that the old ways will see them through. Their conservatism, though, encompasses a fateful error. The company that revolutionizes its supplier relationships, remember, will have lower costs, faster response times, and happier customers.

Other things (like making the right products) being equal, that must also mean higher profits. Or as Bundred puts it, "An open, honest relationship between equal partners in the supply chain is the only way of optimizing the performance of the supply chain." Similarly, within companies "the only way of achieving velocity in design and manufacture is to break down the old barriers and rebuild new relationships" by adopting "simultaneous engineering." That means all functions working together in teams from the start and is "about relationships," not technology.

The denial of new-century management is thus akin to the Luddite resistance to new technology. It's the technology of management that's at stake here. The Luddites of management risk the same fate as the new-technology air conditioners invented in the United States, or the electronic watch movements pioneered in Switzerland. The pioneers abandoned the new-found territory, which was promptly occupied by rivals (in both cases, the Japanese). There are moments in business history when dramatic change breaks with the past—and when those who don't join the future are finished. Variety, velocity, quality, and cost-competitiveness now apply to everything. As a result, the management game has new rules:

1. Expect upheaval: when analyzing your strengths, weaknesses, opportunities, and threats, also analyze those of your competitors—and of a hypothetical new competitor using new technology, new distribution, new pricing, and so forth.
2. Invest in any technology or methodology that promises (or threatens) to create significant change, so that, if and when the moment comes, you are not caught unprepared.
3. Create flexibility, so that the organization isn't locked into a modus operandi that can only be changed after long delay and at excessive cost, which you may not be able to afford.
4. When the moment of change comes, move fast: forget the past and move boldly into the new era.
5. Accept that pain may well result: better to make the sacrifice yourself than to be knifed by the competition.
6. Live by the ideal of virtuality, where quickness of response is of the essence, governing every process and the provision of every product and service.

The fact that much truly revolutionary activity is already going on has its flip side: the activity is usually piecemeal and uncoordinated. One part of an organization may be striding forward, while others are stuck muddily in the past. The task before top management is that of creating an overall context in which all the elements of virtuality are bound together. Davidow notes, rightly enough, that electronics "holds the keys to the virtual revolution." But only good and modern management, based on commonsense analysis, can open the gates.

The Logistics of Desert Storm

5

In 1992, the chairman of British Petroleum, Robert Horton, set going a program, Project 90, to change the corporate culture. Horton had made his mark running the giant BP subsidiary in the United States, and was determined to revamp the parent company in the same dynamic and purposive manner. According to the *Financial Times,* "layers of bureaucracy" were to be stripped away to make the company "more responsive to market conditions."

"Like all reorganizations," wrote the paper, "it has left some people very unhappy." Critics alleged that removing the middle management layers had "isolated top management from other employees and that the company lacks firm direction"—the very opposite of what the culture change was presumably meant to achieve. Real world and ideal had failed to mesh. According to one sensationally successful American manager, that's an inevitable result of "the worst thing a corporation can do," but which boards "insist" on doing. The sin? To reorganize.

The top manager taking this unorthodox view is William "Gus" Pagonis. If the name is unfamiliar, his last managerial achievement is not. Lieutenant General Pagonis ran the logistics side of Desert Storm to spectacular effect. He differentiates between reorganization and ensuring that "the right structure" is in place. Instead of reorganizing, which produces "tremendous challenges from within the organization," the Pagonis team only "tailored." The general believes that "you have to learn to take an existing organization structure and modify it to meet your demands. If you make drastic changes you cannot go back to rely on a lot of other things that you may need later."

In other words, don't throw the baby out with the bath water. By no coincidence, GM and IBM reorganized heavily in their time of troubles—troubles which only got deeper. The possible explanations are that the reshuffles didn't address the right problems; or addressed the right problems too late, by which time they had become the wrong problems; or fell foul of the Pagonis trap, doing at least as much harm as good. The explanations aren't mutually contradictory: all three failures can be observed in both the above cases.

But reorganization isn't the sole prerogative of large corporate managements. Upheaval in small concerns can be equally disruptive, and that's a pejorative word. But should it be? How can you change a culture if it's fixed in organizational cement? What if you agree (and it's hard not to) with the Canadian manager who observed that "The minute you establish an organization, it starts to decay"? If that's so, constantly shaking up the organization sounds like the only way to avoid decay and generate innovation.

The Pagonis answer is that organization and organizational performance are separate issues. The interview he gave to McKinsey's Graham Sharman, published in the consultancy's *McKinsey Quarterly,* deserves careful reading by all managers. No organization suffers more than the military from "the chain of command in the inevitable constraints of a large organization." But that didn't stop Pagonis from using three-by-five cards and "please see me" slots to flatten, not the organization, but the way in which it operated.

Similarly, the organization didn't tell Pagonis how to conduct his literally "stand-up" meetings. No more than fifteen key staff met every morning, and, not being allowed to sit, got the meeting over within half an hour. "Please see me" means that everybody who wants to see the boss has an appointment which will be kept, whatever his rank. The little three-by-five cards convey information and problems: out of a thousand averaged every day during Desert Storm, only sixty got all the way to Pagonis—the rest were handled lower down.

Other hot non-organization tips include holding regular top management meetings that only use charts which people normally maintain: nothing is developed just for the meeting, which is kept to one hour. Then, Pagonis insisted that his "managers" present him with three "ups" and three "downs"—the latter being things that are going awry. The ups that were going right encouraged them to tackle the downs and turn them into ups, thus both improving performance and helping to save Pagonis from unpleasant surprises.

Note that all the Pagonis methods are to do with process, not with procedure, and were dedicated to outcomes, to getting from A to B. The reorganizations of which the general so strongly disapproves are concerned with procedure, not process: with structure, not conduct. In one sense, the reorganizers are right—structure does determine behavior. The paradox is that those who concentrate on structure for its own sake end up with the bad behavior they deserve.

Down the Organization

6

The famous line about heavyweight boxers maintains that the bigger they are, the harder they fall. That certainly seems to apply to many gigantic corporations in these early years of the 1990s. The two largest industrial corporations in the United States, and thus the world, General Motors and IBM, have made unprecedented losses; the two largest securities firms, Salomon on Wall Street and Nomura in Japan, have been humbled by scandal; Italy's three leading European groups, Fiat, Pirelli, and Olivetti, have all been suffering. Are these events, and the many other big-is-ugly examples, linked together by a common factor?

One link is clear—the gap between the aims of big-company organizations and what actually happens in the real world. General Gus Pagonis is evidently right: organizational form and organizational behavior are not one and the same thing. As an example from civilian management shows, if you sincerely want results, you get them, by organizing to do so. What would employees in your organization answer to these questions?

1. What cost reduction are you currently working on?
2. Who is the enemy (i.e., the competition)?
3. Have you met with your management in the past six months?
4. Do you understand the economics of your job?

According to Charles F. Knight, chairman of Emerson Electric, every one of his employees can answer these questions—and the claim appears to be true. His company, an electrical manufacturer with forty divisions, improved earnings and earnings per share every year for thirty-four years: the EPS rise averaged 11.8 percent annually, yielding shareholders an average annual return of 19.1 percent. It's a sophisticated and highly organized business. Yet those questions can be asked, and should be answered, in any firm, regardless of size or structure.

As Knight wrote in the *Harvard Business Review* (January–February 1992), effectiveness is a matter of *process:* the same discovery was made by General Electric when it sought an explanation for the higher productivity of other companies. Knight says that "effective management process" is "what makes us 'tick' at Emerson." He defines process under three headings:

1. Shaping the future by careful planning for improved results and strong follow-up—executing to get them
2. Setting shared values, "including involvement, intensity, discipline, and persistence," to drive the process
3. Establishing policies and techniques, few unique or unusual—but *acting* on them, which "may indeed be unusual"

Within this PFVA process (planning, follow-up, values, and action), Emerson holds to beliefs that are heavily endorsed by my own observations. First, profitability is a state of mind: what you expect, and work for, is what you get. Second, companies fail primarily because "management knows what to do but, for some reason, doesn't do it." Third, the long-term consists of a number of short terms added together, and poor short-term performance makes long-term achievement more difficult. Fourth, keep it simple—which is much more difficult than it sounds.

Long ago, I expressed that third thought in virtually identical language. At its most elementary level, the thought is enshrined in Geneen's Law, which holds that hitting the first quarter's budget targets is all-important: miss them, and you almost never catch up in the next three. Many managers have confirmed this truth, which, since it comes from Harold S. Geneen of ITT, history's most determined exponent of MBB (management by budget), is based on many years of tough (very tough) experience in the field.

The task is to manage to achieve short-term success while building (and never jeopardizing) achievement in the middle and long terms. This Geneen patently failed to do, despite a record run of rises in earnings per share. The higher figures squeezed out of ITT's operating managers concealed a decline in competitive power in the core telecommunications business, plus a host of ill-advised, over-diversifying, over-costly acquisitions, that brought Nemesis in Geneen's wake.

His inquisitorial insistence on financial performance generated a pattern of behavior among managers which was marked by fear and ambition, in roughly equal quantities. Notoriously, one consequence was that, starting the usual three-year assignment, the incoming divisional or affiliate executive would disparage his predecessor's figures. Having established the lowest possible base for his first year, the newcomer would then show spectacular second-year gains. These would be sustained into year three by the same profit-boosting practices as those adopted by the predecessor—like postponing investment or cutting back on the marketing spend.

Like ITT, Emerson is big on charts and presentations, but that's where the similarity stops. The latter's four planning guides are a much more interesting bunch philosophically. The "Value Measurement Chart" looks at "value creation" under two main headings: (1) growth rate and capital requirements, and (2) rate of return, by amounts and by percentages, five years back, current year, and five years forward. The idea is to show at a glance the answer to a question every business and part of a business should answer: *Is the business adding value for its owners?*

The "Sales Gap Chart" analyzes current-year sales in standard form and projects them forward four years to discover whether the forecasts will meet the group's targets: if not, a sales gap will show up on the accompanying line chart, and the operating managers must say how it will be closed. In the process, they must answer some key questions which, in many businesses, are never asked:

In each of the next five years, in money terms,

1. What's the likely rise or decline in the industry served?
2. What's your present and predicted market penetration?
3. What will price increases add to your sales year by year?
4. What sales will you make from new products or services added *(a)* in the previous five years *(b)* in the next five?
5. How will these money numbers translate into percentage growth rates?

The fourth chart is a P&L chart, looking at current year profit and loss, and relating them to the previous five years and to the five years planned ahead. This eleven-year view throws up trends in sales, gross profit margins, operating expenses and margins, capital turnover, and returns both on sales and capital. Its key importance is the long view: if you're managing for continuous high performance consistently maintained, this isn't an optional exercise.

What's done by managers, in a nutshell, must be consistent with what they want to achieve. In organization terms, what General Pagonis calls "the right structure" and I call "the setup" is crucial. As an example from Desert Storm, General Schwarzkopf insisted that one person (Pagonis) be in charge of all logistics, as opposed to the divided responsibility of all previous campaigns. As Pagonis says, "decentralization without somebody being held responsible does not work."

The need, in his words, is "centralized control and decentralized execution"—the organization mustn't get in the way. But neither must reorganization. The three upheavals through which IBM has passed in the last decade, for example, must have left a broad trail of insecurity, confusion, and career destruction (like the GM changes over the same period). That heavy price, moreover, was paid for often highly negative results. It's a most cautionary tale.

Christopher Lorenz of the *Financial Times* tells another about a Swedish IT company, Enacor. It took the fashionable injunction "flatten the hierarchy" so much to heart that it "ended up confused, undisciplined, and directionless." Enacor has brought back central functions and controls in an effort to have the best of both worlds: the flexibility and speed of response that competition (and human satisfaction) demand, together with the control and discipline that are essential to mobilize all the company's material and human resources in the same cause.

If the organization is shown to be inflexible and sluggish in vital processes, its overlords customarily react by pressing the buttons within their central reach: they cut out peripheral or unprofitable operations; they merge, acquire, form alliances, shed managers and blue-collar workers, demand budget cuts, devise new strategies, promulgate new corporate nostrums. However virtuous the approach sounds, it can still have vicious outcomes.

At United Technologies, which didn't save the company from later trouble, CEO Bob Daniell adopted the three-point thrust of flattening the hierarchy, empowering the workers, and getting close to the customers—while training intensively at all levels to do so. Yet one of UT's main subsidiaries, Carrier, lost market share to Japanese competitors in nigh-unbelievable amounts through desperate lags in technology, productive efficiency, and customer satisfaction.

This degeneration began before Daniell's three-pronged initiative and continued after. Nor was the UT malaise confined to Carrier, with the result that, by mid-1993, UT's market value, instead of a respectable parity, was a mere quarter of sales. Did Daniell have anything like Emerson's five-years-back, five-years-forward analysis to show how reality and central perception diverged? What happens in the bad examples follows a pattern that many managers will recognize—and with some pain:

- "Initial management thrusts have wrought great change in your organization, but as attention has shifted to other priorities, old behaviors have reasserted themselves. There is a word for this phenomenon in manufacturing—snapback.
- You have tried to make changes through training or other interventions and found that you have had little or no lasting impact, despite using some of the best internal or external trainers or consultants.
- Staff seem really motivated to behave in a particular (and you

think productive) way, yet for much of the time they actually behave in very unproductive ways."

The writers of that passage, Chloe Cox and Alan Mossman,
observe that "if you have chronic problems with organizational or individual behavior, the chances are that the underlying structures of
your organization do not support the behavior you want—they cause
the unwanted behavior you are getting." General Pagonis concentrated on "resolving behavior," which gets from A to B: in contrast,
the structures created and re-created by the corpocrats encourage
"oscillating behavior," which moves backwards and forwards between
A and B.

The management thinker Robert Fritz, in his book *Corporate
Tides,* describes precisely what happened at IBM. The desire to
change led to changes being introduced, which created a big yearning
for stability, which produced an even greater need for changes—
which only produced another contradictory oscillation. Within this
context, the gains from individual improvements were lost, simply
because the wrong behaviors were being supported by the system.
Remove that support, and the behaviors can change marvelously.

At one operation that I've recently studied, British Airways Engineering, management had previously forced through classic surgical reorganization: thousands of jobs had gone, and control and
discipline had been vigorously imposed on the remaining eight thousand employees. Productivity had risen sharply, but not efficiency.
The CEO was still deeply dissatisfied, not only by the inefficiencies,
but by the atmosphere, or culture, which contributed to the poor
processes and threatened the improvements made by the tough management of the past.

Management decided to tackle the processes, and let the culture
take care of itself. Instead of anything newfangled, the treatment applied was the tried and trusty Kepner-Tregoe method, which is dedicated to the improvement of process:

1. You appraise the situation to sort out the various concerns: you
    analyze the problem to find the cause.
2. You use decision analysis to make a choice.

3. You analyze potential problems to ensure success of the action or plan.
4. You manage involvement to ensure commitment through getting the right people in on the act.

Looking at the great company failures reveals at once that none of these essential stages has been successfully completed—in some cases, not even tried. To cite a single example, Ford's model development time in Europe was quoted in 1993 as *six years.* That's double the time taken by the Japanese, and two years longer than Ford's best performance in the United States. Speed to market plainly wasn't a priority in Ford of Europe. Why not? What was the cause?

The logical procedure advocated by K-T could well have done for Ford what was accomplished for the clients in BA Engineering: a dramatic drop in costs, an equally impressive rise in performance, and a surge of released morale. Note that this wasn't accompanied by "reorganization": the formal structure stayed the same. What was done within the structure changed so dramatically that oscillating behavior was replaced by resolution.

The critical step was for management to descend to the shop floor and, through the consultants, ask the engineers what they needed to improve their performance. Acting on that information (which revealed a tangle of failures) by itself effectively changed an order-and-obey structure to an advise-and-consent one. The engineers were now trusted to use their new tools of analysis and implementation to achieve results. Process had triumphed.

That's why the very same matrix structures (organizing by product, region, and function) that are a recognized cause of grave troubles in Western companies work fine at Japanese groups like Canon—because the processes within Canon's matrix are simply superior. So are Emerson's. For a start, it seeks to make all its systems dynamic, including the "POR," the "President's Operating Report," which updates the expected annual results *every month,* and always covers five quarters.

Continuous cost reduction is equally progressive: each Emerson division has a target, averaging about 7 percent of sales; 70 to 80 percent of the sources of reduction are identified before the year even starts. Such hard-nosed approaches are better than experimenting with softer means, such as appraisal systems. That's not to denigrate soft means: they, too, can have the required element of dynamism.

For example, one GM unit has launched an initiative to tie compensation to the achievement of a one-for-all group culture. But the would-be management reinventors faced a Herculean, uphill struggle—which was none of their doing. The unit, Powertrain, supplies the "big car" group, and, says *The New York Times,* the "new appraisal and compensation plan has *survived three* [my italics] Powertrain reorganizations." Efforts to achieve resolving behavior, in other words, were being made within a violently oscillating context.

By 1994, the swings (especially in the booming car market) were so strongly upward that in October *Fortune* hailed CEO Jack Smith for feats at GM that "rank him with the legendary Alfred P. Sloan." The most featured feat was an $11 billion turnaround, but virtually all of that was the elimination of losses, not the creation of new profits. GM lost market share, and the October strike at Buick City, when overworked employees reacted against "trying to build too much product with two few people," highlighted the defects of downsizing instead of rebuilding, of running a corporation by central edict rather than local initiative, energy, and understanding.

The "worst thing a corporation can do," to use Pagonis's phrase, is to stifle its own energies, and time and again, that's precisely what the reorganizing centralists do. The disorganizing decentralizers are coming into their own. And their ideas make more than sense. They make money.

THREE

The Road to Reinvention: How to Change Cultures

The

Reinventions of IBM

1

In the spring of 1994, more than two years after John F. Akers had launched his latest attempt to "reinvent" IBM, his successor, Lou Gerstner, delivered a damning verdict. The new man's first year in office had convinced him that IBM, having "failed to keep pace with significant change in the industry" and "been way too slow getting new things to the market," had "been too bureaucratic and too preoccupied with our own view of the world." Those were precisely the defects that "reinvention" had been designed to cure.

What went wrong? Was it just IBM? Or is there a fatal flaw in the concept of "reinventing"? The magazine writer who coined the phrase for the American corporate shake-ups of the eighties and nineties struck a rich vein. It put a brave face on hard facts. Some once-great business had become mired in stagnant sales, declining profits, lagging technology, and waning competitive prowess. Now a management reared in obsolete traditions was expected to match, better still surpass, the achievements of the best performers in Japan.

The phrase "reinvent" perfectly suited the situation and the public relations need. The corporation had been "invented" by some founding genius like IBM's Thomas Watson, Sr. Now his heirs had to start, like him, from a blank sheet of paper. They might write off much of the inheritance, they might throw more of it away, just like an engineer reengineering an engine. The end result would be a new corporation, reinvented, free of the lumber of the past and full of the virtues of management renewed and reinvigorated.

The reinventors, in drawing a line between themselves and the past, were by implication stressing the faults of their predecessors and touting their own virtues, something to which managers (including Gerstner) are never averse. Up to a point, the blame does lie with their inheritance. But after a period of grace the heirs are on their own. That period is measured in years—but not eight of them, as at IBM. The mistakes and misdirections of that business as the nineties began belonged wholly to the existing management.

In mid-1992 David Kirkpatrick of *Fortune* delivered his verdict on the latest and most sweeping of the "reinventions" undertaken by the then CEO. Akers was finally attempting to "uproot a structure and culture formed when IBM had no serious competition. . . . But is he pressing the message hard enough to permeate this immense organization? Probably not."

A couple of months were spent interviewing analysts, consultants, customers, employees, leaders of competitors, and top IBM executives before reaching the verdict. How did they rate the widest-ranging reorganization and rehabilitation ever undertaken by a major corporation? The significance lies, not only in the verdict on Akers's reforms, but in the program content itself. It summarizes the conventional wisdom of reinvention:

1. Give more autonomy to individual businesses.
2. Remake the culture.
3. Shift the emphasis from products to services.
4. Emphasize customer satisfaction.
5. Cut back the payroll.
6. Reduce other direct and indirect costs.
7. Share risk and gain expertise through partnerships, where IBM has been extraordinarily active.

An eighth point is more relevant to IBM than other companies: Retain a single nationwide sales force. This plainly has an impact on the autonomy issue, but was heavily endorsed by Gerstner as the new CEO—along with all seven other planks. The ouster of Akers and his replacement by Gerstner didn't amount to rejection of the former's strategy of reinvention. Where Akers had failed, in the eyes of the board, investors, and his successor, was in wrong execution of the right strategy.

That failure of execution emerges clearly from *Fortune*'s overall grading of the reform program: a humble B−. That grade covered a wide range from A− for the handling of job losses to D for remaking the culture of complacency. The verdict was somewhat unfair. The latest and greatest reinvention had begun too recently to take full effect. But Akers had plainly failed to achieve the true object of reinvention: to change, not the organization, but the behavior of those within.

The telltale evidence of failure lies in large gulfs between words and deeds. Kirkpatrick's interviews uncovered plenty. Changing bad habits had been slow. To give one example, "temps hired in one Westchester office got only 45 minutes of work each day. When one asked to do more, she was told to bring a book like everybody else." That example, like most other defects that brought IBM its low grading, sprang from a culture whose faults persisted because of too much reinvention, not too little.

IBM's reinventors had constantly been forced to go back to the drawing board, confronted by clear evidence that the "new" company worked no better than the old. With each successive disappointment, external and internal comments on the reinventions became more grudging and guarded. You can understand the growing lack of enthusiasm of people confronted by a whole string of reinventions: contradictory ones, at that.

The irony could hardly be greater. The first reforms of the Akers reign in 1985 embodied a deliberate policy of centralization. The reformers sought to impose horizontal control across the vertical product divisions—in the fervently held belief that the technology was becoming universal, and that the customers wanted integrated solutions to their information needs. Strange but true, this was the same conclusion to which Akers's successor came in 1993.

That could be ominous. For the 1985 reinvention, intended to build a more responsive, dynamic system, only created a costly, rigid, and rudderless result. So in January 1988 engines were reversed: new reforms were designed to regain control by decentralizing into five product groups. The moves were welcomed around the world as an imaginative response to size and spread. Like the 1985 reorganization, though, the reforms had a limited shelf-life.

By December 1991 the entire scheme was scrapped. The five decentralized product groups became nine, and four overseas marketing and services companies were created. Order, counterorder, and disorder, you might well say. But the reforms all had something in common. They were essentially top-down. The reinventions had devolved some power from the top tier of management to the next. But what about the many tiers below?

The lesser ranks were buffeted about in those winds of change. Their say in these matters was limited to offers they could hardly refuse—of reassignment or "voluntary" departure, with abnormally generous cash sums (for example, two years' pay plus $25,000) to grease their going. To the buffeted, the swift succession of organizational and personal reshuffles could not have made any sense.

They seem no more sensible on a wider view—except on the theory that shake-ups themselves, irrespective of their nature, have beneficial powers. A more realistic view would be that both the new organizations and the people running them had failed in the appointed task of reinvention. There was no excuse. As Gerstner said in the spring of 1994, the problems of slow response and introverted bureaucracy could be fixed, since "they are caused by us and not factors outside our doors."

That had been just as true in 1991, and when Akers took command in 1982, and in all the troubled years between. None of the remedies had worked, because the reinventors couldn't reinvent the most crucial element of all: themselves.

The Rewards of Reengineering

2

Why has reinvention become necessary? It's because the dominance of organized hierarchies, functionally divided and vertically managed, has become counterproductive. Top-down executives still control the business world. But the top-down system is incompatible with the dramatic changes and pressures that have reshaped both markets and managerial requirements. That conflict has resulted in crisis—which can only be resolved by near-revolution.

Reinvention fails when it stops well short of the revolutionary change that's urgently required to accomplish the necessary shift from vertical to horizontal. Organizations are having to shift from centrally controlled, multilayered pyramids to flatter, devolved structures. That's matched by transformation of business systems: the sequential, departmental, vertical division of work is yielding to the concept of the business system—constructed of horizontal processes that cut across traditional divisions.

The road to success in the nineties and beyond lies in improving such processes: and the richest improvements are won, not by working on what already exists, but by reworking, redesigning, replacing, even removing the process: by "reengineering." That's defined by Michael Hammer and James Champy, in *Reengineering the Corporation,* as (my italics) *"fundamental* rethinking and *radical* redesign of business *processes* to achieve *dramatic* improvements in critical contemporary measures of performance, such as cost, quality, service, and speed."

The need has become glaringly obvious—so much so that most managements have taken the point. Just like IBM's bosses and the other reinventors, they claim (in Hammer and Champy's words) to want "companies that are lean, nimble, flexible, responsive, competitive, innovative, efficient, customer-focused, and profitable." Why, then, "are so many . . . companies bloated, clumsy, rigid, sluggish, noncompetitive, uncreative, inefficient, disdainful of customer needs, and losing money?"

This even applies to companies that have both received and acted on the message. The authors conclude, dismally enough, that "most companies that begin reengineering . . . end their efforts precisely where they began, making no significant changes, achieving no major performance improvement. . . . Our unscientific estimate is that as many as 70% of organizations . . . fail to achieve any results."

A McKinsey expert told *Fortune* in like vein that "we did an audit of client experiences with process reengineering. We found lots of examples where there were truly dramatic impacts on processes—60% to 80% reductions in cost and cycle time—but only very modest effects at the business-unit level. . . ." The changes, it turned out, "didn't matter in terms of the customer." But even when the customer does gain real benefits, the overall results of the corporation may not.

There's a fascinating example from IBM Credit, where the operation studied by Hammer and Champy cut a seven-day turnaround of credit applications to four hours, with no increase in numbers employed (which fell slightly), and a well-nigh incredible rise in volume handled: *one hundred times.* This spectacular improvement began when a couple of senior managers walked a credit request through all five stages, asking everybody concerned to deal with the proposal at once. This led to a bizarre discovery: the actual process required only ninety minutes. So the inefficiencies in the system accounted for a whole week's delay.

The solution was simple. Each credit application was thereafter entrusted to one generalist, who handled the application from start to finish, instead of four specialists, one for each stage. There was a backstop to deal with the infrequent more complicated cases. "The old process had been overdesigned to handle the most difficult applications that management could imagine."

The key thus lay in eliminating what Hammer and Champy call "cross-organizational hand-offs." Instead, you either entrust everything to a single individual, or you empower "case teams," groups "who have among them all the skills that are needed" to satisfy the customer: "Typically a case-worker based process operates *ten times* faster than the assembly line version that it replaces." This is admirable, from both the company's and the customer's point of view. It certainly meets the criteria of being fundamental, radical, and dramatic. But why wasn't the whole of IBM performing similar wonders?

There are plenty of other cases where spectacular results have been won in parts of corporations whose overall performance remained awful. Initiatives to reshape businesses and their cultures often founder because top managements, while preaching revolution, actually never go beyond moderate reform. That simply isn't good enough in the external conditions of today's markets. Nor will it meet the internal needs of the corporation. Old bad habits will reassert themselves unless an ax is taken to their roots.

Most reengineering (like cutting Ford Motor's accounts payable costs by 80 percent by eliminating the invoicing stage altogether) consists of what might be called "sub-projects": stand-alone process improvements that involve relatively low-level teamwork and initiative and are not linked to reengineering the entire business. These are the kind of projects that have provided bread-and-butter (and sometimes plenty of jam) for consultants since time immemorial. The benefits are real, but limited by definition.

Rethinking and radical redesign of any individual process will very probably produce dramatic improvement in detail. Is that enough? Employee involvement and morale also benefit greatly from these projects. But lasting economic and employees benefits are won only if the results are not submerged in an overall business system that is ineffective and stultifying. As in information technology, so in manufacturing: "automation" experts have long preached that, before automating, rethinking the factory is indispensable.

Failures in reengineering are thus identical to flops in automation—no rethinking, or wrong rethinking, no or wrong results. Misled managements, as Hammer and Champy observe, try to "fix" processes instead of changing them: instead of focusing on business processes, they appoint task forces on "issues" like empowerment, teamwork, innovation, and customer service. They ignore the fact that successful process redesign will trigger radical changes elsewhere in the business system.

Nor do they involve people and their reward and recognition in the change: they settle for minor results. They give up too early. They limit the scope of the reengineering effort in advance by premature definition of the problem. They let existing corporate cultures and management attitudes get in the way. Cultures resist change instinctively, because managers fear the unknown—and that principle runs right to the very summit.

Consultants know that, offered a 20 percent improvement in a particular process, chief executives will sign on the dotted line. Offer them a great 200 percent leap forward, however, and the sale becomes far more difficult—for that must involve drastic change. In *Fortune*'s words, reengineers in effect ask, "If we were a new company, how would we run this place? Then, with a meat ax and sandpaper, they conform the company to their vision."

Managers are understandably none too keen on being axed or sandpapered themselves; or to accept that their established vision of the company has become irrelevant; or (to bring the issue down to earth) to incur huge, six-figure monthly consultancy bills that threaten to become eternal—for the company will never run out of business processes to reengineer. But these concerns, while substantive, dodge the real issue, which is that the reengineering idea, however labeled, is inescapable.

Management's role includes continuous and fundamental rethinking of the purpose of business processes, so that redesign and improvements can be continuous. But lower cost, better quality, improved service, and greater speed—the targets of business process reengineering—only work their greatest wonders within the framework of a business that has itself been rethought to succeed in its changing markets and objectives.

The most exciting reengineering stories concern companies that went beyond the boundaries imposed by fixed ideas to create a whole new framework for their business processes. These models, moreover, have truly reinvented themselves, not when the business was already in crisis, but by dealing, or rather redealing, from strength—and rebuilding on strength, not on weakness.

At Hallmark Cards, king of the U.S. greeting cards market, management had the wit to see that overall success was concealing mounting problems. Hammer and Champy tell how, to tackle these concerns, the company embarked on "The Journey." The overall destination was "building the organizational capability that will enable Hallmark employees to react swiftly and successfully to continuous unpredictable change."

Before setting its business priorities, the management worked hard to communicate a new set of "five beliefs and four guiding values" to all employees. That provided the context for achieving strictly practical goals; "to get new products to the market in less than a year; produce products and promotional programs that consistently win over both buyers and retailers; and reduce costs with continued improvement in quality."

At Taco Bell, the PepsiCo-owned fast-food chain, the procedure was much the same: rethink and communicate to everybody the entire philosophy of the business—and then radically improve all its processes in that light. Its chief executive, John Martin, noted that "our greatest insight has been our most basic—namely, that everything begins with a simple decision to listen to our customer."

That doesn't differ at all from the message uttered by those countless managers who claim they are "putting customers first," becoming "customer-led," and stressing "customer care." The vital difference is that Taco Bell acted on what it heard: customers hadn't really gotten on the fast-food industry's current bandwagon ("better, bigger, fancier"); rather, they wanted good food at low prices in clean surroundings.

Shifting the company's whole emphasis, from marketing expenditure to value-for-money, was accompanied by specific process reengineering, related to the new strategy, that led to dramatic improvements in cost and speed. Global rethinking is the reengineering that really pays. It is also the hardest to achieve, because it forces organizations and, above all, their leaders to change their minds: minds, moreover, which have been set by decades of practice and apparent success.

In today's markets, however, success can be far more apparent than real—and whether you call the approach "reengineering" or anything else, going back to the beginning provides the only acceptable starting point. You then decide what, starting anew, you wish to achieve. And that search for desired outcomes holds the key to real reinvention.

The most important statement uttered by Hammer and Champy in an important book comes almost as an aside. They mention that "work is best organized around outcomes, not tasks." Success comes only to managements which have clearly decided what business results they want to achieve. Amazingly, this is often forgotten. Indeed, the chief executive of one huge multinational has publicly admitted that this omission from a hugely ambitious and expensive change program lost the company one or two years of precious time.

He confessed that this was his, and his colleagues', greatest mistake. Hammer and Champy embody the outcome principle in an important discussion of how to enlist support for reengineering. They advocate starting with a five- to ten-page "case for action." The case identifies the business problem, spells out the marketplace demands, diagnoses why present processes can't respond adequately, and spells out the cost of inaction. This somewhat negative start is coupled with a positive "vision statement": "here is what we want to be."

The authors prefer short, gutsy visions—literally, in the case of Taco Bell: "We want to be number one in share of stomach." But was it "reengineering" to reduce the chain's marketing expenditure? Or to remove a supervisory layer from the backs of restaurant managers? Those are obvious steps that could also have been taken by a management which (like IBM's) was running hard to move backwards.

Reorienting à la Taco Bell or Hallmark Cards is a different order, not only of magnitude, but of change—for everybody, including top management itself. The commitment of top management to painful change—pain which top managers will fully share—is indispensable. Without that sharing, any work on total quality, reengineering, or any other reform program will fail overall. The push for change must start at the top for more than one reason.

First, only the top people, led by the CEO, can turn process re-design into a way of life, by insistence, endorsement, recognition, and, above all, by example. Then, the broader view that can't be expected from those in the front line is brought into focus by those further away. Their cardinal responsibility is to monitor, update, and, if necessary, reengineer the overall business system or systems which comprehend all other processes. Without that commitment from the top, process reengineering can't work its real wonders.

But you dare not, if you want the best results, pour new wine into old bottles, whether the bottle is an information technology system, a customer service department, an assembly line, or a whole corporation. Of course, you mustn't take seven days over a process that only requires ninety minutes: but that is (and always has been) a continuous management responsibility. The difference today is that the responsibility has to be exercised within a total process—in other words, the entire business.

Hammer and Champy remark that a "company that cannot change the way it thinks about information technology cannot reengineer." By much the same token, a company that cannot rethink its entire being cannot reengineer, and a company that can't reengineer can't reinvent—and vice versa. The lesson of all today's most convincing management thought and action is that limited change is deeply perilous. In organizational reform, reengineering the whole is vastly more effective than attacking its parts.

The Downfall of Digital

3

Long before niche marketing became a cliché, Ken Olsen, a computer engineer who was never noted for his marketing skills, had created its most spectacular example. Long before it became permissible even to question IBM's competence, Olsen not only queried its technological supremacy: he dismissed the Watson culture as regimented, insular—and above all inefficient.

As a graduate researcher at MIT when it gave IBM the crucial contract to develop the SAGE early-warning computer, Olsen acted as liaison at IBM's Poughkeepsie, New York, plant. That added an insider's view to an outsider's perspective. "It was like going to a Communist state," he once said. "They knew nothing about the rest of the world, and the rest of the world knew nothing about what went on inside." Just like the Communist state, too, the monolithic facade covered up dreadful production inefficiencies.

His MIT supervisor recalled Olsen's reaction: "I can beat these guys at their own game." His genius, however, lay in *not* playing IBM's game: or, at least, not playing on the same field. The multinationals who challenged IBM all made the mistake of mounting frontal assaults on the market created by large corporate and institutional customers—like MIT. But IBM showed scant interest in another market, in which scientist spoke unto scientist, and engineer unto engineer.

The market saw several small companies edge into this niche. Of their leaders, the two which settled for multinational takeover (by Honeywell and Xerox, respectively) disappeared without trace, victims of the same large-company disease that Olsen detected at IBM. Olsen's independence of mind, which became celebrated, kept him independent—and created the second corporate phenomenon of the computer age.

Olsen's Digital Equipment, founded in 1957, flourished. By 1986 sales were pushing towards $8 billion. Number two in the world computer industry, the business had taken a clear lead over all other challengers to IBM's dominance. Unlike these far greater firms, Digital had avoided the main battleground, IBM's dominant domain. As an engineer, Olsen could see that many labs didn't need (and often couldn't afford) large, costly mainframes. Digital's machines provided computing on the cheap, made on the cheap.

The start-up capital was only $70,000: Olsen put some lawn furniture and a rolltop desk into an abandoned textile mill in Massachusetts, and kept his designs just as simple, cheap, and rugged. Where IBM tolerated excess costs (because they were translated by standard markups into excess profits), Olsen loathed them. This was only one of many differences. IBM, under the younger Watson, developed and consecrated a smooth, large management structure. Digital's early years were practically free-form.

In one description, "the company consisted largely of bands of engineers who would form fluidly round projects." In 1964, faced with mounting evidence of confusion and overlapping, Olsen found a solution that was again poles apart from the IBM system: what later became known as the "product champion." Full responsibility for a single product line went to a single manager. Reporting direct to the operating committee headed by Olsen, the champion would obtain his manufacturing and sales force support from centralized organizations: but for development, marketing, and producing bottom-line results, the champ and his group were on their own.

Held together by Olsen's hands-on proprietorial style, the system, to judge by results, deserves his own description: "a miracle." For nineteen years, revenue and profits grew by 30 percent annually, as engineers proved that they could be entrepreneurs. New markets and new products fed off each other—and off the strange fact that minicomputer competition from IBM failed to arrive. After surviving some notorious product snafus, Olsen struck paydirt with the PDP series, which became the workhorse of the scientific and engineering communities.

After three years of brilliantly dodging IBM's competition, the thirty semiautonomous operations that composed Digital were generating sales of $1.4 billion and earning a 10 percent net margin. What IBM won in its vastly larger world by economies of scale, by marketing, and by quasi-monopoly, Olsen had achieved by technology. At this crucial juncture, he didn't just double his technological bets: he raised the ante enormously.

The VAX (Virtual Address Extension) range cost billions to develop. But it promised to achieve what IBM had never delivered: the VAX machines, covering all needs from the desktop to lower mainframe levels, would be able to communicate with each other, using identical software throughout the range. At this distance, in a time when computer networking is commonplace, the ambitions of the concept are hard to grasp: they were wondrously sweeping.

Apart from its conceptual leap, the VAX strategy went far beyond Digital's former technological scope. It had never made large disk-storage units, never made microprocessors, never produced the advanced type of software needed to run networks—and never sold to the corporate customers who constituted IBM's fiefdom. Once again, Olsen had to rethink the company. He used a messy process that was deeply painful.

In *Fortune*'s words, Olsen worked his will "by teasing, goading and teaching employees, by sermonizing—and by remorselessly pillorying those who stood in his way." The turnover among executives was extreme: "Not one was fired, but some left wounded, with heart problems, ulcers, or wrecked nerves."

After five years of blood, sweat, and other people's tears, Olsen formally disbanded the product manager organization in favor of a centralized marketing organization similar in function to IBM's. The new Digital was committed to the company's first direct, frontal assault on IBM's business-computing heartland. Yet Digital looked unfit for the unequal contest. Earnings had plunged because of an accounting mix-up, and Olsen had also failed embarrassingly in the personal computer market.

All error was forgiven, however, when the VAX took off. A brilliant success both technically and commercially, VAX produced the first significant bite into IBM's share of the office market. The new range won orders worth $2 billion in 1986 alone. To some, as total sales soared to $7.6 billion, it seemed as if the future might lie with Olsen's company: that he was the new Thomas Watson, Sr. He wasn't: nor was Digital the new IBM—except in the equal extent of the collapse which, in 1993, saw Ken Olsen's departure. What went wrong?

Curing CEO Disease

4

Only a minority of executives ever become chief. But all executives are likely to exhibit some symptoms of "chief executive disease." That's a phrase *Business Week* coined: the stricken bosses (1) can do no wrong, (2) refuse to concede any mistake, (3) spend excessive time away from the company, (4) are surrounded by yes-men, (5) make every decision—often in ignorance, (6) fuss about their incomes, comforts, and perks, (7) seek personal publicity, and (8) hang on to power—often undermining potential successors.

That's a distressing condition indeed—but the word "distressing," of course, refers to the company, not to its boss, who may be perfectly content with himself, his performance, and his business. The self-satisfaction is part of the disease. The great manager is *never* satisfied, for the irrefutable reason that, explicitly or instinctively, he follows the Total Quality philosophy: however good you are, or think you are, you can always do better.

Moreover, today, if you don't seize opportunities for improvement, somebody else will. And their seized advantage will be your diminished profit, reduced market share, and, quite possibly, lost business. The jockeying and jostling in many markets is now so frenetic that relaxation is impossible—even for "market leaders." In fact, the whole concept of market leadership needs rethinking in these circumstances.

You must lead the future as well as the present, and that's sorely difficult at a time when technology is evolving so fast and in so many places: breakthroughs aren't particular about where they are born, and customers aren't particular about where they buy them. Chief executive disease is inimical to this situation. But its symptoms flow naturally from the cult of the hero manager.

That concept runs deep. It's reaffirmed every time a chief executive appears on the cover of a business magazine, jaw jutting or smile fixed, combined with a caption praising the way the hero is "reinventing the corporation" or "blasting the competition" or "building an empire"—or, in Ken Olsen's case, receiving *Fortune*'s accolade as "America's Most Successful Entrepreneur."

More than in any other developed country, business in America places supreme power in the hands of a single individual, and symbolizes and cements that faith by supreme rewards. Europe is still a long way behind in the rewards (despite some earnest efforts to catch up): but both the pay and the faith are anachronistic anywhere. The manager as hero is urgently required: but today's heroism paradoxically lies in forgoing heroic status to tackle the enormous problems and opportunities of Western business. Today's real heroes act as a dynamic, but not omnipotent, part of a brilliant, decisive, interlocking group of people.

That requires a new organizational principle to replace the traditional hierarchical pyramid. Aircraft carriers are known as "flattops": and that's a good word for the urgent necessity of slicing the sharp peak off the organization. The truth is that the hero chief executive cannot cope single-handed with the increasing sheer complexity, not just of products and processes, but of management itself.

What is the company doing about moving to time-based management and activity-based costing? Is the packaging expenditure effectively blended with advertising, below-the-line activities, public relations, and the overall marketing strategy? In that strategy, are distributive or direct channels the more effective? Is there a worthwhile system of further education and training for management? Are inventories too high? Is spending on R&D too low—and does it have the right objectives and correct methodology?

Under such complex pressures, human beings often retreat to the safety of inaction. The classic organization structure encourages the process. The top manager is cocooned from reality by staff and colleagues who share the same preconceptions and pressures. So the disease progresses: worse still, it spreads downwards as well as sideways. Is there a cure?

At many Western companies, the cry is Go East: adopt Japanese-style management practices, which devolve decision-making to local levels and allow designers and production managers more freedom. But since when has devolved decision-making been a prerogative of the mysterious East? Western thinkers, from Peter Drucker onwards, have long advocated such devolution, and pragmatic Western managers have adopted these principles in practice.

At Digital, Olsen certainly showed enviable freedom from chief executive disease when he freed his product champions to exercise devolved power. But there was a difference. In the end, all strings led back to Olsen—and he ultimately pulled them all. An engineer down to the laces on his thick-soled shoes, Olsen ran a technology-led business in a manner which, like its creator, remained rumpled, homespun, eccentric, and unpredictable.

His style, though, was essentially autocratic—and made life unnecessarily uncomfortable for subordinates. Where IBM's Thomas Watson, Sr., made them wait for days outside his office, Olsen kept them for days in committees. Decisions were supposed to emerge by consensus as the issue under review was worn down (like some of the committee members) to elemental simplicity. That suited Olsen's prime management theory: "A good manager never has to make any decisions at all"—because, if the groundwork is done properly, the decision makes itself.

With powerful managers, such theories simply excuse the potentate's own eccentric preferences. The way Olsen dragged out the switch from decentralized product managers to a centralized sales and marketing organization is an example. He could have ordered sudden change. Instead, he undermined the previous system (his own creation) by actions and interventions that made the old way untenable, the new way inevitable, and many other people miserable.

To outside admirers, though, Olsen's eccentricities seemed thoroughly amiable. He worked occasionally as an engineer himself; he spewed out ideas and business "parables"; he seemed to have found a better, if inimitable, way to run a computer company. During the great VAX reshuffle, true, critics thought that Olsen had perhaps succumbed to "founder's disease." In this close relative of chief executive disease, the creator, having hung on too long, pulls his own house down around his ears by insensitive arrogance.

The VAX triumph seemed to clear Olsen of the charge. Persistent clashes with his longtime lieutenants were their fault, not his. They were unable to adapt to external change, to become true entrepreneurs, not proto-bureaucrats. In hindsight, though, the critics had cottoned on to the first symptoms of impending weakness. The Digital brand of management had flourished in conditions where Olsen was in command of his market and leading it all the way. His style was ill-suited to being led by market forces.

In the market-led recession of the early nineties, Olsen's way proved as vulnerable as IBM's. The root technological cause was the same. If mainframes were an endangered species, so were Digital's minis. By 1992, top-of-the-line PC-based workstations rivaled even mainframes in power and capacity. Minis were being challenged for power, and undercut in price-effectiveness, by micros. These challenges were totally inimical to Olsen and the culture he had built. He sought to perpetuate the old order, and chief executive disease protected the doomed attempt.

Laying off employees is no answer to major defects in the system. In three years to mid-1992, twelve thousand Digital employees in the United States lost their jobs, but this didn't end the shrinkage, the corporate crisis, or Olsen's interfering, capricious management style. In the early years, Olsen's autocratic leanings had been tempered by the sage General Georges Doriot, the venture capitalist who originally held 77 percent of the company. In Doriot's late eighties, when Olsen was sixty, the old man still acted as mentor, advising Olsen on delicate issues, like choosing a successor.

With Doriot dead, however, Olsen still had no heir, apparent or otherwise. This was one simple decision that refused to make itself or wasn't allowed to. Consciously or subconsciously, Olsen had seen one potential successor after another off the premises. That's the eighth and literally last symptom of chief executive disease. Other noted exemplars include Harold S. Geneen at ITT, Armand Hammer at Occidental Petroleum, and Harry Gray at United Technologies. In all such cases, the disastrous impact on the companies concerned can be seen long afterwards.

In 1992, Occidental lost $591 million on $8.9 billion of sales; ITT's damage was a loss of $885 million on sales of $21.7 billion; United Technologies lost $287 million on sales of $22 billion. But Digital outdid all three, losing $2.8 billion, or 19.9 percent of its $14 billion revenue. Over a decade, its shareholders had suffered an annual negative return of 3.8 percent compound. The famous entrepreneurship had been swamped in a series of mistakes and miscalculations.

The saga of a spectacularly brilliant recruit, David Cutler, provides an instructive vignette. The VAX onslaught on IBM could not have succeeded without this legendary designer's VMS software. Dismayed by the Olsen brand of office politics, Cutler took his Digital team away from Massachusetts to a haven in Redmond, Washington. The team's work on designing hardware and software round RISC (reduced instruction set computing) chips was well-timed and well-directed. No RISC chip received more praise on arrival than Digital's Alpha.

As described by an Apple man, Cutler sounds like perfect Digital material: "He's an iconoclast and he has rough edges, but he hardly ever makes mistakes." That could once have been said of Olsen himself. By the time the Alpha appeared, though, Cutler and his team had quit, propelled by a decision to build workstations around a different RISC chip. It was Olsen's choice. Digital's many mistakes as its market fundamentally changed proved that the magic touch had fled. More, in a world that has become infinitely more complicated, chief executive magicians are more likely than ever to cast the wrong spells.

The principles of non-magical, disease-free chief executive behavior are quite clear. They've been convincingly articulated by Sir Derek Birkin, chairman of RTZ, the world's largest mining group. His board saw "the need to avoid bureaucracy, which stifles initiative and is not much fun either. It also recognizes the fundamental truth that real authority, the only authority that truly matters comes with respect from below. . . . Even if we wanted to intrude in the management of operations in the field, which we do not, we could not do so to any significant extent."

RTZ does, of course, have annual budgets, closely examines them at head office, and reviews them with the operating units. "But there is not some grand inquisition of each operating unit at a senior level unless things appear to have gone seriously wrong, or unless a subsidiary plans to depart from its strategic plan [which is agreed upon] . . . once every two years. . . . The operating companies, wherever they may be, have to an uncharacteristic degree the ability to run themselves. . . . We are hardly likely to second-guess them in London on day-to-day management. We would be foolish to do so"—and the key points in that statement are surely irrefutable.

1. The exercise of authority is a two-way process.
2. The head office cannot manage sharp-end operations.
3. The shorter the lines of reporting the better.
4. Strategy is the responsibility of those who must execute it.
5. Second-guessing managers on day-to-day issues is foolish in principle and practice alike.

Olsen defenders might argue that a mining group such as RTZ is set up by nature for delegation and decentralization. Each mining project is in its own, usually faraway country, each has its own peculiar characteristics and conditions, each has its own product mix. A clear demarcation line can be drawn around each mine. That's not true of computer companies, which are coordinated across frontiers and across model lines. To achieve crucial economies of scale, components must be sourced globally and shared between different models.

But that doesn't greatly affect the management issue. In any company, each operating unit occupies its own physical and intellectual territory, whether it's near or far; each has its own peculiar characteristics and conditions; each has its own product mix. And if a clear demarcation line can't be drawn around each unit, the latter should be reshaped until the line *can* be drawn.

For all its spread and separateness, RTZ was once no different from Olsen's Digital in the ethos of command. A powerful chief executive headed a triumvirate that not only ruled strategy and finance from London, but intervened constantly in operations through one of its members. This plainly and ludicrously unworkable system could never have coped successfully with the group's current scale. Like Digital's, however, the system could have continued to operate, though with rapidly diminishing returns, long after it had ceased to be fully effective.

Momentum isn't lost all at once—and that was true of Olsen's reign. But his brand of management was subtracting value, not adding it. The latter is a fair definition of the head office function, indeed, of management in general. If managers aren't adding value to the business, how is their pay justified? The general question applies with increasing force the higher their authority and their remuneration rise. The high salaries, the comfortable corporate living conditions, and the prerogatives of power are pleasant possessions in themselves, but accomplish nothing.

Accomplishment is the sole criterion. Winston Churchill, at the height of the Second World War, would, he said, "court-martial" himself every night. What had he contributed to winning the war during the day? The progress of chief executive disease steadily reduces the contribution to break-even point (where the manager isn't subtracting any value, but isn't adding any, either) and then to negative. The object of an excellent management system is to make that process impossible, to ensure that the whole company becomes worth more than its parts by enhancing their value.

It's axiomatic that the CEO can't cure the disease of which he is the cause and the carrier, however hard he tries. In that situation, the harder they try, the harder they fall. Olsen's execution of seven vice presidents at one swoop in May 1992 was only the prologue to his own departure that October. His successor, Robert Palmer, had only joined Olsen in 1985, coming from semiconductors. His career had blended two strands that now dominate the industry: the rise of the microprocessor to universal supremacy, and the necessity to inject new entrepreneurial blood into bureaucratic veins.

Palmer's effort to accomplish a fourth great revolution in Digital's style, this time to customer-based profit centers, was compromised, many thought, by an addiction to hiring ex-IBMers for the task. Given the difficulty of Digital's strategic situation, that task was always going to be mountainous. By mid-1994, with a fourth successive operating loss looming, the mountain was beginning to look too high to climb. Regeneration had been left desperately late, even though Palmer's approach to the after-effects of chief executive disease had seemed so promising.

That approach entails, first, injecting new leadership from outside the company and outside its traditional business. Second, reducing the tiers of top management. Third, pushing through wholesale reorganization. Fourth, making the most of a highly symbolic personal break (like Olsen's departure) with a glorious but increasingly irrelevant past. What the new regime apparently lacked, though, was the same ultimate attributes that, during his long success, had once given Olsen, the maverick in minis, his true greatness: ruthless tenacity, and the ability to change direction—ahead of need.

When the old order changeth in markets, the old order of the corporation is doomed. And so is the rule of chief executives whose disease blinds them to new truths and binds their companies to the past. It's the future and the customer that hold the key to continuing success.

The Mayhem at
General Motors

5

In management, as in medicine, the cure can sometimes be worse than the disease. The conventional reaction of managements faced by falling indicators is to become "leaner and fitter." The leanness takes precedence in the pairing: surplus factories are shut, blue- and white-collar employees are dismissed, businesses are sold, and products are delisted. After the initial heavy "rationalization" costs have been absorbed, fitness is thought to follow automatically. Even if the company is only producing the same output, fewer assets and people are being employed. Productivity and profitability will soar accordingly.

General Motors, the world's largest industrial company, is a case in point. Between 1992 and 1995, GM is set to close twenty-one plants in all, removing a fifth of its entire North American capacity and dismissing 74,000 workers. Nor was this the first cutback. When the cuts are complete, GM will have *half* the labor force of 1985. Its management must call to mind the old-time physicians who drew blood from their patients, thus weakening their resistance, observed the deterioration, and prescribed more of the same—until the patient died.

The true position was summed up by Alex Taylor III, writing in *Fortune:* "While *productivity*—the number of cars produced per worker—will improve, *efficiency*—the number of worker hours required per car—will not." In other words, GM was tackling the symptom (low productivity), but not the cause, which was inferior efficiency. This misdiagnosis merely repeated earlier failures. Under threat were plants that "were built new or completely renovated in the 1980s at a cost of $1 billion each." They were built under the misguided belief that GM could invest itself out of its shortcomings.

The true sickness is that GM was organized brilliantly by Alfred P. Sloan between the wars to cope with circumstances, common to most companies until the 1960s, that will never be seen again. Market shares used to vary little over time; competition was domestic and played largely by the rules. You made money by maximizing production runs to get the longest possible service from capital equipment and design expenditure. This meant extending product life-spans and production technology to the limit.

Marketing was seen primarily as an exercise in distribution and selling—the former to shift the product of those unceasing production lines, the latter to change the product into cash as rapidly as possible. Economies of scale, rather than economies of method, were the target of top managements. To obtain those economies, centralized control was essential. Individual businesses and brands existed mostly in name. The corporation itself was the real business, and it created a whole caste of managers who served only management itself.

In today's conditions, all that sounds like a remote dream, an improbable fantasy. The modern business, of any kind, has to cope with the following scenario:

1. Market shares are highly volatile: even when overall shares move slowly, segments within markets are now far more important, and may fluctuate wildly.
2. Competition has become global, and may come from sources inside or outside the industry or the country—from new players who break all the old rules.
3. Variety has totally altered the manufacturing game, replacing

long runs and homogeneous products with short runs, marked differentiation, and shorter life-cycles.

4. The technology of both product and process is changing rapidly and generating sudden and decisive shifts in competitive advantage.

5. Distribution has become a crucial component in the ultimate price to customers, whose changing demands are leading production and altering the nature of selling.

6. Economies of method and exploitation of powerful "brands" (for which read "market recognition") are the joint keys to superior profitability.

These six profound changes have made the old GM style of organization as obsolete as the horse-drawn carriage. John Smith, the current chief executive, knows that well. He made his reputation, after all, at GM in Europe, where spectacular strides have been made, not just in competitiveness, market share, and financial performance, but also (which enabled the turnaround) towards new-century management. The advances have been revolutionary, though they came late in the day.

The Omega executive car, launched only in 1994, was the first GM Europe line entrusted to multidisciplinary teams, with all ten disciplines, from product engineering and finance to marketing and service, forming product development teams for all thirteen areas. Whether it was seats or wiring, bumpers or engines, the teams worked together to give customers what they wanted, as determined by thorough research.

Omega pre-production cars were also the first to be assembled on the shop floor, so that production workers could contribute to the final decisions. Most important of all, this £720 million project was the first where final approval rested with the top management in Europe, and not in Detroit. The ultimate bosses in Michigan, led by Smith, had of course approved this delegation of authority. But why was Europe finding so straightforward what the North American operations have found so tough? Throughout GM's world, what kind of modern machine can replace the antique—one that, in its own time, will achieve equally spectacular results?

Resurrecting the Dinosaurs

6

The excruciating problem of GM suggests an interesting analogy from Detroit's prime. All the Big Three manufacturers (as noted in Part One, Chapter 2) concentrated on the so-called dominant design—the rear-wheel-drive, separate chassis, engine-in-front machine. The dominance didn't spring from customer preference, as was shown by the soaring rise of the rear-engined VW Beetle to fourth-largest-selling brand in the United States. Rather, it suited the economics of Detroit to continue with the dominant design until long after competitors and, more important, the public had turned to other approaches.

The dominant organizational design, with its centralization of decision-making and its hierarchical relationships, can't generate fast enough reactions to cope with—let alone anticipate—rapid external change by swift internal initiatives. The center is too far from the market or the factory floor, separated from both by too many layers, which in turn are reproduced in the over-dependent subsidiaries. If the latter also embody brands, the lack of independence jeopardizes the vital brand identity.

The difference between the dominant design and twenty-first-century management is charted exactly by a questionnaire which the English psychologist Mark Brown uses to differentiate between "dolphins" and "dinosaurs." Score your organization from 0 to 6 along the distance between the two extremes:

1. Those around me "yes, but" new ideas to death......................Those around me encourage new ideas

2. We are geared to providing what we want to provide.............We provide what the customer wants

3. My organization is focused on solving problems ....My organization is focused on opportunities

4. Many of our people are mentally retired ....Our people are highly motivated

5. The match between individual values and those of the organization is poor ....The match between them is good

6. People feel disempowered ....Individuals show high levels of initiative

7. People's minds are fairly set ....People are very good at "thinking afresh"

A score of 21 marks the dividing line between dolphins and dinosaurs. Brown also adapts the questions for personal grading ("*I* feel disempowered .... *I* take a lot of initiatives," etc.). He points out that you can be a dinosaur in a dolphin organization, or a dolphin living within a dinosaur. The latter situation, very uncomfortable, must be that of the best managers inside organizations such as the GM: for it's doubtful whether many of its denizens would give the company even a half-best score of 21.

In any event, nothing less than an all-dolphin score of 42 can be praised. Look again at the seven opposed extremes: the ideals all embody "natural" and rewarding ways of behaving, while the zero scores result from unnatural, cramped conduct—as do the faults at GM. Reversing them gives an excellent guide to the new necessities of dolphin management in organizations of any size.

First, *design the organization to meet the needs.* Never, for instance, have design and research heads who don't report to the main business; never have that reflected lower down by designers and scientists who don't work with the engineers.

Second, *"rationalize" continually in the true sense of the word*—acting rationally and eliminating unreason. That way you don't (a true-life GM example) produce three different products and import a fourth, all more or less to the same specification: nor do you lose output of a hot product by being forced to stop the line that it shares with a sales laggard.

Third, *"always reward merit and never let a fault go unremarked"*—sage advice which comes from Seisei Kato, once the sales supremo of GM's biggest rival, Toyota. So you don't reward bad mistakes with promotion—for example, advancing the manufacturing head for a make-or-break project, after a production fiasco during the launch, to the rank of vice president. Don't be like IBM, either, and conclude that failure results from not firing enough incompetents. Rather, success comes from insisting on and using the competence within everybody, and providing the conditions from which competence flows.

There are other common failings that uncommon management avoids. It's essential today to *cherish the brands.* GM used to milk the middle market with three makes (Buick, Oldsmobile, and Pontiac) that shared much engineering and were differentiated only by badge and image. In the new markets, that technique doesn't work. Customers want genuine product advantages, and will pay accordingly. However, their negative reaction to perceived poor value outweighs several tons of perceived advantage: thus customers with bad experiences of your product or service bad-mouth you with eleven other people—those who've been pleased pass the good word to only six others.

Fifth, *benchmark all the time and act on what you find.* The old GM was 40 percent less productive than Ford, with twenty assembly plants that took 35.7 worker-hours to build a vehicle, against Ford's 21.6. Redesign took GM forty-two to forty-eight months: nine to twelve months slower than the Japanese. GM spent 20 percent to 25 percent more than Ford on getting factories ready for production—partly because of lags on designing and engineering tools and dies.

Even in 1992, it cost GM $486 more than Chrysler and $795 above Ford to make a car: partly, no doubt, because 70 percent of its components were still made in-house, more than double the Chrysler ratio. In 1993, a bundle of inefficiencies caused GM's third-quarter output to fall short by 95,000 vehicles. Where Chrysler renewed its models at five- to six-year intervals, GM's replacement cycle averaged eight years. Today's markets simply don't allow long-term survival with significant diseconomies in fundamental costs and processes.

Finally, *emphasize opportunities, not problems* (which is Brown's advice to his dolphins): solving problems creates opportunities—provided that the problems are actually solved. According to one industry consultant, that didn't happen at GM: "They have programs that are going to solve every problem, but they never get solved." He describes the "biggest problem" as "to get the organization actually to do something." But that, of course, is only half the battle: doing it right wins the war.

A company's problems can be divided into two varieties: the things that weren't done, and those that were. The first set spring from lack of creative responsiveness: the second from imperfect mechanisms for making decisions. The genres are different, but their remedies combine. Use creativity to improve the decision-making, and you don't get (to quote GM again) $77 billion of investment, much of it excessive and ill-executed. This monumental program was intended to cut labor costs; but (as every systems engineer knows) you improve the systems *before* the investment, and the improvements, rather than the investment, are decisive.

Every organizational consultant also knows that you don't add management layers (as GM did when combining its North American car interests into two groups): you eliminate them. All these sad errors (and others, like foolishly investing a sky-high $3.5 billion to produce the low-priced Saturn) have a common theme: an instinctive preference for taking action at the center rather than the periphery. The center can order massive investments, buy other companies, reshuffle entities, close plants: but it can't increase efficiency, delight customers, raise morale, and beat the competition.

Those essential ends can only be achieved by penetrating to the true nature of the organization and giving it the systemic treatment it requires. The heart of the matter is that organization provides a framework of discipline. The discipline gives creativity its direction and its constraints. For example, the great comedy director Preston Sturges, after an unbroken run of moneymaking hits, broke with Paramount over his increasing irritation at front office imposition of its authority. This was enshrined in strict rules, like shooting three pages of script a day, which Sturges found irksome. But after his escape to freedom, Sturges made nothing but costly flops.

By throwing money at its problems, confident that the money would never run out, GM not only spent itself into the biggest loss ever made by any company: it took away a vital constraint. Had the Saturn team been told to produce a world-beating car for half the money, they might well have created a better (and profitable) car in half the time. But task forces and similar groups, within such constraints, also need the freedom to decide for themselves how the task should be tackled.

The constraints usually applied, though, are not helpful. They're totally obstructive. Gifford Pinchot III points out that three hundred large corporations account for 85 percent of all R&D spending in the United States (a pattern which is probably typical of other countries, too). Yet the big outfits produce less than half the major innovations. This isn't because they lack inventive power: that's enormous. Rather, they fall down on the implementation. That's readily avoided, if you

1. Don't focus on the short term
2. Don't have multilevel approvals
3. Don't cut discretionary time to useless amounts
4. Don't expect home runs every time
5. Don't operate rigid planning systems
6. Don't allow turf battles over who does what
7. Don't become fearful of making mistakes
8. Don't oppose individual initiative
9. Don't allow authoritarian traditions to rule

As with Mark Brown's dolphin qualities, the positive attributes are far more attractive and natural than the negative: exploiting constraints, rather than succumbing to them. An intriguing book entitled

Getting It Right the Second Time by Michael Gershman recounts some of the uphill struggles survived by some of today's best-selling brands. Clarence Birdseye launched his first frozen food company in 1923. It promptly went bust. After further vicissitudes, General Foods, set up to exploit Birdseye's inspiration in June 1929, finally made a profit in 1937. How? By facing up to a seemingly fatal constraint—housewives wouldn't buy frozen food.

The answer was to tackle the institutional market—hotels, restaurants, hospitals, and so forth. Success there filtered back into the retail market. The Second World War, which sharply boosted the demand for convenience foods, did the rest. Another example is Hoover: from 1910–17 sales rose from 2,140 cleaners to 48,878, the major constraint being that busy retailers couldn't demonstrate the machines. After Hoover put its own demonstrators into stores, sales quintupled; the big breakthrough came with door-to-door canvassing, which had a fantastic 31 percent success rate.

More interesting even than such anecdotes are the conclusions that Gershman draws from his studies. He found it "safe to say" that, as a group, the heroes

- Took total responsibility for their products, because only by controlling the variables that had tripped up their predecessors could they improve them
- Were committed to doing the job right—no matter how long it took or what it entailed
- Looked on failures as part of the process and learned something from each one

On that last point, the author quotes Thomas Watson, Sr., the founder of IBM: "Remember, that's where you'll find success. On the far side of failure." For that to happen, however, you must face up the reality of failure and its true causes. At GM, the *causes* of its problems were not too many plants and workers. Those are severe symptoms. They spring from plants and workers making the wrong things in wrong ways because of bosses managing the wrong things in wrong ways. Unless that condition is remedied—which is far less expensive and painful than closures and redundancies—all other "cures" will merely lead to recurrence of the disease.

What Jack Smith has already accomplished at GM shows how sick large organizations can become. There are now 2,500 corporate staff where once 13,500 earned large paychecks. That's an astounding 81.5 percent cutback—or, the other way around, a previous bloat of 5.4 times more people than were actually required. Eight models have been removed from a sixty-two-model lineup, which plainly leaves far deeper cuts to be made. Basic car and truck platforms have been more severely cut from eighteen to ten. But correcting such inherited errors is housekeeping. Can Smith rebuild GM's stately mansion?

It's no less stately after the most drastic of Smith's opening gambits: the merger of all GM's domestic businesses, formerly a cat's cradle of bureaucracies, into a monolith called North American Operations. That loss of eleven thousand corporate staff in fact exaggerates the pruning: for half the eleven thousand joined NAO. Still, real gains can flow from centralization. Another single unit, the North American Strategy Board, has replaced what *Business Week* called "a tangle of executive committees." The result is "quick decisions in what Smith likes to call 'real time.' "

Decisions on car prices that "used to wend their way through five committees over weeks or even months" now take "a matter of days." Again, that's an improvement. But should pricing decisions rise that high? Shouldn't the people responsible for making and marketing cars be competent to decide their prices? During the previous regime, I was regaled with the story of how a new model, aimed at a carefully selected target market, had the targeted price raised by the committeemen—and promptly flopped in the market (for which, no doubt, the division was blamed).

NAO is a symbolic move away from the old GM, a psychological removal symbolized physically by suburban, open-cubicle offices that bear no resemblance to the downtown HQ—a famous temple to bureaucracy and corporate elitism. The new system, too, is a long way from the dinosaur days when GM managers held pre-meetings and even pre-pre-meetings to ensure that the main meeting went smoothly. But the present system is also far removed from the dolphin culture. GM, *Business Week* said flatly in November 1993, "is still sinking under the weight of its own bureaucracy."

In the critical area of new product development, where GM has lagged so conspicuously, the magazine even found one man, E. Michael Muchler, who described the failing process with notable pride: "We definitely are not going to radically change it." In this process, members of new product teams, the magazine reported, "have rigid areas of control and the right to overrule other members on key issues." Quarrels and false starts are inevitable under a system that simply denies the well-established principles of synchronous engineering and true teamwork.

The issue is more than assembling engineers, designers, accountants, purchasing people, manufacturing experts, and marketers and placing them under a single project leader. It's more than making him (and thus them) responsible for start-to-finish performance— right through to success (or failure) with the customers. It's also insistence that the team operate as a unit, committed to each other and to the project. It's understanding that teamwork functions through give-and-take and mutual respect.

The effectiveness of undiluted teamwork has been endlessly proven, not just by the Japanese, but by Chrysler. Yet Muchler thinks that "the school's still out" on the Chrysler approach. At the time of speaking, he was the boss in charge of all GM's North American car platforms, and both his attitude and his eminence show that the corporate psychology of GM, and the obstructive weight of the "way we do things round here," are still in need of radical change. They're probably more dangerous to GM than are its competitors, Ford, Chrysler, or the Japanese.

The success of GM in Europe, where it came from far behind Ford to lead the Continent in profits, remains a good omen. But the most hopeful sign for the Smith regime at GM lies in words that his wife had etched onto a copper plate as part of a desk ornament: "A leader is best when people barely know he exists. Not so good when people obey and acclaim him. Worse when they despise him. But of a good leader who talks little, when his work is done and his aim fulfilled, they will say, 'We did it ourselves.' "

Those admirable sentiments come, not from the twentieth-century Mark Brown, but from the philosopher Lao-tzu, who wrote six centuries before Christ. The dinosaurs, of course, lived many thousands of millennia before that. But without that philosophy—helping people to do it themselves—the dolphins will never take over. With that help, organizations can swim anywhere, and as fast as they want.

FOUR

Breaking Away—and Out: How to Divide and Conquer

The Electronic

Breakouts

As the twentieth century closes, the magnetism of capitalism rich and triumphant is still one of the strongest cards in America's technological hand. Allied with a restless search for achievement, the lure has generated an unprecedented and productive migration of people between companies. What, for example, do Tangram, Digital Equipment, GRiD Systems Corporation, Adobe Systems, Cauzin Systems, Apple, Metaphor Computer Systems, 3-Com Corporation, Acorn Computer, Data Point Corporation, and Microsoft have in common, apart from some whizzing and wonderful names?

All are evidently information technology firms. But that's not the significant connection. These companies are the 1988 business residences of men who created the personal computer inside the Xerox Corporation. Most of this incomparable team left Xerox after it turned down their wonderful invention: maybe the most wonderful of the entire century.

Several of these aces co-founded their new companies. Their start-ups had many contemporaries of similar origin: breakaways led by brilliant people seeking to exploit their brilliance under their own control. As Irwin Federman, semiconductor boss turned venture capitalist, noted, "Silicon Valley is a technology crucible. Every engineer in the valley has at the back of his mind that if he comes up with an interesting product, he can start a company."

Federman was quoted in a *Financial Times* article, by Geoffrey Owen and Louise Kehoe, which observed that "the hyper-competitive atmosphere of Silicon Valley, with its *adaptable giants* [my italics], cheeky spin-offs, and ambitious start-ups, is an American asset which no other country has yet been able to match."

The "adaptable giants" are companies like Hewlett-Packard, with its rare capacity for renewal and recovery, and Apple Corporation, whose versatility enabled it to survive potentially fatal technological isolation. It was Steve Jobs of Apple who saw the astounding results of the PC work done for Xerox at the Palo Alto Research Center, picked up the ball that Xerox fumbled, ran with it, and produced the Macintosh computer.

By absolutely no coincidence, three Xerox émigrés ended up with Apple, including Alan Kay, the genius who once uttered an immortal line: 'The only way to predict the future is to invent it." Another distinguished trio of inventors of the future moved to Digital Equipment: Butler Lampson, Bob Taylor, and Chuck Thacker, the great pioneers of "distributed processing," in which linked computers are located throughout the organization.

Nobody on the list joined IBM. The insularity of the industry leader seems to have extended to recruitment of both top technologists and managers. Others have poached liberally from the giant. Compaq was founded by three breakaways from Texas Instruments, but crucial roles were played by IBM refugees. Even more conspicuous was the IBM breakaway Gene Amdahl, whose large mainframes, given Fujitsu's major stake in Amdahl's success, could be described as Japan's Trojan horses.

The IBM of the late twentieth century tried to cover every technological bet, like a roulette player covering every number. That was ironically beneficial for the breakaway movement. Cutbacks in the group's own personnel encouraged thousands of able IBMers to invest their financial payoffs in start-ups or join former spin-offs. At the same time, many lesser firms, backed by IBM funds, were exploring the countless promising byways and labyrinths of the technological revolution.

The breakaways weren't all technologists. The most famous escapee was a salesman, H. Ross Perot, the future presidential gadfly and billionaire. He became super-rich by seeing and seizing a business opportunity which IBM let pass. Perot was superbly successful at selling computers, but noticed that his customers, ostensibly sold solutions, actually purchased problems.

In the mainframe era, making best use of expensive new computers, or even making an effective return on the investment, plagued users. Perot's idea was to open a new stream of income by developing workable systems to run on the computers. When IBM showed no interest, Perot left and started up Electronic Data Systems. He could easily afford the move, thanks to another quirk of the giant corporation.

Once, Thomas Watson, Jr., had filled his year's sales quota on its very first day. Admittedly, he had Wall Street for his territory, where being his father's son helped. Admittedly, the record was achieved "when U.S. Steel Products, an account that had been thrown into my territory to make me look good, came across with a huge order." But nobody stopped Watson from carrying on with the good work.

Not so with IBM salesman Ross Perot. He hit his annual quota in a few weeks; and promptly ran into a roadblock. Top management had decreed that nobody could outearn the chairman, the same Tom Watson. With his stunning performance in Dallas, Perot had reached the ceiling on his earnings for the year. He had every incentive to quit.

In his new career, Perot showed equal common sense in another matter: equity. The older Watson never held more than 5 percent of IBM's equity (worth $2.5 billion, though, even in the already reduced circumstances of mid-1992). Perot clung to four-fifths of EDS and duly made billions from its sale to General Motors. Significantly, many other individuals in the computing industry made more millions than its ruling family, the Watsons.

The giants dominated the highways. But the multiplying byways of computing still held out the prospect of fast capital gains. The giants unthinkingly passed on their own marvelous opportunities to others. This was doubly ironic. Maybe IBM's most lasting and greatest contribution to the electronics revolution that will change the world rests outside its own walls, where the breakaways are booming, flourishing in ways that large, rigid corporations are trying hard, and with too much difficulty, to imitate.

Freeing the Intrapreneurs

2

The many ironies of the electronic era include its mainspring of inspiration, the Palo Alto Research Center. PARC wasn't a breakaway or a start-up in a garage, but a richly financed operation of a mighty multinational, Xerox Corporation. No large established electronics manufacturer (and no start-up, either) could have matched Xerox's serendipitous assembly of the manifold talents whose work underpinned all future development of the personal computer.

Xerox was creating a new, costly lab in a research field where nobody had a presence. Existing computer companies all owned powerful scientific and technological establishments, mostly geared to mainframe-driven needs, rather than to invention of brave new worlds. Because it was doing something "wrong"—investing billions in a blue-sky effort unrelated to existing business—Xerox did everything right, including the choice of the Palo Alto site, where West Coast mores nurtured an unbuttoned, unencumbered, loose management style.

The research, however, was focused tightly and with uncanny

accuracy. In March 1970, Xerox CEO Peter McColough had unveiled a truly amazing vision before an audience of security analysts:

> The basic purpose of Xerox Corporation is to find the best means to bring greater order and discipline to information. . . . Even a casual examination of Xerox reveals that we already have most of the raw materials of advanced architecture of information technology: computers, copiers, duplicators, microfilm, communications devices, education techniques, display and transmission systems, graphic and optic capabilities, heavy research and global scope.

McColough asked his audience to "think for a moment of combining those raw materials with the talents of some 55,000 people throughout the world. In the years since then, the importance of forming a "vision" has been drummed into corporate managers with mounting intensity. Innumerable "vision" statements have been composed. None has surpassed the vision that Xerox's CEO, no technologist himself, laid down long before the inventors got together at PARC.

The later breakaways had no trouble in learning the visionary lesson. New-century management needs a guiding star, an understanding of the environment, a determination to stretch the bounds of the possible, always with practical intent and within practical boundaries. The team assembled at Palo Alto brought McColough's vision down to earth, or to desktop. They used his cornucopia to turn their own vision into reality: personal computing.

That is a second modern management theme: the direction of vision towards achieving pre-determined business results. Tragically, PARC's work didn't create a business for Xerox (a story superbly told in *Fumbling the Future* by Douglas K. Smith and Robert C. Alexander). There were many reasons. They included PARC's isolation, geographic and spiritual, from manufacturing, head office, and the existing Xerox markets. Lacking business-minded leadership themselves, the inventors lost out to those who held commercial power.

In one sense, their isolation was extremely productive. It created a highly innovative, focused climate, free of the constraints which dampen endeavor in corpocracies. But the best of the breakaways have shown that you can have your cake and eat it, too: high creativity coupled with driving commercialism; low-cost and defect-free manufacture with rapid spawning of new products; freedom of action with disciplined pursuit of objectives. Moreover, the successes show that the *combination* of these contrasts is the crucial factor.

The breakaway millionaires owe much to the brilliant solutions devised at PARC. These meant that when its PC moment belatedly arrived, IBM could put together a machine without any recourse to its own labs. Its engineers could design and assemble a world-class product cheaply from commercially available components. Non-IBM engineers, however, could do likewise. And the components themselves provided a mass of other opportunities for manufacturers with small resources. They could compete on equal terms with billion-dollar multinationals.

A parallel effect sprang from PARC's masterstroke of placing software on programs contained outside the computer itself. Innumerable software houses sprang up with no allegiance to anything but their own packaged programs—and their customers. The experts in distributed processing who went to Digital from PARC also helped to rupture the status quo. The VAX line of computers, able to intercommunicate fully and freely, opened the door to networking. Here, too, new companies rose to exploit new opportunities.

Everybody took pieces out of the hide of the established leaders, meaning mostly IBM, and punished them for lagging behind the PARC pace. It's a much-repeated lesson of technology, ignored at dire peril. The highest levels of technology may not make the largest sales: but unless the market leader holds the commanding heights of technology, its leadership is in danger.

The brightest hope for all U.S. industry, therefore, lies in the faith that the commanding electronic heights are safely and collectively based at home: that "Silicon Valley" is a unique resource, a fount of technology and enterprise, with a "rich infrastructure of electronics engineers, subcontractors, venture capitalists, public relations advisers, headhunters, and lawyers": an environment where you can generate new ventures by placing a call. "I could start a semiconductor company on the telephone from my home," as Wilf Corrigan has said.

Corrigan, chairman of the semiconductor company LSI Logic,

is another epitome of the breakaway boom. Both he and Andrew Grove, chairman of microprocessor king Intel, were employed by Fairchild Camera. Sherman M. Fairchild had inherited a large line of IBM stock. A playboy investor, he financed the breakaway of Robert Noyce and colleagues from Shockley Laboratories (founded by William Shockley, who invented the transistor at Bell Laboratories).

Fairchild reaped large profits from the Noyce group, which formed Intel after the parent's managerial gyrations proved unbearable. The new start-up changed the world, not just Silicon Valley, with the invention of the microprocessor. But Intel's own impetus has been maintained by more than its own inventiveness; its competitors—like Jerry Sanders of Advanced Micro Devices—are a continual threat, spur, and goad.

In 1986 AMD was singled out by *Fortune* as prime examplar of the "glamorous company." Today, even sober-sided businesses are advised to make it "fun" to work for them. The Silicon Valley glamour boys, though, exploited the fun formula from the very beginning:

1. *Celebrate success.* Sanders's parties of the early eighties were legendary: for one bash, four thousand attendees, several rock bands, lavish food and drink, and a bill of $750,000. You needn't go nearly so far. But regular and irregular small parties boost morale, create acquaintances, and breed community and communication.

2. *Encourage individual initiative.* Everybody is potentially creative. Their potential can't be exploited if ideas must struggle through bureaucratic processes, internal memoranda, and repeated meetings. Talented people working independently are strengths, not nuisances, if their talent is allowed expression.

3. *Apply a firm hand with a light touch.* This balancing act is the hardest part of the formula: staying very close, but keeping your distance. One dominant figure in a software house has done that literally. He's moved his base to the Bahamas, applying the firm hand electronically from thousands of miles away.

4. *Create a unique and powerful corporate culture.* That provides the essential environment for points 2 and 3. Individuals aim themselves in the direction encouraged by the culture. The cul-

tural norms provide a means of control without whips. And the celebrations (point 1) help strengthen and develop the culture.

5. *Achieve real, continuous, two-way communication.* Meetings of all employees are one effective method: but each culture develops its own ways of achieving mutual understanding. Every piece of paper is a potential means of communication. One company neatly gives everybody the same desk diary, with a suitable message on every page.

6. *Manage for the long term.* According to Sanders, running an innovative company is like growing asparagus, which takes three years to mature, as do some new product ideas.

7. *Accept the permanence of impermanence.* Product strengths and markets alike can vanish overnight. So can staff. The breakaway environment encourages others. Sanders has suffered from the phenomenon; some of AMD's best designers walked out in the mid-1980s. Their company, Cypress Semiconductor, has become yet another force in the Valley.

Sanders thought in 1992 that Cypress would "never become an important global competitor." Maybe so, maybe not. The power of being biggest has commonly been exaggerated, and the long-term viability of start-ups underestimated, throughout the industry's history. But even if competition stays local, it can be more than an irritant—as Intel found to its cost when Chips and Technologies, a total newcomer, stole a march on the champion. PCs use several semiconductors in addition to the (usually) Intel microprocessor. The small company simply packaged the other devices in "chip sets," taking away much of Intel's non-microprocessor sales.

"In retrospect it was a simple thing to do," Intel's Grove admitted. "They thought of it, we didn't." In a field of burgeoning, vital technologies and ideas, monopoly of thought can never be achieved. The newcomers keep on coming—and coming on strong. That's the raw stuff of the competitive, dog-eat-dog free market. From that strenuous dialectic, according to capitalist theory, technological and economic advance most readily flows. If that theory holds, so does American supremacy in the Olympic Games of technology.

But doubt has been cast on the theory, or at least the practice, from the Valley itself. There the problems now loom as large as the opportunities, to judge by a 1992 report on the region. *Silicon Valley: An Economy at Risk* announces the title of the document, produced by the Center for Economic Competitiveness at the SRI International consultancy. A self-styled wake-up call, the report was intended to arouse Valley businessmen to the erosion of their competitive prowess. For once, the fearsome Japanese weren't to blame; the Valley's alleged wounds were self-inflicted.

The Valley has suffered recurrent bouts of self-doubt ever since its initial explorers turned their newfound lands into established world powers. But that's what they are: established, powerful, global. Since 1938, when Bill Hewlett and Dave Packard set up shop in a rented garage, Hewlett-Packard (like other top companies) has evolved into a global maker and seller of highly complex product lines: Hewlett-Packard makes everything from reduced instruction set computing chips to the electronic instruments with which the partners began (selling first to Walt Disney).

Beneath the leaders, a host of middle-sized companies also boasts international presence. Most are breakaways: just as Apple, now a veteran, was an early-stage breakaway from Hewlett-Packard. Steve Jobs was only a summer employee: his co-founder, Stephen Wozniak, had worked for the company. Hewlett-Packard's lack of interest in the enthusiasms of Wozniak's "Homebrew Computing Club" made the young engineer susceptible to Jobs's notion that they should father their own little computer, which became the Apple I.

Hewlett-Packard itself was actually a closet computer company. As Hewlett explained, his researchers "came up with the idea of a desktop calculator. It really was a computer, but we didn't want to call it a computer, because every customer company had a computer guru and all they wanted was IBM." The inhibition about IBM may well have governed Hewlett-Packard's further development. Although computers provided the largest share of its $14.5 billion revenues by the early nineties, growth had been won well away from IBM's data-processing heartland.

Most of the Valley had grown the same way: either steering clear of IBM, or operating around what were once its fringes (personal computers, scientific hardware, etc.), or becoming an indispensable supplier to the colossus. As IBM expanded into nearly every market (whether successfully or not), sought out new suppliers, and stumbled in its own growth, the Valley's breakaways, old and new, were bound to feel the effects.

But their overall stability in such an unstable environment points to the power of the Freedom Formula. Of course, the formula depends on maintaining your technological prowess and progress. That goes without saying: to recover from the mid-eighties recession, AMD launched one new chip *every week.* If there is a "dark side" to "employee autonomy within a strong corporate culture," as *Fortune* worried, the anxieties, by and large have not been borne out.

The "potential for elitism bordering on hubris" did look dangerous, though. "Dazzled by their own success and recklessly confident that it will continue, the people in key jobs at glamorous companies may fail to notice critical changes in the marketplace." They may indeed miss opportunities—like Intel in the case mentioned above. But the century's end abounds with main chances. In a truly opportunist corporate environment, the ones that got away won't be decisive.

The ones that are got make the difference. In 1982–92, AMD had the tenth highest growth rate (30 percent compound) for earnings per share among the *Fortune* 500: profits as a percentage of sales (16 percent) were tenth highest in 1992 and return on assets sixteenth highest. Intel did even better. In so volatile a business, such fabulous returns can't be guaranteed every year. But that's another century-end necessity: to recognize that growth over the long haul, not just next year, is the true corporate objective.

So the "warning signs" noted by SRI in 1992 are ominous. As reported by Louise Kehoe, they included "slower employment growth, a decline in venture capital financing, slowing growth in precompetitive research and development spending and a shortage of skilled workers." As she observed, however, several of the "problems" ascribed to Silicon Valley "are common to all high technology regions in the U.S." She saw no need (although the report did) for joint private and public initiatives to turn the Valley into an "American Technopolis": "The Valley has its problems, but it has spawned more new ventures and more important new technologies than any other place on earth. It ain't broke and it doesn't need fixing."

The Valley, anyway, is shorthand for an American Technopolis that already exists: in the report's words, "a dynamic community that supports technology enterprises and retains value-added manufacturing, employment, and wealth." In other words, the whole United States. It matters little where the members of the technopolis settle, whether they are start-ups by kids from school (like Microsoft) or breakaways from breakaways (like NeXT, where Steve Jobs has spent frustrating years trying to create a new Apple).

So long as a cluster of like-minded firms gets together within easy reach of a first-rate academic campus, the technopolis can expand and flourish. When one European PC firm wanted to locate a new plant in Europe, an American consultant wisely advised these clients to follow this same prescription. Instead the firm expanded at the existing site, close neither to other high-tech businesses nor to academics.

The management's choice was much the cheaper, but similar decisions by indigenous Europeans explain why the European Technopolis has failed to compete with "the Valley." America's has proved endlessly extendable. Witness the example of James B. Moon, who, on one account, had every reason "to be loyal to Silicon Valley."

"He grew up there, studied there, and joined Intel Corp. Then in 1979, Intel moved his operation to Oregon. . . . During the 1980s . . . Moon watched dozens of technology companies spring up and succeed in the Northwest. In 1986, he started his own company to make portable patient monitors. That company, Protocol Systems Inc., nearly doubled its sales last year, to $23 million, and went public in March."

Moon's saga is only a tiny part of what *Business Week* billed as "High-Tech Heaven" in the Pacific Northwest. In mid-1992 the region housed 3,200 high-tech operations, of which 2,100 were in electronic hardware and software. Bill Gates's Seattle-based Microsoft, while by far the biggest, is just one of 1,500 software companies whose main concentration is in the eastern suburban "technology corridor." Yet the region is only one among several existing high-tech heavens—and others are waiting to be born.

The Global Technopolis is developing fast: and America's valleys will remain its heartland. They won't be all-American territory in any sense: the Japanese have moved into the valleys in force. The technology is global, and can't be kept exclusive. But the management style of the electronic pioneers—their receptiveness to new ideas, jaunty conviction that brains beat size, hatred of hierarchy and formality, and reliance on the independent spirit of man: *that* is special.

It can be copied, but it's too rarely imitated outside the valleys. That's a serious error. In any business, in any sector, the opportunities are greatest for managements and managers who accept that the breakaway culture, just like a PC or even a microprocessor, can be cloned, and who, knowing that, dare apply the Freedom Formula to become their own breakaways.

The Odd Apotheosis of AT&T

3

The greatest triumph of the modern trustbuster came in 1982. The Justice Department had taken aim at American Telephone & Telegraph, modern America's nearest approach to the classic monopolies. These were built on restrictive control of the market—like John D. Rockefeller's hammerlock on the means of transporting oil, or AT&T's decades of monopolizing America's telephone lines. Its Bell System was a foundation stone of latter-day capitalism—and the trustbusters dug it up.

The great telephone company capitulated. In a settlement which the company's own chairman called "exactly what the Government wanted," AT&T lost, not just some of its domestic local-call monopoly, but all; even the remaining long-distance business was opened to powerful competition. For their part, the seven so-called Baby Bells were set totally free from Big Mother, and left to find their own destinies. Mother herself had to seek her future in long-distance and international telecommunications.

But the year of antitrust triumph also saw the Justice Department's greatest defeat. IBM walked away unscathed after a case that had lasted thirteen years. The failure to break up IBM was especially galling because at the beginning, so chairman Thomas Watson, Jr., wrote, "I was willing to split IBM in two"—large machines and the rest. His sticking point was the trustbusters' wish to impose a settlement similar to AT&T's. Rather than be busted into seven segments, IBM fought the government with no holds barred.

Ranged against "the most powerful corporation in the world," which "fought tooth and nail for the continuation of that power" as it "spent lavishly on its defense," the government trial team, "never able to match" that spending, wrote Richard Thomas DeLamarter, felt themselves to be leading a crusade. DeLamarter was one of the crusaders. His book *Big Blue,* published in 1986, is a unique study from the inside of an antitrust case brought against a major corporation. The crusade was against, to quote his subtitle, "the use and abuse of power."

DeLamarter, in an eloquent and worrying passage, admits that the U.S. laws under which his colleagues labored are an unsure defense against monopoly of the kind then exercised by IBM: a monopoly that rested, not on the traditional overweening size of market share, but commercial and technological practices. What DeLamarter—and for that matter Watson—failed to spot was that those very practices were undermining the quasi-monopoly (a more accurate description of the reality of the mid-eighties).

The author began his analysis with "a few facts about IBM" that make strange reading today:

1. IBM "is the most profitable company in the world."
2. "IBM continues to dominate the computer business and is well on its way to dominating everything that is connected to and/or operates with these computers."
3. "IBM faces no significant domestic or foreign competition that could threaten this dominance."
4. "The antitrust laws, designed to police such unequal competition, are of little use."

Half a dozen years later, only the last of these points is still valid, but wholly irrelevant, given that IBM's profits, after degenerating into multibillion-dollar losses, show no sign of ever regaining, or even approaching, the 13 percent net margins of 1985; given that its market shares in most major product lines, and its overall share of the computing market, have fallen dramatically; given that competition, both foreign and domestic, has burgeoned at every point.

But meanwhile, what had happened to the broken-up AT&T? By mid-1992, the phone giant's shareholders had seen the total worth of their investment rise by 279 percent: the paltry rise of 66 percent for IBM at that point was subsequently wiped out by big dips in the share price. In April 1993, the stock market valued IBM at $31.6 billion. AT&T alone weighed in at $80.4 billion, while the five largest of its eight dismembered parts took the total to $192.7 billion. That makes IBM's antitrust triumph seem like the most unfortunate of victories.

But that's not the worst, or the best of it. Not only have the Baby Bells rapidly established cultures and management successes of their own, but AT&T, once a byword for bureaucratic stagnation, has been transformed. *Fortune* writer David Kirkpatrick (who took a very cold-eyed view of IBM's efforts at reinvention) stated that the phone company had "uprooted its complacent, sluggish, inward-looking culture" since Robert Allen took over as CEO in September 1991.

Lord Acton wrote that "power tends to corrupt and absolute power corrupts absolutely." Paradoxically, the stripping of its monopoly power from the old AT&T set it free to develop new and badly needed competitive powers that met modern needs. The undivided IBM, while it remained "the most powerful corporation in the world" in its industry, never had absolute power. It had more than enough power to corrupt its own competitive ability.

Taking It from the Top

Science progresses by formulating hypotheses and conducting carefully controlled experiments. Management can't do this. You can't find identical organizations and make one try Theory A while the other stays unchanged. Even if you could and Theory A produced wonderfully better results, that wouldn't prove the theory for other, different companies. Comparisons from published results and reports, of course, are even less scientific. But sometimes conclusions are so striking that it's unwise to ignore them.

The contrasting experiences of AT&T and IBM after their respective federal antitrust cases can be regarded as a Great Experiment in a real-life management laboratory—and the outcome looks very convincing. In giving its verdict on Robert Allen's AT&T, *Business Week* waxed even more lyrical than David Kirkpatrick about the change this CEO had wrought upon "one of the world's most entrenched corporate cultures." The encomium succinctly lists the way to bust the most rigid of trusts, the internal monopoly of a single management view:

1. Shatter the old icons.
2. Clean out the deadwood.
3. Lure in outsiders.
4. Infuse "a sprawling empire with a simple, overarching vision of the future."

To eradicate the old culture, Allen used a new corporate tool: a five-man team (the heads of the four operating divisions, plus the chief financial officer), which acts as a collective chief operating officer. Like the Swiss presidency, the leadership of this group rotates. The object is to achieve real synergy and total understanding between corporate components whose interactions are becoming more and more decisive.

That can stand as a symbol of what is happening in the management world at large: interactive management. Team-working is more than a trend; it's a necessity. It has become vital to organizational effectiveness—Allen's essential concern. He has strictly pragmatic reasons for driving the culture from "very control-oriented and top-down" towards "an atmosphere of turning the organization charts upside down, putting the customers on top." The people "close to the customer" must be "doing the key decision-making." That's for one of those pragmatic reasons: because a whirling, converging marketplace demands an AT&T that's "quicker on our feet."

So Allen seeks two-hatted leaders. Wearing one hat, they represent their businesses. Under the second hat, they "help me make decisions that cross business unit boundaries." Under either hat, executives spend an unusual amount of time discussing the "core values": respect for individuals, dedication to helping customers, and adhering to the highest standards of integrity, innovation, and teamwork. The commitment to the values leads to the end-result sought by Total Quality practitioners: "sharing the vision" throughout the organization.

These "soft" values have not stopped the hard profits from rolling in: 1992's record earnings of $4 billion doubled the 1988 figure. The twenty business units into which Allen split the group are expected to meet several hard targets, financial and non-financial, on a tough, "or-else" basis. The units' success has financed his ambitions, which in turn are creating a new leviathan. Hot on the heels of the $7.5 billion purchase of NCR, Allen broke that world record with the $12.6 billion bid for McCaw, the leader in cellular phone services.

The deals seemingly make a mockery of the 1982 settlement, but the essential point remains: the antitrust breakup gave AT&T the focus vitally needed for the new world of telecommunications. The breakup cut away, along with the Baby Bells, the underpinnings of the old culture. That didn't happen at IBM, a comparison of which Allen is acutely aware. In everything from the recruitment of outsiders to the devolution of decision power to those responsible for execution, Allen showed far greater speed than IBM's bosses in an essentially similar situation.

As one of his executives observed, "Much of the world saw the problems that have afflicted some other big companies for as long as fifteen years." The managers of those companies didn't see. An undivided AT&T would quite likely have been just as blind. The trustbusters had attacked the right of any organization, however benevolent or well-run, to exclude competition, by fair means or foul. In doing so, the Justice Department inadvertently proved that a large corporation, thus protected, can become too large for its own good—and that of all other interested parties.

IBM had won its power by different means than AT&T. The Watsons had no stranglehold over either the technology, the productive apparatus, or the channels of distribution. So what explained its quasi-monopoly—and its blindness? In the unfolding of the Computer Age, IBM simply combined its power in all three areas to create a profound control over *customers*. The latter, primarily the big businessmen of America and the world, could have turned safely to the many competitors following in IBM's wake. The Watsons bent their energies to preventing that turn.

In the fifties and sixties, the sheer success of IBM in selling to the corporate market bred still more success, still more dominating market power. The capitalist model gave the prize of market dominance to those who best used the combined powers of technology, distribution, and marketing: and that spelled IBM. As these powers were strengthened and applied, lesser competitors fell away, increasingly unable to exercise their prime economic function: to provide a viable alternative, profitable both to the customers and to themselves.

As Damon Runyon wrote, "The race isn't always to the swift, nor the victory to the strong. But that's the way to bet it." The Justice Department tried to change the odds, to argue that capitalist success could be too extreme, that society, via the government, could and should intervene to cut the branches of the tallest tree—if its shadow stunted the growth of others.

The suit threatened to destroy not only the IBM system, but the philosophy behind the structure. IBM offered its corporate customers, spread across a multitude of industries, a platform for safe one-stop shopping. It took the inherently kaleidoscopic technology of electronic data processing and shook it into a pattern that formed one unchanging configuration: IBM.

In the nineties, however, the kaleidoscope is being shaken so violently that no pattern lasts for long. The issue of dominance, fair or foul, becomes irrelevant. But IBM was imprisoned by the earlier rout of its mainframe competitors. That had confirmed the image, held internally as strongly as externally, of IBM as the high-tech leader that used unbeatably large investment in its products and processes to compound the impact of equally powerful investment in its marketing.

That image, true or false, has become as obsolete as the old-style mainframe itself. No dominant design can cover all the multiplying ramifications of the century-end market. Nobody's future is secured any longer on installed bases of expensively acquired office machinery and software. Corner the large corporate market, as IBM could and did, and you once cornered the industry. But an industry of many markets and many technologies defies the dominance theory.

True, in 1992 IBM accounted for 28 percent of the sales of the world's seventeen largest computer and office products companies. The figure is massive, but exaggerated. It doesn't count the billions of sales included in conglomerates like Hitachi, Siemens, and AT&T (which now owns NCR), and that's only three. Even using the narrow definition, the 28 percent represents a sharp fall from the 39 percent equivalent share enjoyed three years previously. No great market leader, no star of such size and brightness in the corporate firmament, has ever suffered so abrupt a descent.

Many other managements, though, have slipped, in most cases because of an identically erroneous view—the idea that successful competition meant maintaining leadership by preserving the status quo. That's why, for example, the tire industry resisted beyond the point of no return the new radial technology introduced by Michelin. Powerful forces inside the electronics giants resisted first the personal computer, and then its full implications, for the same reason: the new technology upset the old order.

What are those "forces"? They are human beings, professional managers. They rise through staff and line jobs, where they often have technological responsibility, but lack great knowledge. Some inevitably end at the summits of organizations employing hundreds of thousands of employees. The higher they rise, the more they become prisoners of the system; but they also control and modify the system. Their power to create, or enable creation, is great. So is their power to obstruct.

The obstruction often takes the form of resisting the rise of new, upsetting technologies. The large corporations of America are mostly driven by non-technologists. That needn't be decisive; AT&T's Allen is among their number. But most CEOs have risen by selling rather than producing, managing rather than making, and too few can generate visions that rise clear above such limited backgrounds. IBM, a salesman's foundation, naturally fits this pattern. It wasn't perceived as typical, because its products and achievements were technologically high.

Closer examination of the power structure and reward systems in this technological cornucopia shows that selling ruled IBM; technology was subservient. Subjecting technology to market disciplines, and to managerial expertise, is indispensable. But that doesn't demote technology. A prime role of management is to finance, enable and ensure technological leadership: to see that wherever the company chooses to compete, its products and processes equal or surpass the competition, both in satisfying the market and in timeliness.

Sometimes this means giving genius its head. IBM failed with Gene Amdahl, the mainframe wizard; the former SmithKline French succeeded with Sir James Black. That brilliant British pharmacologist proceeded to discover Tagamet, the billion-dollar anti-ulcer drug. Pharmaceutical companies like Merck, which years ago replaced IBM as America's most admired corporation, know the rules of the high-tech game.

Speed to market with market-leading products is the vital formula for such firms, which are often (like Merck) led by top-class researchers. Similarly, success after success in information technology has been won by leaders whose leadership began in development: Bill Gates of Microsoft in programming, Ken Olsen of Digital in computer engineering, Robert Noyce in semiconductors. In new industries, high technology and high management acumen often go hand in hand.

Virtually all Detroit's pioneers were automotive engineers, from Henry Ford downwards: in other industries, founding fathers were mostly technological founders as well. It doesn't follow that all manufacturers should be led by techno-executives. The genius of world-shaping entrepreneurs can lie in spotting emerging technology and jumping on the bandwagon, like John H. Patterson with the cash register, or his star pupil, IBM's Thomas Watson, with punch cards. Thomas Watson, Jr., saw and exploited the potential of the digital computer. Two other IBM chairmen, Frank Cory and John Opel, played the godfather to its personal version.

As these men proved, IBM had (and has) all the resources needed to turn technological vision into rich reality. So have most large corporations. So why was so much leadership in so many industries lost to small and foreign competitors? IBM's legendary PC team suggests the answer. The Dirty Dozen shot to fame (but not to personal fortune) as a group of engineers powered by their own drive. They owed the corporation two things only—one irreplaceable, the other not.

Without IBM's brand name and reputation, the PC wouldn't have struck the market with such a thunderclap. Given its product advantages, the PC would have prospered under any name—but not so fast, nor so furiously. The second contribution, finance, was available elsewhere. IBM's PC depended on a microprocessor from Intel, itself a venture capital creation. A continuing strength of the U.S. economy is its ability to mobilize large development capital outside the big-time corporate world. Whether independents would have had the courage, or felt the pressure, to force the PC project through in a year is another matter: but it's not impossible.

Where the PC led, others could have followed. Within any Western car company, the talent lay ready, for example, to reduce model development costs and lead-times to the Japanese standard. The four-year Western norm was conventional wisdom with no technical or economic justification—except that, on outdated accounting principles, the longer basic models and engines ran, the more money you seemed to make. The fact that competitive power was steadily eroded carried no weight. It literally wasn't taken into account.

Who is to blame? The technologists don't call these shots. That privilege is reserved for top management. "Strategy" is determined by the corporate strategists, which doesn't mean the staff experts who do the strategic analysis and present the cases. The strategy that ultimately controls the pyramidic layers of management is that of the senior group. Their strategy is not subject to checks and balances, especially if it seems successful.

The cause of major management problems, in firms of any size, is often the concentration of strategic and operational power at the top. In big businesses, even if all chieftains were competent technologically, thoroughly versed in strategic principles, familiar with the business and its personnel, expert in all relevant management disciplines, concentrating on the right priorities, and rewarded only for their success in achieving the top priority aims—even then, the size, range, and complexity of modern corporations would put the task beyond the reach of any one individual.

As it is, too many have been left behind by technologies they never understood; have no experience and no present knowledge base in strategy; are remote from most people and parts in the business; have done little or nothing to refresh (let alone expand) their management knowledge since business school days; and spend more time on internal politics and external entanglements than on the vital business of their company.

They are rewarded, not for any achievement that relates directly to their efforts, but simply for occupying their posts. Their power to create is paralyzed because of the above-mentioned remoteness from the markets in which their people compete—and from those people. Their power to frustrate is enormous, though. Overnight, as a whole decade of decline showed at both GM and IBM, decision or indecision at the top can waste the destiny of products, plants, and people.

If customers wanted the old quasi-monopolies, the old ways would make more sense. But customers in all markets increasingly favor diversity. Businesses must become more diverse in management and in marketing to meet this fragmentation. The corporate center can contribute nothing to market-centered businesses save a number of non-operational but priceless elements. The first is to set the overall "strategy," intelligent and communicated, which covers broadly the choice of destination and the means of getting there.

Within that general framework, the center sets minimum and high standards; represents investors in seeing that each business is earning excellent returns on their money—and will do so into the foreseeable future; facilitates ambitious plans with money, advice, and connections (including interconnections with other group businesses); appoints excellent top managers, and insists that they recruit excellently; and looks after relations with outside agencies, including governments and other corporations, that need handling centrally.

The list, closely akin to the principles that Bob Allen has applied at AT&T, could go on. It's demanding enough to provide plenty of occupation for men at the top—for which read "the topless top." Once top people start giving orders to their appointees, the game is over. The bureaucratic silt builds up again. The best people quit in hope of finding a better environment: and the personal initiative on which corporate success depends dries up.

Through the internal and external blockages created by its top-down policies, IBM may have retarded rather than defended progress in information technology. As AT&T's Allen has recognized, the information industry's exceptional volatility demands freer-form, fluid management. Established corporations with rigid traditions and set procedures are not about to change their habits easily. They'll never do so under the leadership of men who, having risen under an old system that buttresses their power and privileges, won't let go of the reins until retirement.

The Lessons
of Lexmark

Something like the old maxim *de minimis non curat lex* (the law doesn't care about little matters) applies to huge companies: corporations tend to lose interest in little businesses. The trouble is that a little business in corporate terms may be colossal by other standards—like the two-hundredth largest company in the United States.

That was the size of Lexmark, once IBM's typewriter and printer business, when, in spring 1991, the owner divested itself of the bauble. That was a rare event in itself. The company had sold off the Rolm phone exchange business: but that had been a recent and unwise acquisition. IBM had created its typewriter interests. More, it had built the division into a market leader whose prestige reinforced the group's status at the top end of the business equipment market.

Its electric typewriters, perceived as the best, carried the highest prices. It was no use grumbling: if you wanted to recruit or retain a top secretary, she got an IBM. It was the Mercedes-Benz of the executive suite. Every typewriter paraded the name and fame of IBM before the secretary's bosses. And they were often the very customers whose multimillion-dollar orders for mainframe computers built the profits and progress of the main IBM business.

What misfired? Disproportion was a factor: the typewriter business, with "only" $2 billion of sales, seemed insignificant in a corporation waxing rich on mainframes. The latter machines, being vastly expensive, were also bound to take precedence among the salesmen. But that wasn't the real problem. The managers of the typewriter business had other sales outlets, actual and potential. It was management's neglect that ruined one of America's best businesses.

That neglect is all the more remarkable because the worst damage occurred where IBM should have been strongest: technology. In the progress of typewriter technology from manual to electronic, IBM won big in the electro-mechanical stage. It added ingenious ideas like the golfball font to the basic principle of operating keys by electric power. Yet the world's greatest powerhouse of electronics technology mishandled the next and crucial stage: adding electronics.

Memory functions were given to the typewriters, making them even costlier. But the Japanese were allowed to take the lead in producing all-electronic machines. They shattered the price structure and took typing into a new era. The old leader still had a chance to recoup. The word processor, the ultimate in electronic typewriters, was an early life-form of the personal computer—yet this market was left to Wang.

Its progenitor, An Wang, used money made from IBM (for inventing core memory) to launch his own instant-hit product. IBM must have noticed the flood of orders, $1 million in all, taken for Wang's product on its 1976 debut at a New York trade fair. The lack of reaction to such basic changes can partly be explained by the typewriter division's relative unimportance to its great parent. A second factor was surely lack of cross-fertilization, taking expertise from one part and injecting it into another.

A third and fundamental factor was that, instead of the corporate system helping, it positively hindered. Size, centralization, and control mechanisms simply got in the way. With the creation of Lexmark, the surviving employees moved into a luckier way of life. Its breakaway management wasn't headed by some external genius. CEO Marvin Mann had worked for IBM for thirty-two years. Yet he knew exactly how an entrepreneurial business should be staffed and organized.

After a major shakeout, half the former numbers were employed in manufacturing, administration, and development. By dividing the business into four separate units (printers, keyboards, typewriters, and printer supplies), Mann exchanged focus for the fuzziness that clogged the previous information flows and marketing. Selling was entrusted to a dedicated salesforce. Meetings and formal presentations were slashed even more severely than the workforce, and executives at meetings no longer needed to overload themselves with all the transparencies they might need to answer questions from their superiors.

Mann emphasized the importance of people "working in units where they feel they can make a difference." He dismantled a superstructure that was subtracting value in both tactics and strategy. The strategic damage was the greater. The typewriter division was neither given its head nor integrated into the group's mainstream strategy. Otherwise, IBM might have broken into the PC market far earlier.

A clear technological path ran through electronics and memory. Had it been followed, the PC wouldn't have started life as a sideshow. IBM might also have avoided the trap of leaving its system wide open to imitators. That's hypothetical. The unleashing of Marvin Mann and Lexmark's powerful abilities, which had been bottled up inside IBM, was no hypothesis. Sell-off shouldn't be the only method of unbottling such talents. There has to be a better way—and there is.

6

Parenting
Corporate Children

The Lexmark case raises basic issues of organization. A *Wall Street Journal* writer saw the early experiences of the liberated typewriter and printer business as a good omen for the reorganization launched by chairman John F. Akers (and then aborted by his successor): it might "turn out to be a model for the quasi-independent business units that are at the core of IBM's plans to decentralize."

There was nothing halfway about Lexmark's independence, though. The vendor retained a 10 percent stake and a boardroom seat. But the shots were ultimately called by Clayton & Dubillier, the investment firm that arranged Lexmark's leveraged buyout. For five years Lexmark had the right to the IBM trademark, an asset of incalculable value. The old owner remained by far its largest customer for printers, keyboards, and so forth. Otherwise Lexmark was strictly on its own.

That independence was a virtue. One consultant observed that, as a business unit, the future Lexmark had everything ("a factory that was state of the art"), except the ability to escape from an imposed problem: "that the parent is busy and neglects the kids. . . . Also, the overhead costs of any organization that big is a tax that burdened their ability to play in the low-end commodity price business. They couldn't compete effectively. Something had to give."

The key word there is *parent:* "the parent is busy and neglects the kids." The parental analogy is used very effectively by Michael Goold, Andrew Campbell, and Marcus Alexander as the governing metaphor for *Corporate-Level Strategy: Creating Value in the Multi-Business Company,* their investigation of how multibusiness companies seek "parenting advantage." As they note, the parent (the corporate center or holding company) makes choices no different from a small shopkeeper's: what lines to stock, push, and drop.

So might parents decide which children to keep in the family business, which to send forth. In the multibusiness company, that translates into which businesses to keep, back, or sell. As the authors stress, though, the parental role is not passive. How well or badly the parenting is done affects the outcome. With Lexmark, IBM's bad parenting had spoiled a perfectly good child that might profitably have stayed at home.

The first fruits of rebirth, a new range of laser printers, make the point: aimed straight at Hewlett-Packard, the printers were well praised. IBM had long been at least HP's equal in technology, but it had lost in the marketplace, where the concentrated HP salesforce had run several rings around the opposition. As usual, the latter's salesmen represented a range of products. In setting free other, much larger units, would IBM destroy the unified salesforce that was once the envy of the office machinery industry?

The question could be put another way. Should companies fragment themselves at all? Few management issues are clear-cut, but the answer to this fundamental question shouldn't be ambiguous. Either scale has economies, or it doesn't. Believers in the bigger-is-better formula could allow that beyond a certain point, disadvantages of size outweigh its advantages. The small-is-beautiful brigade, however, would always pitch that point far lower—thinking in hundreds of employees where the rival school thinks in thousands, or hundreds of thousands.

Fragmentation has no fears for these advocates, or for the rampant privatizers in John Major's British government. The nationalized railways, prior to planned sale, were carved into two dozen passenger

franchises, operating services on lines run by Railtrack, which was itself split into ten geographical zones. Zonal managers, to quote the
Financial Times, were "given a high degree of devolved power to run
their businesses," aiming at quarterly targets set by HQ, "with financial rewards geared to the degree of success."

Devolution and incentives are the essence of fragmentation theory. It makes sense, moreover, to separate rail infrastructure from the
rail services. The costs of a network can never be fairly allocated
among users, for the network is a sine qua non: no network, no services. With the network separated out, the economics of separate services can be intelligently assessed.

Fragmentation theorists go much further. They claim a recipe
for universal success. Break down the organization, any organization,
into discrete components; place each component under a single manager; hold said manager entirely responsible for the success or failure
of this devolved enterprise: reward or remove leaders accordingly.
The idea has flourished before; in the sixties it was called giving a
man "a business like his own." But success was scant.

Lou Gerstner, the new man wrestling with IBM, explained why
in a *Fortune* interview. "I don't think getting the economics right in
a business is necessarily the same thing as decentralization. There is
a misconception that small is always more beautiful than big. Just
fragmenting an organization does not create conditions sufficient for
success." If it did, small- to medium-sized corporations would always
outdo the large. But they don't.

Fragmentation is simply one form of parenting. How far can the
parent analogy be taken? For a start, good parents are always loving
and tolerant: at times, reasonably firm and justly critical. In terms of
parental strategy, they

1. Encourage offspring to aim for achievably high standards: help
   them to develop strengths and eliminate weaknesses
2. Use connections within the family and outside to improve the
   offspring's prospects and performance
3. Make their own knowledge, know-how, experience, and abilities
   available to the offspring
4. Release the apron springs as soon as children are ready to leave
   home

These parental behaviors equate with four main influences which, say Goold, Campbell, and Alexander, parents may use to create value in business units: (1) influencing stand-alone performance, (2) forming linkages, (3) supplying functions and services, and (4) changing the portfolio. They show brilliantly how parents have vacillated around these four variables since 1960, when diversification became a driving force. By 1969, over half the *Fortune* 500 had diversified, most into "related" businesses. The relationships were sometimes strange: gas supplier BOC even owned King Harry Pizza, reasoning that gases froze the pizzas!

Not surprisingly, by the seventies many diversifiers "were beginning to encounter performance problems." The executive suites didn't blame the problems on their own parenting. Instead, they turned to "portfolio planning." The Boston Consulting Group devised its simplified matrix methodology, based on growth rates and market share. It showed parents which children were "stars," which "question marks," which "cash cows," and which "dogs" (to be done away with).

The matrix system helped tidy up many a mess. It did nothing to improve the parental, and thus the corporate, performance. The predators of the eighties did plenty: and not only by ousting failed parents. They stimulated other, frightened managements into "restructuring." Cash cow or star, question mark or dog, all were grist to the restructuring mills. Between 1974 and 1987, diversifiers fell from 63 percent of the *Fortune* 500 to 41 percent.

That report comes from Constantinos Markides of the London Business School, who concluded, alas, that "companies that restructured to reduce diversity were . . . characterized by [relatively] poor performance." Hence, in the latest phase, the parent concentrates on "core businesses" (those left after restructuring), or "core competencies," and relies on "sharing activities and transferring skills" (in Harvard professor Michael Porter's words)—the object being to achieve profitable synergies and better performance.

As *Corporate-Level Strategy* points out, this goes right back to ideas originated by Igor Ansoff in the conglomerating sixties. The wheel has come full circle, but the vehicle isn't moving. The parent has two tough tests to pass. The first is, Does the business perform better under the parent's care than it would independently? The three authors, though, think this test doesn't go nearly far enough. Hence the second test: Does the business do better under the parent's care than it would under that of any other parent?

While that latter test may sound hypothetical, it certainly places corporate parents on the spot. They must decide how to achieve the authors' "parenting advantage." What insights can they contribute to improve the value of their businesses? How do they behave as parents, and what businesses fit this behavior? What is their "heartland"—the business or businesses where they feel most comfortable?

There are other issues. The fit of strategy with markets matters as much as the fit of parenting styles. Whatever Gerstner says or does, for instance, any solution attempted at IBM will tend towards fragmenting the monolith into stand-alones. That's simply because its markets have fragmented, greatly altering the economics of the businesses. That's why one of the few remaining mainframe competitors, Unisys, has made two huge businesses (consulting services and open systems) more independent.

Unisys is "trying to achieve the advantages specialized companies have," says chairman James Unruh, "without losing the advantages of economy of scale and the breadth of market of large companies." Never sneer at scale advantages—not when it comes to reducing overlaps and surplus numbers. No theoretical or practical gains in managerial vigor, speed of response, faster communication, or any other benefit of smallness, can match the once-for-all economies available from merging two complementary organizations.

Equally, efficiency gains made through devolution (as on the British railroads) may be offset, even swamped, by the diseconomies of fragmenting services that would otherwise be central. But the fact remains that whatever the arguments in favor of fragmentation, CEOs have found amalgamation much more attractive. The history of strategic fashions reviewed earlier can easily be read as a series of justifications for central managements—for parents.

The post-war wave of mergers and acquisitions, each adding power and pelf to a parental organization, has been interrupted only by recession. Unisys, after all, put itself together (with the merger of Burroughs and Sperry) before starting to take itself apart. Though many mergers have disappointed—Unisys made huge losses for four years—that doesn't disprove the principle: other things being equal, the bigger the company is, the greater its opportunities to maximize profits by sharing costs.

What must be equal? First, if overheads rise in step with turn-over, that defeats the object of the exercise, which is to push more revenue through the same pipeline of costs. Second, companions in misery are no happier for being larger: the two Unisys components were about to pass from decades of domination by IBM to years of agony adjusting to a post-mainframe world. Third, the turnover must be reasonably homogeneous, so costs can genuinely be shared.

The homogeneity question raises the issue spotlighted by Goold, Campbell, and Alexander: diversity versus concentration. Totally ho-mogeneous, one-product companies look vulnerable: therefore, stra-tegic diversification is the only answer. But Coca-Cola rightly sold off its only major diversified acquisition, Columbia Pictures, and has enjoyed an unprecedented run of success founded on soft drinks. Royal Dutch–Shell has managed its homogeneous oil business with conspicuous, consistent excellence: but in the early nineties its chem-ical business fell, yet again, into the soup.

Oil companies have generally failed in the chemical industry. Managing outside petroleum simply isn't an oilman's parenting skill. Managing diversity is a skill in itself, a skill not easily acquired. It has, however, created some gigantic businesses. Diversified, con-glomerate giants abound, although the genus has become so unfash-ionable that they mostly hide under other labels. To take three ur-conglomerates in the *Fortune* 500, Hanson Industries NA shelters under mining, Textron under aerospace, and Litton under electronics.

Under any name, their scale offers few economies. They enjoy no managerial certainties akin to oil's. Their basic principle is frag-mentation. Each unit is supposed to have the "high degree of de-volved power to run their businesses" reported above in respect of Railtrack. The latter's quarterly targets set by HQ, too, are the method with which Harold Geneen created ITT's conglomerate leg-end: and "financial rewards geared to the degree of success" are meant to make parental supervision a breeze, almost superfluous.

Similar thinking lay behind IBM's creation, in September 1992, of a separate PC Company, with responsibility for R&D, manufac-ture, and marketing all under the same roof. This reversed the his-toric destruction of independence that ended the original saga of the

PC start-up. When marketing was removed from the start-up's control, it ripped the heart out of the Boca Raton operation. That removal was ordained by the same parent, John F. Akers, who now ordered a transplant.

Nothing had really changed in the intervening years, except that separation of PC marketing had failed. In an anti-bureaucratic industry, the corpocracy had taken charge. The typewriter syndrome rode again: the parent's "size, centralization, and control mechanisms" simply "got in the way" and retarded PC sales and profits. But centralization of marketing is the essence of IBM's parenting. Remove it, and what's left? A much better question is, What's taken away? The answer, in one word: Overhead.

Asking children to bear the costs of the parent—an offer they can't refuse—is the foundation of bad parenting. With centrally imposed overhead separated out, the economics of business units can be intelligently assessed. Not a few dogs and cows will then star. The $10 billion IBM PC Company would make still better sense without its continuing heavy central overload. Even so, increased independence swiftly improved financial performance, market share, and morale. Bucked-up PC executives even talked (prematurely—they had a disappointing 1994) about rebirth of the start-up spirit: the comeback of Camelot.

Behind the new deal in PCs, and Lexmark's separation, lies a half-perceived but vital need to create a new kind of parent. The best pointer to the requirement lies in IBM's joint ventures with Apple Computer and Motorola, aimed at producing startling new operating software (Taligent), PowerPC microprocessors (Somerset), and dynamic multimedia software (Kaleida). The partner images contrast sharply: the white-collar salesman, the quality-conscious engineer, the Silicon Valley whiz kid. Their parenting styles vary accordingly.

It could be an appetizing mix. According to *Business Week,* the culture evolving in the units, each with a few hundred employees, leaned towards that of Apple: "The style is pure Silicon Valley: flexible hours, small teams, and pizza bashes to build team spirit." At Kaleida, started with a former venture capitalist Nathaniel Goldhaber in charge, IBMers can no longer rely on marketing staff. Their hardest challenge, he said, "is to take on more responsibilities. . . . Engineers meet directly with customers to hear what's needed in new products." In modern management, that's standard practice.

Nor is there anything revolutionary in the formula proposed by Joseph M. Guglielmi, the IBMer who set up Taligent: "Put smart people in charge, motivate them, and get out of the way." Bad parents never apply that simple recipe, never appreciate that real and deep difference has to be achieved by different parental conduct. Every manager has a fatherly or motherly role. More and more, the test of excellence is the test of parenthood: a happy, healthy, self-fulfilling, growing child who is rightly the parent's pride and joy.

FIVE

Champions of Change: How to Shift Organizations

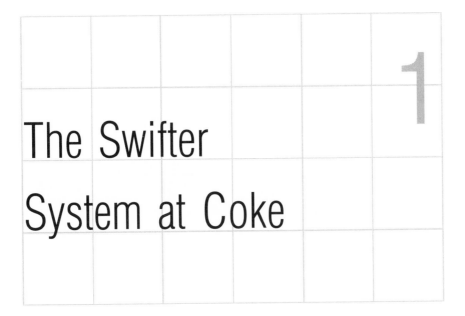

The Swifter
System at Coke

"Coke had one of the great names when he took over. But there were a lot of other great names back then too: Sears, IBM, American Express, Bank of America, Eastman Kodak." The speaker, a Coca-Cola non-executive director, is extolling the company's chief executive, Roberto C. Goizueta.

In a fascinating account in *Fortune,* John Huey tells how Goizueta was picked by "The Boss"—Robert Woodruff, richest of all the Coke millionaires around Atlanta. Offered the chair, Goizueta asked if he could appoint his own president. Woodruff's reply? "You are running the company, so you can do whatever you want. There's no sense to talk any more. Goodbye. I'm going to take a nap."

The principle is plain. For any job, back whomever you believe to be right and only intervene (and then decisively) as soon as it's clear that you were wrong. But the issue which Goizueta raised is as vital as that of delegated, true responsibility: partnership. The introverted Goizueta knew that he couldn't both rethink the company and at the same time run a sprawling multinational operationally. He needed his extrovert president, Don Keogh, to galvanize operations in a stirring way that Goizueta could never have managed.

On the other hand, Keogh wasn't the man for the rational diagnosis that Coke also required. Every manager manages better if teamed with a complementary talent. The weakness of one-man bands is that they *are* one-man. Psychologists believe that the greatest single human intelligence is invariably surpassed by the sum of several intelligences working together. The success of bosses thus depends on their ability to mobilize others—and that includes picking a second-in-command who genuinely shares command.

The natural division between partners is Coke's—between strategy and operations, or framework and content, or setup and performance: the military equivalent is the distinction between field commander and commanding general. If the latter's plans are mistaken, the armies in the field can't win. When starting any new project, any new job, any turnaround, action must be preceded by effective organization.

To get new and desired results, you need a new system. Goizueta installed one. It was the first evidence that The Boss had chosen right. How do you know if an appointment is wrong? Look at the system for repeated, systemic errors. A single flop is no evidence: Goizueta and Keogh, after all, deservedly took the blame for the disaster of New Coke, a misguided attempt to revamp a brand that didn't need it. Not only did the board refuse to punish their error: the two men got a special bonus, which may have taken forgiveness too far.

Look rather for persistent gaps between effort and achievement. For instance, research and development is widely believed to be the powerhouse of corporate growth. So who are the biggest R&D spenders? In the United States, only General Motors and IBM are above the $5 billion mark: they each spend three times as much as Hewlett-Packard, with its far better recent record in the profitable exploitation of new technology.

The same curious relationship applies outside the United States. The ten biggest R&D spenders include Siemens (the only other $5 billion spender in the world), Philips, and Fiat, the latter two deep in the corporate doldrums. Philips outspends Canon three to one: but in 1992 the Japanese company earned the same profits on half the sales. Large R&D budgets are apparently a function of size: but size, equally, threatens to make the spending relatively ineffective.

The same is true of another aspect of innovation: design. Its value as a business weapon is proved every year—for instance, by-products like the Apple Powerbook, which won billion-dollar sales after late entry into a well-occupied laptop PC market, on the strength of differentiated design. Once again, the design leaders are the leviathans: GM and IBM have won more Industrial Excellence Awards than Apple since 1980. Both giants are in the top three. Which prompts the famous question: If you're so good, why aren't you more successful?

A consistent pattern of such shortfalls is one giveaway. Then, repeated U-turns or aborted initiatives in policy show that the appointees don't know what they are doing. Above all, hope constantly deferred is a bad sign and deeply counterproductive. The new man at IBM, Louis V. Gerstner, expressed this well, a month after taking over: "The adjustment period that IBM has been going through in trying to deal with changes in its markets is now carrying into its second or third year. The longevity of that change is as dysfunctional as the seriousness of the change."

In other words, the longer you take to implement a change process, the more likely it is to be overtaken by events. "The Boss" would certainly have removed Goizueta if the latter, in making serious changes at Coke, had followed such a protracted, uncertain course. The other great company names mentioned in the first paragraph of this chapter were guilty of the same error as IBM. In management, he who hesitates is sometimes saved. He who procrastinates is almost always lost.

Adding Value to

Management

2

What makes one CEO succeed while another fails? And can whatever makes CEOs succeed apply to all managerial work, right down the organization? The secret ingredient plainly has terrific power. The issue of R&D results, raised in the previous chapter, points clearly to the ingredient's nature.

The values adopted by R&D winners apply here. R&D winners tend to

1. *Concentrate* on areas where they are already strong
2. *Work concurrently* by bringing all affected interests together at the earliest possible stage
3. *Decentralize* the task to the business units
4. *Go truly multinational* by bringing different nationals together
5. *Go cross-cultural* by using leaders from foreign cultures
6. *Plan up-front,* and thoroughly, before starting any projects
7. *Forget protocol*—and encourage good "unauthorized" projects
8. *Invest in success* by backing good projects to the hilt, but ...

9. *Identify the weak projects* early on—and put them out of their misery
10. *Remove barriers,* so that good ideas aren't blocked by vested (or dumb) interests

These Ten Rules of Innovation have immediate relevance to big-company success or failure. Coke's management is *cross-cultural:* CEO Goizueta is Cuban by origin; when he turned up to open a bottling plant in Prague, his party included a Greek, an Irishman, a Turk, and John Hunter, who is Australian. The latter's *decentralized* initiative revolutionized Coke: Hunter persuaded its Atlanta HQ to spend $13 million to buy control of its Philippines bottler. His argument was that nothing else would reverse Pepsi's two-to-one market lead.

The success of the experiment (reversal indeed—a two-to-one lead in the Philippines) reversed Coke's historic policy of leaving bottling to the bottlers and selling only the syrup. That's the single most important reason for Coke's stupendous rise from $5 billion of market value to $60 billion under Goizueta. But the latter also rigorously followed Rule One, *concentrate.* Although he bought Columbia Pictures, he also sold it (at a profit). Initially, he concentrated Coke by applying Rules Seven and Eight in the highly planned up-front way recommended in Rule Six:

"You make a chart. Across the top you put your businesses. . . . Then you put the financial characteristics on the other axis: margins, returns, cash flow reliability, capital requirements. [Some], like concentrates, will emerge as superior businesses. Others, like wine, look lousy." The latter, naturally, you sell. Goizueta followed up this simple approach with another. All the remaining operations would be judged by their "economic profit" or EVA (economic value added)—that is, operating profit after not only tax, but also a charge for capital employed.

A traditional company, if especially thorough, will have a financial perspective built from five components: return on capital employed, cash flow, project or product profitability, profit forecast reliability, and sales backlog. Few firms include Coke's economic profit—although here the results are rich in more than one sense. For instance, Coke's share price has multiplied fourfold since 1990; in another case, the rise is 3.5 times since 1988; in yet another, 14 times in twelve years.

The concept has one supreme virtue: elemental simplicity. Its elementary proposition is that a business must earn more than the cost of its capital. That's obvious in the case of debt, although many companies, often unwittingly, do commit the cardinal sin of earning less on their debt than it costs (quite a feat, considering that the interest attracts tax relief). But even companies that appear to be handsomely clearing their interest costs may truly be consuming their capital.

That was painfully true of Coke. Because the company never borrowed but financed itself on equity capital, Goizueta's predecessors had never bothered about the "cost of capital." But equity has to be serviced, too. At first sight, equity seems like very cheap capital, and if you look simply at the cost of the dividend, that's true. But EVA advocates argue that the cost of equity is much higher. The money entrusted to your care by shareholders could have been invested elsewhere, and it will be if your returns becomes less attractive.

"Returns" here means not only dividends, but capital gains. Lumping both together, U.S. shareholders, according to *Fortune,* can expect to better long-term government bonds by six percentage points. The average cost of U.S. equity at the end of 1993 was therefore over 12 percent (the cost is far higher for volatile stocks, and lower for stable ones). The weighted average cost of equity and debt is the true cost of capital.

At Coke, the cost of equity worked out to around 16 percent. Since Coke's profitability was 8 to 10 percent, it was eating its own flesh. Basing strategy on the cost of equity did more than impose realism on the financing. It forced managers to concentrate on keeping down capital employed by managing inventories and costs intelligently.

These two considerations are basic. First, that the key financial statistic isn't the gross margin on sales, but what it helps to achieve: the margin between the cost of capital and its return. Second, that managers who aren't held responsible for their use of capital won't use it to the best advantage of the business. The two fundamentals apply to any business—the reasons for the large-scale corporate downfalls certainly include the same damaging propensities that Goizueta identified at Coke.

Reliance on the traditional return-on-capital-employed figure is open to two grave criticisms. The accounting definition of capital may grossly understate the funds actually being employed, and thus overstate the rate of return (even if—a *big* if—profits are stated accurately). Second, comparisons with the cost of capital will be invalid and misleading unless all its costs are taken into account, which must mean equity as well as debt. But that doesn't end the EVA figuring: what's the capital?

Under EVA, capital includes not only fixed assets and plant and equipment but also "revenue investment": that is, expenditure on essentials like R&D, training, and even marketing (of which more later). How you account for revenue investment seems a fuzzy area. But that makes no difference to the power of the concept, which is both strategic and operational.

Strategically, it demonstrates to top management whether the positioning of a business is viable (Coke) or not (its wine business). If EVA is negative—that is, after-tax operating profits don't cover the cost of capital—the business is ultimately doomed. At IBM, you can clearly see the writing on the wall. EVA started to decline in 1985: by 1987, it was minute: in 1988 and 1989, EVA turned negative.

The upward blip in 1990, to a positive figure, was merely the prelude to the billions of losses and EVA deficits in 1991 and 1992, both years in which the company still showed profits at the operating level. The EVA told the true story: capital was being savagely eroded *before* counting the massive costs of redundancy and reorganization. Small wonder that investors preferred to put their money somewhere else. Small wonder that high and low EVA and high stock market performance show a close correlation.

Operationally, the concept has two virtues. It gives top management a way of measuring the value of individual operations, and the achievement of their managers, while still, as bosses, keeping their proper distance from the operators. At the same time, it directs operational managers towards the right actions and away from the wrong. Also, it enforces a close look at the organization to ensure that capital is properly allocated to those who use it, thus sweeping away the confusion that in many businesses makes proper measurement and direction impossible.

AT&T was only typical in holding at group level all the capital used in all long-distance services. Today, these businesses have been broken down into forty units, each with its own capital. An individual unit can then work out its own EVA by deducting cost of capital from after-tax operating profit. If the result is negative, the call to action is immediate and compelling.

At the strategic level, the response may be negative, too: close or sell the offending operation. But operational managers can also respond positively and profitably. At CSX, freight trains whose negative EVA was $70 million came to generate a positive $10 million thanks to greater utilization of fewer locomotives and less rolling stock.

Cutting back on total capital employed is the most effective way of raising EVA in an unrestructured business. But restructuring to eliminate negative operations and to reinvest in highly positive ones is also miraculous. That's why Coca-Cola shifted its emphasis overwhelmingly to soft drinks, which largely explain its 29.4 percent return on capital. Goizueta also smartly reduced the average cost of the latter by putting the unleveraged Coke into cheaper debt: his cost of capital promptly dropped by a quarter to 12 percent.

That's an excellent example of how a well-directed CEO adds value. I've no hesitation in urging extreme attention to the EVA performance—not because it's a management panacea (there's no such thing), but because it uses one clear financial ratio to focus attention on the realities of the business. The worries arise about lumping in revenue investment with capital costs, given that the thrust of EVA is to minimize the latter. Managers should be encouraged to invest in innovation, training, and marketing—not discouraged.

Marketing investment is a case very much in point. In strong theory, marketing expenditure should be treated as an investment, because (like R&D) it purchases a future benefit. Nobody questions that a brand is a capital asset. It's illogical to recognize this capital value but to treat the marketing money which created the asset as a lost expense. The market-leading Marlboro between 1967 and 1989 spent cumulatively some $1.5 billion on advertising—double the outlay of Camel and Kent. It ended the period with four times their market share.

Is this a chicken-and-egg issue? Companies commonly allocate marketing expenditure as a percentage of sales revenue. So a firm whose sales are soaring above the competition will automatically outgrow the rise in their marketing money. That doesn't weaken the argument. Rather, it stresses the essential truth: that present marketing investment creates future sales and profits. Cutbacks, equally, jeopardize the future, a point which managers ignore at grave peril.

I was once asked by an advertising agency to meet one of its clients, a brewer who (to the agency's understandable distress) had challenged the value of a multimillion-pound spend. His profits from beer were far lower than those made by the owned premises which (among other catering services) sold the brew. Didn't it make sense to divert his marketing millions to improving the outlets?

If owned premises had accounted for all his beer sales, that strategy might have been reasonable. But the brands sold nationally in many other outlets—and it didn't prove necessary to argue about the effectiveness of advertising to dissuade the brewer. Who, I asked, had the largest market share? And was this leader's proportion of beer advertising greater or lesser than that share?

The answer was "greater," which promptly ended the argument. There's a *Harvard Business Review* study that cites—oddly, as a *good* example—Hawaiian Punch, which, after years of massive spending, cut back and virtually stopped its advertising in 1987–90. The business was successfully sold to Procter & Gamble in 1990, but not before sales had "eroded." That's really a bad example. The management wasn't adding value by boosting profits in this easy way. The article is on much firmer ground when it says that "considering the time and effort needed to get customers from awareness to loyal usage, when companies willfully disrupt a message or fail to reinforce it consistently, they shoot themselves in the foot."

Building a brand or building sales (which are one and the same thing) is a long-term investment that should not be jeopardized by short-term decisions. During recessions, however, that's precisely what most managements do. That only gives more astute companies the opportunity to increase their share of voice and ultimately their share of market. The question for managers is not what percentage of sales is appropriate for the marketing effort: rather, what spending is required to meet the marketing objectives—those that will pay off in a high and rising EVA?

What would the brewer have found from analyzing his EVA? Did his beer truly offer a worse return on capital than his outlets? Probably not. Both EVA and the concept of marketing as revenue investment stress the crucial importance of looking at the business anew and making it come to fuller and richer life by applying the results of that different viewpoint. If you're using the wrong map, don't expect to reach the right destination.

It doesn't have to be a purely financial map. The importance of financial numbers is obvious: but their management value is currently under attack for many reasons. For a start, the most-used financial measures look objective but are only approximations to reality. Second, accounts can measure the results of past management, but that doesn't add up to "helping managers to manage"—the telling Japanese phrase for "management accounting." Third, the financial figures are an outcome, the result of decisions and actions that are inherently non-financial.

Hence the newish concept of the "balanced scorecard," in which financial performance is only one of the elements. At Rockwater, the American underwater engineering and construction company, the scorecard consists of four "perspectives": customer, innovation and learning, internal business, and financial. To illustrate their nature, "customer" includes the customer satisfaction index, and "innovation and learning" takes in the staff attitude survey; while "internal business" means aspects like levels of rework—taking rejects back and rectifying the defects.

These three elements will also be found in Total Quality programs: some corporate TQM practitioners, in fact, use the balanced scorecard, too. It expresses the same principle as bonus schemes in such companies: the "financials" that dominate most management appraisals form only part of the assessment. Non-financials (naturally including the manager's success in quality work) may actually outweigh the financials.

Like Total Quality, too, the balanced scorecard starts with a "vision" or "mission." Writing in the *Harvard Business Review,* Rob-

ert S. Kaplan and David P. Norton describe a process that has four
stages:

1. What is my vision of the future?
2. If my vision succeeds, how will I differ
    (a) to my shareholders?
    (b) to my customers?
    (c) in my internal management processes?
    (d) in my ability to innovate and grow?
3. What are the critical success factors (on each of the four above
    counts)?
4. What are the critical measurements (again on the four counts)?

The fourth question gives you the balanced scorecard. Advocates claim that it links measurements to strategy. To quote a vice
president of FMC, the U.S. conglomerate, "If you're going to ask a
division or the corporation to change its strategy, you had better
change the system of measurement to be consistent with the new
strategy."

That's another argument against relying solely on monetary
measures, especially the familiar, established ones. They are rigid
and unchanging in concept. Any business, no matter what it is, or
how dynamically its environment is changing, is placed in the same
straitjacket as all other businesses. Since WYMIWYG (what you
measure is what you get) applies, a central task of top management
is to pick those measures which will best enable the company to
meet its objectives, financial and non-financial.

Equally, the job of all managers is to work out what truly drives
the business and to demand timely reports that measure how the
drive is progressing. That's tougher than it sounds. The customer satisfaction index, for example, is an expensive way of comparing
polled opinions with previous measurements. The important result is
the trend, the measure of improvement or decline. But on its own the
index won't reveal what customers want that you're not providing,
how likely they are to repeat their purchases, how they rate you compared to the competition, and so on.

Apple Computer provides a handy example. Its balanced scorecard was intended "to focus senior management on a strategy that

would expand discussions beyond gross margin, return on equity, and market share." Did management really have such limited vision beforehand? If so, it's easy to understand how the company, maybe fatally, persisted in maintaining a closed, proprietary stance. Opening its admirable Macintosh technology to others might have partly forestalled the very real threat now posed by Windows from Microsoft, which offers similar features.

It's hard to see how the "balanced scorecard" would have prevented or corrected this strategic error. While the scorecard's principles are fair and good, it seems a cumbersome way (to quote the same FMC man) "to streamline and focus strategy that can lead to breakthrough performance." Apart from anything else, the scorecard aims only at management. Breakthroughs are unlikely to be achieved without some means of mobilizing the full forces of the business, of which management is only a part.

Without doubt, though, it's well worth attempting the exercise of going through the scorecard questions in a management workshop, finding those factors and measures which truly measure progress, and thus portraying the business in the round. But the process runs the danger of persuading managers that, by going through more elegant motions, they are playing a better game.

Therein lies the answer to the question posed at the start. What makes one CEO succeed while another fails? The successes insist on having clear responsibility, and giving it to others; they pick the best, complementary partners, and share power; they choose powerful, accurate, quick performance measures that they, their colleagues, and the corporation can live by.

In all that, they use action-oriented philosophies—like those embodied in the Ten Rules of Innovation—to add value for all parties. And they do so within the shortest possible time-frame. That's the way you make a great company in the first place—and keep it great in the second.

The Fumbling
of Ford

3

Ford Motor occupies a unique position in the annals of both industry and management. The first Henry Ford invented the mass-production techniques that dominated the evolution of world industry right into the second half of the twentieth century. With the assembly line and vertical integration went vertical management. When that profoundly influential system all but collapsed early in the reign of the second Henry Ford, he initiated a post-war reformation that still reverberates today.

The modernization of his grandfather's outdated and crumbling edifice, entrusted to Ernest R. Breech, gave the world another management innovation: the whiz kid. That nickname typified a new force in management: scientific method. Whiz kids Tex Thornton (later founder of Litton Industries), Robert McNamara, and their fellow brains had been recruited en bloc from the U.S. Air Force to apply the same methodical, logical techniques that had helped to win World War II.

For all the brilliance of these men, the Ford Motor Company never shook the supremacy of General Motors, where Alfred P. Sloan had constructed a far more durable and effective vertical organization. Ford continued to recruit and train acute intellects, but the company retained many of the emotional characteristics of an imperial court. The emperor's name, as he liked to say, was "over the door," and the imperial defects lay behind that door.

The years since Henry Ford II relinquished power, years marked by GM's decline, have seen some notable surges from Ford, especially on the back of the Taurus success. But original management sin still seems to lurk within the company. The poor results are epitomized in an interview which Lindsay Halstead, then Ford of Europe head, gave to *The Times* in Britain in 1992. Motivated by his division's money-losing performance (where once Europe had been the mainstay of Ford's worldwide business), Halstead made the following discoveries:

1. "An investigation" showed that 40 percent of the 21,000 white-collar workers were "indirect" workers, mainly clerical, legal, and administrative.
2. The corporate structure of seven management layers was too weighty, time-consuming, and bureaucratic and had become out of sync with assembly lines slimmed down to improve efficiency and output.
3. Reaction times were too lengthy: "We are too slow to report and we just have to find a better way to respond."
4. Senior executives, including Halstead himself, were asked to confirm decisions, about which they had little or no specialist knowledge, by subordinates unable to act on their own initiative.
5. The new Escort, which ran into severe criticism and poor market reception, was probably "over-researched" by some of these seven management layers instead of leaving decisions on styling to the designers and engineers.

Halstead now wanted to remove two layers of the bureaucracy that was gumming up his works as part of a review that would apparently require two years of voluntary job-losses. Three questions leap out from all this soul-searching.

First, why was an *investigation* needed to discover the over-supply of white-collar indirects—and why weren't such basic manpower issues the subject of continuous analysis and control? Second, why had the apparently blatant obstructiveness of the "paper-pushing" bureaucracy only been recognized under the pressure of poor results? Third, why was the remedy to take so long?

One thing is certain: any reform undertaken over so protracted a time will confront a different situation at the end than at the beginning. The reorganization runs the risk of applying the right solution to what then becomes the wrong problem. Part of the Ford malaise in general appears to be sluggishness itself. How else do you explain what *Business Week* called the "trouble under Ford's hood" in late 1993?

This time the trouble wasn't only in Europe but in the United States. According to Salomon Brothers, in the third-quarter of 1993 Ford barely made a profit on its vehicles: just $40. That was shaming in itself. But Chrysler turned shame into disgrace by earning *twenty-five times as much*. On one estimate, overall profit margins at Chrysler would double Ford's for the year as a whole.

The explanations were no more complimentary to Ford. True, in addition to the obligatory new cars and trucks, it was spending capital heavily on new transmissions and engines. But part of that expenditure reflected false economies in the past. In both transmissions and engines, competitors moved ahead when Ford held back on spending in the eighties: so the new Mustang, for example, has an eleven-year-old engine. Even after a two-thirds increase since 1987, Ford is still under-spending Chrysler at $988 of capital per vehicle against $1,039 for the smaller company.

Even worse, Chrysler has stolen a lead in the vital business of new product development. Simultaneous project teams at Chrysler, hauling together all necessary disciplines from the beginning, have achieved results like the thirty-one-month launch of the Dodge Neon for $1.3 billion. Ford did take only four months longer over the Mustang, and only spent $700 million: but that compares the wholly new Neon sub-compact, which needed a new stamping plant for the body, with a sports car that uses a high proportion (25 percent) of its predecessor's components.

On a per vehicle estimate, the Neon came in 17 percent under the Mustang's cost. But those numbers dwindle into insignificance compared to Ford's compact "global car." Selling as the Mystique in the United States, that cost an astronomical $6 billion, a heavy burden on a group already suffering margin trouble from a badly scrambled product mix. Chrysler reaps large profits from minivans and sport utility vehicles; Ford's efforts to exploit the same boom were restricted. Why? The answer again lies in under-investment. Ford's truck plants came right up against their capacity limits.

As in Europe, so in the United States: the questions leap out of the facts. Why couldn't Ford's management in Dearborn see that under-investment was bound to create competitive disadvantage? Given that the trend towards minivans, and so forth, was obvious long ago, why didn't Ford anticipate its future development more successfully? Worst of all, the power of Japanese-style teamworking in new product development has been famous for years—and Ford knew that power from its own experience.

The CEO wrestling with Ford's problems in the mid-nineties is the same man, Alex Trotman, who in 1990 as an executive vice president started to attack the departmental barriers by forming a single team of fifty line executives representing all the Ford functions. He also put twenty young designers, engineers, and product planners together as a "skunk works" team to speed up development of the new Mustang, aiming, wrote *Fortune,* "to cut costs by speeding communication and reducing confusion."

Yet the Taurus and Sable models, largely responsible for astonishing gains in U.S. market share, had been celebrated for their teamwork way back in the eighties. Those successes made a business idol of then CEO Donald Petersen, whose feet of clay were exposed when the board forced his early departure in early 1991. That was a clear and sharp response to the corporation's deteriorating performance. But when Trotman took over from Harold "Red" Poling in 1993, confusion and poor communication still reigned and the comparative numbers were even worse. Why has it taken Ford so long to catch up?

Mastering

the System

At Ford Motor, in both the United States and Europe, the obvious question is what top managers were doing, and where they were looking, while the European silt was building up (or refusing to wash away), and while the North American business was being locked into low profitability. Probably, top men like Don Petersen and Red Poling were doing the very things of which ex–European boss Lindsay Halstead complained—pushing paper, making decisions on inadequate knowledge, and second-guessing people who are paid and qualified to eliminate the guessing and get it right the first time.

Sir Derek Birkin, the RTZ mining group chairman quoted in Part Three, Chapter 6, expounds a far better approach: "Even if we wanted to intrude in the management of operations in the field, which we do not, we could not do so to any significant extent. We maintain short chains of command to give us an ability to act quickly. . . . Once we have agreed [on] strategic and financial guidelines with our chief operating units, they are left to manage themselves. . . . Accountability at all times matches the autonomy, but we do not have massive volumes of data flowing back and forth between Head Office and the operating units. . . ."

At Ford of Europe, the stultification began right there, in head office itself, where the management levels multiplied, and the model interference reigned, under the board's nose—and with the directors joining in. Across the world, Ford was and is an impressive apparatus for designing, building, and distributing complex pieces of machinery that generally work well and reliably. The management machine, though, sputtered, stalled, and sometimes broke down completely.

Ford managers in Dearborn must have known about the dangers of delaying new investment. Right under Ford's nose, Lee Iacocca had made a similar error, condemning Chrysler to a drastic later shortage of new models by firing thousands of engineers to cut payroll costs in 1979–80. There was an excuse: the urgency of the crisis, the need for sheer survival, made Iacocca's retrenchment appear inevitable, whatever the consequences.

The discovery that the secondary effects can nullify the primary objectives is among the major contributions to management understanding made by MIT's Peter M. Senge. "Shifting the burden" is his phrase for treating the symptom rather than the underlying disease, and thus making the latter worse. That's probably the most common infringement of Senge's Fifth Discipline, which is that of thinking about the whole system, not just the primary problem that immediately confronts you. Senge propounds eleven disciplinary laws:

1. *Today's problems come from yesterday's solutions:* witness Ford's shortage of new transmissions and engines.
2. *The harder you push, the harder the system pushes back:* the more output Ford tried to squeeze from its truck factories, no doubt, the higher costs rose.
3. *Behavior grows better before it gets worse:* misguided policies (as above) will show good initial results.
4. *The easy way out usually leads back in:* if the first round of job cuts doesn't work, try another (which happens more often than not).
5. *The cure can be worse than the disease:* accepting lower profits per Ford in the eighties might well have meant much higher figures in the nineties.

6. *Faster is slower:* why do so many high-growth start-ups run into high-octane trouble?

7. *Cause and effect are not closely related in time and space:* manufacturing problems may not arise in the plant at all—but in design, marketing, or somewhere else.

8. *Small changes can produce big results—but the areas of highest leverage are often the least obvious:* changes in reporting systems can radically improve management performance.

9. *You can have your cake and eat it, too—but not at once:* low cost and high quality aren't incompatible, but eventually go hand in hand.

10. *Dividing an elephant in half does not produce two elephants:* artificial boundaries between functions and departments cause all parties to under-perform.

11. *There is no blame:* outside factors such as recession (like that which "caused" Ford of Europe's problems in the early nineties) aren't what damaged you and your organization—like Ford, you did it to yourself.

The laws help greatly to explain the ultimate failure of radical changes designed to achieve the opposite result. Thus in November 1988, a *Wall Street Journal* headline read "Campaign to Cut Bureaucracy, End Insularity Starts to Pay Off"; this was "history's second great experiment in *perestroika* and *glasnost* . . . showing results that the other *perestroika*'s architects would envy. IBM's earnings will be up about 14% this year and probably at least that much in 1989."

A year later, falling prices had forced IBM to incur $2.3 billion in restructuring expenses to save $1 billion in annual costs. Another ten thousand people were to go, prompting a grim joke about the "retirement" program, known as "7, 7 and 1." In working out benefits, the dismissed had seven years added to age, and seven to length of service, and got one year's pay as bonus. One employee sardonically added another "1 and 2": "you have one minute to think about it, and you have to take two people with you."

That 14 percent earnings growth for 1988 vanished into a 40 percent decline. But there's an interesting correlation. When IBM's employment peaked at 405,000 in 1984–85, so did earnings: as jobs fell by 12 percent to 1991, the earnings trend also dropped, culminating in that year's $2.8 billion loss. At the same time, share of market (defined as all computer hardware, software and services), as calculated by the Gartner Group, fell from 40 percent in 1984 to 23 percent. And still observers were caught by surprise.

The *Wall Street Journal,* in March 1991, reported that the company "dropped an earnings bomb" as a result of problems "which arose so quickly they stunned analysts" and which affected most product lines and most of the world. Plainly, the symptoms hadn't responded to treatment, which must mean that the disease, far from improving, had probably become worse.

This would be no surprise to Senge, whose stimulating book provides acute analysis of why managements get into trouble—and how they can avoid it. Every company, he points out, works in a "limits to growth" structure: when growth halts, or goes into reverse, you know that the limits have been reached. So far, so very obvious. What's less clear, and demands extra-careful analysis, is why. What are the true limits?

If the company has been stimulating demand by progressive price cuts and discounts, for example, management will tend to stimulate sales by more of the same. This may have a short-run effect. But if the explanation is different—if, say, the company's service and product range are at fault—the new price cuts will have no impact on the underlying adverse situation. Similarly, if excessive costs arise from poor processes, cutting worker numbers will reduce the wage bill, but overall costs will remain stubbornly and disappointingly high.

Worse still, the sloppiness may increase; the excessive numbers are often needed to make inefficient processes work at all. Mass cutbacks in staff, moreover, are seldom selective and often deeply counterproductive; the best employees, who will most easily find new and better jobs, are the quickest to seize their money and run. That will intensify any service and sales problems, especially since morale is inevitably damaged by the redundancies.

The "limits to growth" are sometimes all too clear, like Ford's shortage of U.S. truck capacity. But sometimes they are hidden in apparently worthy aims. For example, IBM's master strategy for the century-end was "growing with the industry." It sounded modest, but was plainly impossible. Had the 40 percent market share of 1984 been maintained, the company would have *doubled* its actual 1994 sales: the additional sales required would have equaled the turnover of four Hewlett-Packards or Digital Equipments, which is a blatant absurdity.

The strategy of "growing with the industry" was bound to fail, at least under the centralized system operated by IBM, and should never have been attempted. Loss of market share, of course, is hard for any management to tolerate. But unless the causes of lost share are properly understood, intelligent responses cannot be devised. Senge quotes an industry-leading manufacturer of industrial goods which found the right answer. An MIT team of "system dynamics" experts used computer models to uncover the truth: "Because it cost so much to store its bulky, expensive products, production managers held inventories as low as possible and aggressively cut back production whenever orders turned down. The result was unreliable and slow delivery, even when production capacity was adequate."

The "unreliable and slow delivery" readily explained the decline in market share. In fact, the computer predicted that the delivery problems would even worsen if demand turned down in a market slump. In the recession of 1970, the firm took MIT's advice, maintained output, improved delivery performance, and won back market share from satisfied customers. But "during the ensuing business recovery, the managers stopped worrying about delivery service": when the next recession came, they returned to the old policy of "dramatic production cutbacks."

Rather than mocking their stupidity, it's important to note that this reversion to type is common among companies (and individuals, for that matter—look at all the fat ex-dieters and recidivist smokers). Senge blames the "mental models" held in this firm: "Every production manager knew in his heart that there was no more surefire way to destroy his career than to be held responsible for stockpiling unsold goods in warehouses."

This same "inertia of deeply entrenched mental models" applies at Ford. That's why it has been slower than Chrysler to adopt "platform teams" for simultaneous engineering of new models: that's why at General Motors senior executives were still challenging that proven principle in 1993. But forming teams, or even dividing the whole corporation into self-contained businesses subject to less central control, isn't enough. As Senge emphasizes, without changing mental models, nothing will be achieved.

In a culture that's not tolerant of mistakes, for example, managers will protect themselves by referring decisions upwards. If that's ruled out, they will put off the evil day by procrastination. The delay is likely to produce grave secondary effects in an age which is increasingly intolerant of slow reactions. But faced with a choice between external requirements and internal anxiety, fearful managers will opt for their own perceived interests every time and leave the customers (and thus ultimately the company) to look after themselves.

The problems faced by Ford in Europe and in the United States look amenable to specific action. Tackling them one by one, though, will lead to further problems down the line. Only general reform of the entire corporate system will remove the difficulties. What about the set of management misdemeanors listed below? Would you describe them as symptomatic or systemic?

1. "Filtering" of instructions and intentions from on high, so that they never penetrate to lower levels of management, or do so in diluted form.
2. Plenty of good excuses for bad results (Field Marshal Montgomery memorably defined this process as "inventing poor reasons for not doing what one has been told to do").
3. An internal perception of quality as excellent which is not echoed by the customers.
4. Too many meetings at all levels of management.
5. Too little urgency and too much "waiting to be told what to do."
6. Low priority to issues of operational performance.
7. Lack of focus on each distinct business.
8. Toleration of low performance and low performers.
9. Excessive numbers of people in key areas.

These failings, to which all organizations are prone, were singled out by CEO John F. Akers in the diatribe to a group of senior IBM managers quoted in the Introduction. Evidently, none of the faults represents a self-contained system. All are symptoms of much wider breakdown. The whole IBM system's defects have been exposed by the limits to growth. The dramatic loss of market share, in Senge's language, is a "balancing process," bringing the company's sales into line with its true ability to serve the market.

In such circumstances, shifting to a totally different system is essential. The route to that system doesn't lie in reshuffling the organization (though that may be a necessary adjunct). The true road runs back from the customers to rethink the way the company serves them within the industry structure—whatever form that takes. The rules of rethinking are as follows:

1. Always look for the underlying cause of any problem, and make sure that you treat both the manifestation and the systemic cause.
2. In choosing and monitoring treatments, check Senge's laws to make sure that you're not about to prove them right.
3. The "Just Around the Corner Syndrome," in which promised renaissance is continually postponed, is a sure sign that Senge's laws are at work.
4. Watch the long-term trends when analyzing short-term problems, and when short-term trends surprise you, realize that something more than a reporting system is seriously wrong.
5. Always ask, What are the limits to growth? And concentrate on extending those bounds, without exceeding them.
6. If at first you do succeed, reinforce success: never reinforce, or return to, failed policies.
7. Find out (you may need outside help) what "mental models" govern organizational behavior, and if they don't match what the market wants, change them: don't just change the organization.

In rethinking the organization, as part of the system, some of the principles are established and universal. One is simply physical: keep the head office small both in numbers and dimensions; size limits stop the otherwise inexorable process of expansion. The second essential is to keep lines of communication short, with no "relays" who pass on instructions and information without adding anything (except possibly confusion).

The third necessity is to ensure that jobholders (from chief executive downwards) know how and where they can add value, and to achieve a culture (for which read "set of mental models") that will insistently achieve that value. John Kotter of the Harvard Business School writes perceptively about cultural transformation and large companies like Ford and IBM. In *Fortune*'s words, he "concluded that corporate insiders like Akers can seldom transform an organization beset by inertia."

To Akers's credit, he invited Kotter to discuss his research with top IBM executives at the annual corporate strategy session. Kotter "confronted them with some really tough stuff": however, the now-deposed CEO came up to him afterward and said, "You've done exactly what I wanted today." Those who (like me) have engaged in similar exercises will recognize the remark. It's what they nearly always say.

The overriding issue is not what they say, but what they, and all those managing the system, will do to change the system by deeds, not words—no matter what the cost to themselves, their privileges, and their authority. There's the rub, and there lie the roots of failure. The fumbling at Ford couldn't be corrected by the arch-fumblers themselves. Unfumble the system, and the fumbling has to stop.

The Culture

Change of Jack Welch

5

One corporation has always been preeminent in the realm of putting management theory into practice: America's General Electric. GE thus led the way into formal corporate planning and then out of it. It pioneered "portfolio planning," which winnowed out the attractive and profitable "strategic business unit," or SBU (its name for the discrete businesses, built around their markets, to whose managers the corporate executives delegate effective powers).

Now GE is seeking better ways of animating that decentralized structure, after making a disturbing discovery: that companies with better productivity growth concentrated on the *how* rather than the *what*. Get the process right, in other words, and the performance will follow. If the process is wrong, all efforts to raise performance will fall short, if not fail completely. GE's financial controls had faithfully recorded good scores by big-company standards: but they only recorded—they couldn't vitalize or revitalize.

One of the many academics hired to help GE's current vitalizing drive has said that "this is one of the biggest planned efforts to alter people's behavior since the Cultural Revolution." Changing corporate cultures is notoriously difficult, with the emphasis on the "notoriously": the difficulty is much exaggerated by the notoriety. While that's true, it's also true that a huge gulf exists between traditional management and chief executive Jack Welch's brave new world.

Welch is quoted as saying, "We've got to take out the boss element." In his vision, reported *Fortune,* "21st century managers will forgo their old powers—to plan, organize, implement and measure— for new duties: counseling groups, providing resources for them, helping them think for themselves." As Welch puts it, "We're going to win on our ideas, not by whips and chains."

Neither this general approach, nor the specific programs that GE is adopting, will be strange to exponents of what I've called "the management consensus." Like Welch, the gurus of the consensus (meaning virtually every guru) believe you should:

1. Involve employees at all levels in making decisions.
2. Adopt "best practice" ideas and methods from within and without the organization.
3. Attack every process and procedure in the company with the aim of simplifying, compressing, economizing, and improving.

The actual initiatives at GE reflect every part of this triple prescription. An example is work on projects like mapping and redesigning the manufacturing process for a jet-engine shaft. Here GE workers were able to turn a total tangle into an orderly pattern, and to double production speed, by their own intelligent efforts. GE calls this "Process Mapping"—and it's a very powerful, basic tool.

Much the same analytical technique can redesign entire "business systems," after finding out where cost and time are most spent and most wasted. You can then design detailed plans for reducing or eliminating both cost and time. Process Mapping, though, by no means exhausts GE's new participative tool kit. It also uses "Work-Out" to uncover specific proposals for improvement from anything between forty and one hundred people, nominated by management "from all ranks and several functions."

The Work-Out participants turn up for a three-day informal, off-site conference. Under the guidance of an external facilitator, they form some half-dozen teams, each given part of the broad agenda laid down by the boss: say, to eliminate unnecessary meetings or forms. On the third day, the teams present their proposals, which is where an equally interesting innovation appears.

The boss, who may have a hundred or so proposals on the table, must decide on the spot whether to (1) agree, (2) refuse, or (3) demand more information—appointing a team to deliver the data by an agreed date. The psychological pressure to agree must be heavy: in one quoted example, only eight of 108 proposals were turned down by a plant services head. His own boss was present for the Work-Out: but the boss lurked out of sight behind the manager, who thus couldn't seek for signs of approval or disapproval.

In this case, the results were worth having, but not huge: $200,000. No doubt, the Work-Out cost as much—but this is a teaching and learning process, rather than a prime technical tool. Teaching and learning, though, are the foundation of Jack Welch's new world, and of organizational change. Organizations can't learn. But their members can. That body of individual collections of knowledge, passed on like some great library from one employee generation to the next, constitutes much of what's known as corporate culture. Within it lie the keys to the kingdom of twenty-first-century success.

Progress
Through Processes

6

The hardest question I am ever asked (and it's asked often) is to name the best-managed company in the world, or the country, or the industry. The latter is much the easiest, since even in an industry full of misguided managements, one will be the evident leader. Even on this surer ground, though, selectors must tread cautiously. To outsiders, management can only be as good as its current manifestation, and today that can change for the worse with shocking speed.

But General Electric has consistently shown the ability to renew itself, to find new leaders—like Jack Welch—who aren't content with the old ways, and who don't practice management by lip service. Thus GE is currently demonstrating the greatest good sense (naturally enough for a hard-nosed company) in following a golden rule: in changing culture, actions speak louder than words. To put it the other way around, if more effective actions producing much better results are not flowing, the culture has not been changed in any meaningful way.

Words do have an important role to play. In *The Super Chiefs* I remarked on the long-term performance of twenty companies that were committed verbally to "values." They had expanded their net income twenty-three times, while America's gross national product had managed to rise only two and a half times in the same period. But the proof of the pudding is in the numbers: values that don't add value, you might well say, are valueless.

That's axiomatic to the Welch regime. Like Robert Allen of AT&T, this CEO is an old company hand: you don't have to be an imported turnaround ace to turn a culture. Alert veterans of companies (and returned veterans) have an advantage in leading revivals and renewals: they know where the bodies are buried, and their own experience enables them to see the weaknesses in the old cultural system. Much nonsense is written and talked about "culture," though—largely because quite different concepts are thrown into the same pot.

The problem starts with the word itself. "Culture" in the sense of the organizational norms of a business has a very recent meaning: the word used to refer only to "improvement or refining by education and training," coupled with "the intellectual side of civilization." Every company does have a distinctive nature, a set of traditions, often dating back deep into its past, which can only be broken by sharp discontinuity. These traditions are only harmful if they become embedded in obsolete or inefficient systems.

Organizations have no culture: people do. As in all societies, traditions are handed down, while physical assets (factories and offices no less than cities and landscape) influence how people behave. But behavior is the crucial meaning of culture. You may talk about "a high degree of attention to the customer, sensitivity to the individual inside the company, dedication to quality." But these are meaningless concepts unless translated into, and proved by, behavior.

IBM's Louis V. Gerstner mentioned the above trio as aspects of its culture that he valued and had "created" in his previous roles at American Express and RJR Nabisco. He added, though, that "I'm not interested in the part of the culture that defines processes as opposed to values. I don't want anybody to tell me about the processes." The truth is that processes enshrine culture. By changing the process by which operational managers were judged, for instance, Roberto C. Goizueta (Chapters 1 and 2 of Part Five) radically changed Coke's culture.

Look back at the ten rules for R&D winners in Chapter 2, and you see example after example of process change. Many IBMers in the research "culture" once had as top priority "being published in scholarly journals. Now they have to specify how their work will help the company." The result, says *Business Week,* is that research labs are now picking up their own developments and running with them: controlling a start-up in 3D supercomputer graphics, for example, or actually manufacturing special lasers for telecommunications.

That's a clear case of process changing culture and doing so for the better. Look at service champions. What does "high attention to the customer" mean? Process. There's a marvelously effective store operation in the United States that has demonstrated the point while growing its earnings per share by 42.5 percent annually for ten years. The processes used for this do-it-yourself chain, Home Depot, include the following "cultural" features:

1. *No commissions,* so that small customers are treated with as much consideration as large
2. *Shares for all employees*—they win them instead of discounts on purchases, get at least 7 percent of salary in stock (over and above their pay), and can purchase stock at a discount twice a year
3. *Training* in corporate principles, like always selling customers the lowest-cost solution—if it's the best
4. *Customer research* to ensure that purchasers are indeed satisfied
5. *No part-timers,* because they won't see the business as their career
6. *Above average pay* coupled with . . .
7. *Stock options* down to assistant store manager
8. *Meticulous recruitment* that rejects 98 percent of applicants
9. *Consistent low prices*—no seasonal sales
10. *Top-level involvement:* the chief executive, Bernard Marcus, spends a quarter of his time in the stores. He and president Arthur Blank devote a day a month to indoctrinating all new store managers *and* assistant managers

There's a further cultural element: Marcus and Blank are *partners;* in fact, with the same inspirational-analytical combination as

Goizueta and Don Keogh at Coke. Their no-commission rule stands in total contradiction to practice in the big company (where the sovereign dominance of commissions has been a well-known obstacle to change). In other respects, though, most giants could subscribe to Home Depot's cultural principles—like training, meticulous recruitment, and having employees as shareholders.

But such cultural elements can't make enough difference without another vital ingredient: "atmosphere." The word was used by Field Marshal Montgomery to describe what others might mistakenly think to be the sum total of culture. In the right atmosphere, people are bound to the company by love of their jobs and loyalty to the culture—as they were at IBM when Tom Watson, Sr., used every device, including corny songs at pep rallies, to boost morale.

The Home Depot bosses do the same: at six-thirty one morning every month, *Breakfast with Bernie and Arthur* is relayed live over closed-circuit TV to nearly all the 45,000 employees. The dominant refrain is to contrast "Where do you go if you want a job?" with "Where do you go if you want a career?" (enthusiastic screams of "Home Depot"). The razzmatazz conceals a deep truth about management priorities: the difference between a job and a career is fundamental. Putting people and their lives first has to come first, because nothing can be executed save through people.

"Right-sizing," for example, will be far better done if the employees are involved, not as a final thought, but as a first. In one high-tech company, job cuts were approached culturally, as a Total Quality exercise. The object was to ensure that only dispensable posts went; that all necessary strengths were left intact; and that everybody agreed with the decisions and their implementation. That's a *process,* but one that helps to create, nourish, and sustain a creative culture. Management's over-arching priority is to do precisely that.

The other way around, bad processes create a bad culture. Quaker Oats, for instance, used to follow a common practice in fast-moving consumer goods, known as "trade loading." The plants pumped product into the trade irrespective of retail demand. Such methods boosted the quarterly profits, on which managers' bonus payments were based: but the price was an unacceptably high capital cost in filling warehouses and holding inventory.

When the economic-value-added technique, discussed in Chapter 2, was applied, it revealed the terrible cost of a practice which had become embedded in the organizational culture. When the bad habit was broken, the results were spectacular. One Quaker plant which employed fifteen warehouses and had $15 million in inventory found it could move much more product with ten warehouses and 40 percent less stock. The critical cultural move, though, wasn't the cutback, nor even the EVA analysis. It was the readiness to change.

That readiness can never be taken for granted. Take unnecessary meetings and (which is just as important) unnecessary attendance at meetings. One consultant had a client company that suffered badly from the "He's in-a-Meeting" Syndrome. He wisely suggested that all executives be given a rubber stamp. On receipt of memorandums or agenda convening meetings, they would be free to apply the stamp. It read "I see no reason for me to attend this meeting. Please let me know if my presence is considered essential." Top management was interested; but it didn't buy any rubber stamps.

The consultants also suggested that senior management should agree to come to the office every Monday, with no meetings scheduled all morning, and doors open. Everybody could then be certain of making contact, and with luck getting needed answers and decisions, for at least that one half-day every week. That brainwave suffered exactly the same fate: nothing doing. Processes like GE's Work-Out expose that kind of organizational, bureaucratized kneejerk in so naked a fashion that the jerking becomes impossible.

Such processes build a key idea into people's consciousness (and thus the corporate culture): that making and accepting practical suggestions is part of the way the company manages. That happens, not by exhortation, but by example. The best example, of course, is that of the best practice: another vital part of GE's vitalizing kit. The process involved selecting companies that were outgrowing GE's own productivity and then exchanging management ideas. The approach is so simple that its neglect (and not only by GE) is amazing.

Other companies offer important lessons from which you can benefit. Not Invented Here should be a recommendation, not a cause for rejection. As noted earlier, GE's major discovery was that winners concentrate on process (*how* you manage) rather than on function (*what* you do). But the comparisons also established some other crucial culture-cracking points:

1. Look for continuous improvements, most of them small, rather than quantum leaps: this could have been learned long before by superficial observation of best Japanese practice, but needs qualifying—quantum leaps are also available, and must be taken.
2. Executive job rotation, traditionally the best practice for developing managers, is counterproductive in new-product introduction. Without question, much else suffers from the excessively short stints of rotated managers.
3. Processes cut across departmental boundaries, which means that they need "owners" who can do the same.

In a multibusiness group, though, the problem is also how to cut across the boundaries between businesses. Transfer of ideas, on processes or products, from one part to another is notoriously difficult. But virtuous chains can be created: GE's Montreal appliance plant adapted job-shop ideas from a New Zealand company, Fisher & Paykel, to speed operations in ways now adopted in the Louisville plant—which sent two hundred-plus managers to Montreal.

The resulting program, Quick Response, has halved the production cycle, reduced inventory costs by over 20 percent, and made Louisville the Mecca of other Best Practice seekers from GE. All well and very good, but have these efforts changed the culture at GE? Not according to Welch himself. He believes that ten years will be needed to alter an established hierarchical culture into a horizontally organized grouping. GE will then employ participative, successful people to whom change is a natural order, in which the role of managers is to facilitate rather than command and control.

Ten years? Is that long haul unavoidable? Are cultures truly that resistant? To repeat, so-called cultural change is actually concerned with specific processes, with what Kalchas, the London strategic consultants, calls "Total Organization Capability." This shows itself in the effective ordering of priorities, the quality of decision-making, and the efficiency of execution. Inadequate capability shows itself in observations like these from senior managers:

- "I will tell you why I cannot get things moving. I can never get the right people together at the right time, and when I do, the action step is another meeting, or let us set up a working committee or something, but I can't get action."

- "I have so many people to speak to to get a decision that it takes ages and I'm exhausted at the end of it. I can't do that on every issue."
- "I have got two major problems in trying to get to grips with the business myself: I cannot get the right data, and when I do, eventually, force what I need out of the system, it's inconsistent or unreliable."

These fairly standard complaints or gripes, as Michael de Kare Silver of Kalchas points out, really indicate "process roadblocks." The moans reflect obstacles in the way of prioritization, decision-making, and efficient execution. Remove the roadblocks and you change the "culture"—and improve the total organizational capability. Kalchas found a wholly different, much more effective culture at another business in the very same industry, which generated managerial quotes like these:

- "We don't have meetings that are not decision-making."
- "Everyone helps out if someone is behind on a profit target, as we'd all suffer otherwise."
- "I cannot recruit any additional manpower without the approval of the president of the company."
- "It's simple—we all know what we're shooting for and what our individual responsibilities are in getting there."
- "I have to control every nickel."
- "Profit is our goal."

The last two quotations sum up the guiding principle around which all else revolves: staff skills, style, symbols, systems and controls, and the shared values are all directed towards the profit objective. Kalchas found that in this company, "before we do anything," three questions are invariably asked:

1. Do I need to do this?
2. If yes, how can I do it at no extra cost?
3. Now it's done, how can I do it at less cost next time?

The questions are excellent, although I would improve the first: as phrased, it invites the answer no. A more positive rephrasing is, Why do I need to do this? But the trio establish what kind of capability the company seeks (the ability to achieve optimum cost-effectiveness), and everything else supports that drive. For instance, managers are rewarded with money for achieving profit goals; they receive public recognition for cost efficiencies; they suffer public embarrassment for cost inefficiencies.

The first, woolly organization studied by Kalchas also had profit as an objective, but in the form of return on net assets. The consultants did some process mapping to show that RONA comes at the end of two chains or trees. One is rooted in market size and share (from which trading profit stems). The other stems from the number of sites, the plant, and the land and buildings (leading to net assets employed). At every point along the branches, results are determined by individual actions. That suggested eight simple process improvements:

1. Set managers' primary goals that can be personally and directly achieved.
2. Keep the number of goals to six at most.
3. Weight goals by importance.
4. Change goals if priorities change.
5. Link compensation packages to goal achievement.
6. Have defined time-frames and clear targets.
7. Communicate other managers' business goals to everybody else who needs to know.
8. Speed up decision-making by *(a)* restricting meetings to one and a half hours at most and to no more than six people, *(b)* forbidding three proposed meetings a month, *(c)* encouraging informal discussion by telephone and corridor, and *(d)* using action teams with seven-day deadlines.

Obviously, the installation of these eight approaches would enormously change the "culture." But acceptance is the greatest change of all. Somebody, or some group of people, has to determine that "we're going to change." Thereafter, change is readily accomplished by instituting new processes like those above, or the Welch innovations at GE. That corporation's culture includes the fact that each new chief executive, promoted from within, has imposed new concepts of what GE should be and how it should be managed.

There's always a gap, of course, between "should be" and "is." What *Fortune,* in September 1994, called "Jack Welch's Nightmare on Wall Street," the $350 million of profits allegedly conjured out of thin air by Kidder Peabody trader Joe Jett, raised grave questions over strategy, personalities, and control—not at Kidder Peabody, but in GE's head office. The magazine printed a "litany of sins," five previous major catastrophes whose unifying theme was mostly greed.

The greed backfired into costly penalties. Its latest Wall Street manifestation inspired *Fortune* to write of "a disturbing chronology of bad business decisions and a cavalier disregard for normal operating procedure." Just as bad, the profits don't seem to have materialized. Great at cutting costs, GE seemed less good at building sales, which in 1993 fell by 0.9 percent. For all his high reputation, therefore, Welch still has plenty to prove in the here and now; the corporate hereafter will be even more testing.

Paradoxically, Welch will only have succeeded if his successor in ten years' time breaks the GE tradition of reforming CEOs—if the culture, in other words, has become self-generating and self-regenerating. That's the ideal of the management consensus. It can be realized—but only through process, not by preaching.

SIX

The Sharper Edge:
How to Stay
Competitive

The Realities of Japan

1

In a straight bet between Japanese and American companies, bettors who know business history would surely favor the East—with one major exception: computery. But even here, fight commentators have always swung between two extremes. On one side are the naysayers who chant what *Business Week* described as their mantra:

The Japanese do not understand marketing.
The computer industry moves too fast for the Japanese.
The Japanese can't write software.

As the nineties unfold, opinions remain divided on the strength of the Japanese challenge. Computer optimists maintain that the United States still holds all the hardware aces; its labs are the supreme fount of new technology; its installed base of computing power around the world dwarfs all competition; and its hardware makers still lead the market in current sales in almost all sectors. In software, the U.S. supremacy is uncontested, and soft power, not hard, will dominate the future.

Since these facts are mostly incontestable, what can explain the following Jeremiad? "We have this inexorable drift toward being a techno-colony by the end of the decade." Nobody could accuse the speaker, Andy Grove, of ignorant defeatism. He's chief executive of Intel, whose 286, 386, and 486 microprocessors (now joined by the Pentium) have been synonymous with the explosive growth of the personal computer in numbers and powers. No Japanese company has yet has dared enter the lists against Intel. Intel's chip designs are shining symbols of the industry's success. Its leadership in world semiconductor sales has forced the Japanese into becoming also-rans.

What explained Grove's dismal prognosis? The answer was spelled out in the *Chicago Tribune* in an article by R. C. Longworth. Its burden was statistical. In key sectors (like Intel's microprocessors) the United States led comprehensively. But overall figures showed broad retreat.

America's lead in hardware (78 percent against a mere 11 percent for Japan in 1984) was still substantial: but the gap had narrowed by 1990 to 59–25. The trend pointed to a crossover in the reasonably foreseeable future. Nor could the Americans rely on new inventions to rebuild their position—ominous data for portables and laptops (the newest and fastest-growing sector) showed Japan with 60 percent of the market.

For flat panels the picture was even bleaker: Japan had 95 percent of the market in a technology invented by the Americans (which U.S. companies have been striving, with some difficulty, to improve). The Japanese author and politician Shintaro Ishihara (author of *The Japan That Can Say No*) put the issue neatly, if obviously: "Brilliant breakthroughs in the lab are useless until engineers and lathe operators turn them into products."

If chips are taken as the products, the Japanese had converted a 57–27 disadvantage in 1982 to a 50–36 advantage ten years later. In one technology, that of dynamic random access memory (DRAM), the Japanese share was 60 percent against America's 11 percent. Two-thirds of silicon wafers are Japanese-made: the United States, with 2 percent, barely has a look-in. In ceramic packages, the United States does a little better: 3 percent. The rest of the market belongs to Japan.

In other words, true market share (percentage of all hardware sales) is being picked off by well-armed and trained guerrillas. Increasingly, American firms are battling each other with Japanese ammunition. Longworth cited Compaq's LTE laptop, made largely by Citizen Watch. His article carried a photograph of Apple's former chairman, John Sculley, holding another laptop, the Powerbook, reliant on Sony.

Personal laser printers sold by Hewlett-Packard are Canonmade. There's a Sony disk drive in workstations sold by Sun Microsystems. Note that the latter market, for powerful PC configurations used originally by engineers, but now spreading to managers and others, is one where the United States reigns supreme. But the colossal growth won't be in these top-end products. If that supergrowth, as expected, is based on miniaturization, the Japanese are in the lead position.

Actually, the race looked like a foregone conclusion as the nineties began. Companies like Citizen Watch treasure the engineering talent that has brought the national fascination with miniaturization into the forefront of a great industry. These skills are not widely matched in the West, and it would be unrealistic to expect speedy catch-up from this point, however hard the awakened strive. Much of the industry, though, has yet to pull its head out of the sand.

One of Longworth's interviewees, a software manager, used the language of bereavement counseling to express the industry's state of mind—"still in the denial stage." Compared to other markets, true, the penetration of Japanese brands in computing has been small and slow. But that's not the whole tale. The Cassandras can point to the Japanese edge in chip-making tools, memory chips, and six other key technologies, and to their rising sales of components everywhere, and of both PCs and mainframes in the United States.

Fujitsu, maker of the world's fastest conventional supercomputers, the lightest laptops, and the largest memory chips, has the world's second biggest sales of computers, topping Digital Equipment, Hewlett-Packard, and Unisys. By buying into companies like International Computers, Ltd., in Britain, Amdahl in the United States and Nokia Data in Scandinavia, Fujitsu has heavily reinforced its market-leading strengths in Japan. Hydra-headed and far less conspicuous, Japan, Inc., has become the largest, though not the leading, force in the world computer industry. Its American competitors need to recite a new mantra:

The Japanese understand marketing.
The Japanese are moving as fast as the computer industry.
The Japanese can write software.

That's the reality. Anything else is self-delusion.

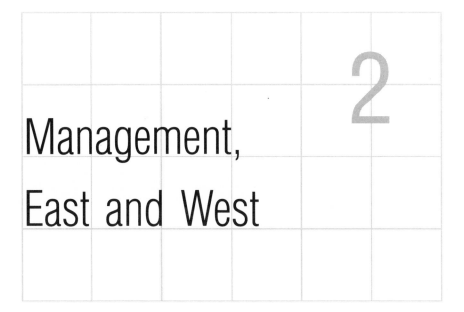

Management,
East and West

A fascinating struggle is going on between East and West, not just in world markets (though that war is crucial), but in the kingdom of ideas. After long and damaging resistance, Western management preachers and practitioners are accepting the obvious: Japanese practice offers examples and methods which the West can ignore only at its peril. In consequence, virtually all the new approaches now being urged on Western managers are old hat in Japan. From Total Quality to time-based competition, the West is following in Japanese footsteps.

Nobody proposes that American or European companies should convert themselves into Japanese clones. Rather, the intellectual war is between the perceived Asian style, based on custom and obedience, and the Western effort, building on the old foundations of Douglas McGregor's Theory Y, to create a new kind of company and management. Jack Welch's latest initiative at General Electric is part of this pattern, one of liberating the voluntary energies of individuals and guiding them towards a common end.

The cynic might describe this as doing the hard way what comes naturally and thus easily to the Japanese. But the idea of "a free association of like-minded men and women," a phrase used by Sir John Harvey-Jones when reforming the culture and performance of ICI, is very attractive to Western minds. So are the basic assumptions that led McGregor to savage Theory X (that people only work when made to) in favor of the Y alternative:

1. Work is as natural as play.
2. Self-discipline is as effective as external disciplining (and by implication more so).
3. The psychological rewards of achievement motivate people towards attaining corporate objectives.
4. "The average human being learns, under proper conditions, not only to accept but to seek responsibility."
5. Imagination, ingenuity, and creativity are widely, not narrowly, distributed among people in organizations.
6. Most companies don't utilize the full potential of the people employed.

The problem for those seeking new Western solutions based on these eternal principles is that modern Japanese practice follows them so faithfully. Take the first and most important: work is as natural as play. The late Soichiro Honda came close to using McGregor's very words in a startling passage from his biography. In his earlier days, Honda was a Theory X manager par excellence: "A bolt that had been tightened by a young worker made a few more turns when Honda did it himself. 'You damned fool. This is how you're supposed to tighten bolts,' shouted Honda, as he hit his employee over the head with a wrench." Not surprisingly, industrial relations at Honda were poor.

According to biographer Tetsuo Sakiya, the boss got angry with workers who played baseball in the plant grounds, and put far more effort into the game than into work: "In collective bargaining they complain about having to work too hard. But when it comes to playing baseball, they do it until they become completely exhausted, even though baseball does not bring a single yen to them. What kind of men are they?" Then he answered his own question (my italics): *"I must recognize that man achieves the highest degree of efficiency when he plays."*

Unlike McGregor, Honda could put this perception (which neatly encapsulates the whole of Theory Y) into practice. "I must," he told himself, "create a workshop where everyone will enjoy working." In other words, the famous Japanese enthusiasm for good business and effective management isn't simply a product of the national culture. It's also the result of excellent managers applying principles which can be translated perfectly into Western language—and which are echoed in the West.

Yet you still encounter the old ostrich attitudes that caused Western companies so much damage. They failed to respond adequately to a challenge whose force they refused to acknowledge, often arguing that to emulate Japan is impossible because of its peculiar culture. Bad Western habits, like investing too little in productive capacity, new products, training, quality, and marketing, are hardly cultural—not unless bad business economics are built into Western mentality.

For instance, recessions are generally shorter than new-product development cycles. So cutting back during recession guarantees that innovations will miss the first and very probably the second year of upturn. Culture comes into the equation in only one way—if everybody else is doing likewise, no competitive disadvantage will result. But in a global economy, that breathing space has disappeared.

For Western competitors, the Japanese economy outside Japan is a basic threat. Its managers have shown repeatedly that their domestic methods can produce equal or better productivity and market penetration in foreign cultures. These methods are no more culturally determined than the technology of the internal combustion engine. Just as McGregor's principles make sense in any language, so do those of productivity.

George B. Stalk, Jr., and Thomas Hout of the Boston Consulting Group, in their *Competing Against Time,* compared two manufacturers of an automobile suspension component: "With one-third the scale and more than three times the product variety, the Japanese company also boasts total labor productivity that is half again that of its American competitor. Moreover, the unit cost of the Japanese manufacturer is less than half that of the U.S. company"—even though the direct workers in Japan had lower productivity than their American counterparts.

The simple explanation is that the Americans employed 135 indirect or overhead workers, a bigger total than directs; the Japanese had only 7. I'm often tempted to believe that the most important rule in business economics, and thus in management, is the simplest: KEEP DOWN THE OVERHEADS. You can be sure that, in their expansion across the world, now concentrating more on Europe than America, the Japanese are following this precept and many others of like simplicity and power.

That helps explain how Nissan, assembling cars at Sunderland in Britain, produces over three times Rover's cars per employee. Rover, however, is a full-scale manufacturer. A fairer comparison is with General Motors, whose Vauxhall employees assemble 40 percent fewer cars apiece than Nissan. The latter will be outshone by Toyota's projected performance in Derbyshire, where it plans to produce 35 percent more cars per employee than Nissan—and over twice as many as the GM plant.

This greatly shocked union leaders, who calculated that Rover, the last British-owned competitor until it fell to BMW in 1994, would need only two-fifths of its labor force if Toyota's methods were adopted. So what is this magic methodology? It includes

1. Complete flexibility between crafts
2. Daily and changing production targets
3. Stopping production if faults appear
4. Insistence on achieving the day's production targets even if the assembly line has had to stop temporarily
5. Longer work weeks—thirty-nine hours against thirty-seven

That involves no waving of wands, and little fundamental Japanese innovation. The same down-to-earth approach that dominates the factories governs the hunt for technology. Missing strengths have sometimes, alas, been stolen. Mostly, the technology has been begged, borrowed, and bought, in two senses. Straightforward licensing has given Japan essential technology. But so has acquisition of all or part of companies with valuable technological resources.

By 1992, some 363 high-technology U.S. firms were in Japanese hands: in computers, they hold 87 out of 133 American businesses bought wholly or partially by foreigners. "There's an economic war on, and we're losing it" was the grim verdict of Papken Der Terossian, chief executive of a chip maker, the Silicon Valley Group. Is the war being waged on equal terms?

The Japanese ability to buy up key players isn't matched the other way around. Japan's capitalism doesn't create hosts of buyable businesses: American capitalism does. The Western approach is a marvelous method of starting up new businesses and rapidly developing their markets. But the transition into medium scale (let alone major size) is far less easily achieved.

That is a crucial challenge to American management. Start-up stars may well find that the optimum time to optimize their personal wealth comes shortly after the first moment of fruition, when the company is still riding high on its initial surge. At that stage, the entrepreneur either goes public, or sells out, perhaps to the Japanese. The long buildup that created Hewlett-Packard, Digital, IBM, and so forth has become much harder to finance.

Most Silicon Valley start-ups rely on venture capital. That's quite patient money. The funds usually run for a ten-year period, but their purposes is to yield abnormally high gains on investments. For these yields to materialize, profits must be taken; the rule of thumb for a successful investment is ten times your money after five years. At which point the successful investor looks for an exit, via public flotation or outright sale.

For every head lopped off by these market forces, though, at least two more have grown. Every day new developments testify to this vitality. In *Business Week*'s 1992 list of fast-growing companies, half the top twenty were engaged in the broadly defined computer industry. They ranged from A to X. Artisoft stood at number one: after three years of 171.3 percent annual growth, it had $64.3 million of sales, precisely a thousandth of IBM's. The company made both hardware and software for networking PCs by "peer-to-peer" links, which do away with the need for powerful "servers," such as a mini or workstation.

Number twenty was Xilinx (sales growth 39.9 percent to $94.3 million over three years). Its reprogrammable chips had doubled profits in three years. As the A to X companies flourish, innovation bubbles up from the bottom. So far, efforts to direct it from the top have foundered. This is a serious problem for the leaders of Western industry: these leaders are too often being led. So, true, are the Japanese—witness the humiliating collapse of their project to mimic human intelligence with the fifth-generation computer.

The temptation to crow over such failures, while understandable, is dangerous. It never pays to underestimate your competition, especially if it's Japanese. Western competitors have a tendency to create comforting myths. In cars, the myth was, first, that Japan couldn't compete with Detroit or European engineering. When that comfort failed, it was styling at which the invaders were doomed to flop. When that myth collapsed, it was luxury executive cars that were beyond Japanese competence—today, try telling that to the buyers of Toyota's Lexus or Nissan's Infiniti.

These cars set the seal on the eighties as the era of Japan, the age when Western management reputations, and some managements, were swept away by the tide of Japanese success. But have the seeds of its own decay begun to sprout within that success? Japan never was immune to the general run of either history or economics—and the country's rocky introduction to the nineties seems to confirm the fears (or hopes) of its critics.

In 1993, not a day passed without evidence that the Japanese are all too human. Criticism of their weaknesses has swollen to loud accusations that, stripped of benefits like cheap raw materials and money, Japan's managers are no more effective than anybody else's. Rather, they are just as ineffective. When Nissan was riding high, instead of losing billions of yen, nobody bothered about its excess of components (86 different steering wheels, 173 different steering columns, etc.) or models (29 in all).

Those unbothered by Nissan's negligence included not only its management, but outside observers. The failures of Japanese automakers were hidden by successes on very obvious and important points: such as manufacturing costs, product quality, delivery performance, and market share. What you look at is what you see. What you don't look at, by the same token, goes unobserved and without criticism.

The Japanese policy of lifetime employment, for instance, was universally admired. In hindsight, it's obvious that, combined with vigorous competition for graduates, it must result in steady bloating of the executive ranks. Many aspects of Japanese management, including the large number of minds brought to bear on debating and deciding issues, reflect this inflation. But who cared, so long as sales and profits rose?

The proliferation of models and components arose because Japanese car firms matched their product strategies to the domestic market. Its booming growth allowed too many manufacturers to compete across the board. They prided themselves on the manufacturing genius which enabled them to produce an excess of models at remarkable speed, which suited the boomtime market. As soon as domestic demand reverted closer to the worldwide norm, the strength became a weakness.

In hindsight, piling up product upon product seems strange. One Japanese food manufacturer, cited in the *Financial Times,* is *reducing* its lines to 2,500: that looks even weirder when you learn that two-fifths of its products provided only 3 percent of sales. One cardinal difference between East and West remains, though: finding sin, most Japanese react swiftly to achieve virtue. That's the best reason for supposing that Japan's idols may return to the pedestals from which they fell, pushed by their own unnecessary failings.

In any event, the Japanese remain tough, resourceful competitors, even if their relative edge is being eroded. In the U.S. car market, for example, domestic and Japanese quality are now, in many cases, on a par, while Chrysler has succeeded in launching a new sports model (admittedly, on a short production run) within a Japanese time-frame. In other words, the occasional best of Westerners matches the fairly standard practice of Japan.

If best practice is the criticism, in fact, the nineties can also be seen as Japan's era in management and competitive terms. Exported competition, far more than exported goods, is what has galvanized the more alert Western competitors into learning new lessons. In cars alone, nearly 250 American parts companies are wholly or partly Japanese-owned. The mistake for Western managers would be to identify Japan's macroeconomic troubles with its microeconomic potential.

Japanese managerial prowess hasn't followed the plunge of the Tokyo stock market. That prowess, true, may have been exaggerated.

Like high-riding companies, soaring national economies encourage misplaced belief in superior quality of management. While the performance of Japan's overseas operations appears to endorse that quality, so did that of America's European affiliates in their time: set up shop on a brand-new, "greenfield" site, back local management with all the parent's resources in money, technology, and expertise, and if you don't win, you should be ashamed.

Nobody, however, is more shamed by bad performance than a good Japanese manager. The reaction—outdo yourself—was admirably demonstrated when the virus of the soaring yen triggered a previous epidemic of blue-chip blues. The crucial issue is whether Japanese management can demonstrate this celebrated resilience all over again. If that happens, any time lost while the Japanese are bandaging their wounds will be time most grievously wasted.

Even if no further thrusts forward are made, the penetration already achieved makes these Japanese managers the team to beat—and that includes the broadly defined computer industry. They won't be overcome without applying the same techniques, or finding new and improved approaches, to the vital business of achieving more with less: more output, more on every attribute of importance to the customer, but with less cost, fewer man-hours, and less error.

Oddly enough, even though Japanese management methods are mostly founded on Western insights and precepts, most CEOs and executives in the United States and Europe persist with puzzling reluctance to practice what's preached in Western sermons. For instance, Total Quality Management is a largely Western concept that was developed by the Japanese and imported back into the West, only to be bad-mouthed by local managers. Total Quality, though, is essentially about creating and maintaining far better managed businesses.

There Japan still leads, like it or not. Dr. Michael Cross wrote to the *Financial Times* in December 1993 to report on a long search for world-class manufacturing operations. Out of 1,039, classified on the criteria used for the Malcolm Baldrige Quality Award, no less than 675 were Japanese. North Americans owned 221 operations in the world class, but only 113 were in North America. Nearly five times as many of Japan's world-class plants (510) were in Japan.

In other words, Japan's relative strength is greatest where its manufacturers lack the innate advantage of greenfield plants and imported technology. They simply have the advantage of superior management. Five to one is a formidable gap. But Westerners with a world-class will have one large, bright, hope: Japan's management technology is no secret. It can be begged, borrowed, bought; and even—with perfect impunity—stolen.

The Fallen Idol
of Innovation

3

Opinion researchers who in 1993 helped *Fortune* to compile its annual list of Most Admired Corporations tried an interesting new exercise. They used multiple regression analysis to discover whether admiration paralleled financial performance. Sure enough, it did. If you want to be admired by your peers, above all produce excellent figures for ten-year annual return to shareholders (in capital gains and dividends), return on assets, total profits—and stock market value.

A prize tautology leaps from that list. Stock market value is a function of admiration, so you're admiring the corporation for being admired. That's an important point to remember when contemplating the catastrophic decline in reputation of superstars like ITT. Fame is exaggerated because it feeds on itself. But note that the numbers for total assets and single-year earnings growth feed fame the least. In other words, how you use your assets and sustain financial performance over the longer term is crucial.

The *Fortune* ratings, which result from polling several thousand business executives, are by no means dominated by money, however.

They judge the 311 largest companies in the United States on eight criteria, only three of them financial. The full list is quality of management; quality of products or services; innovativeness; value as a long-term investment; financial soundness; ability to attract, develop, and keep talented people; community and environmental responsibility; and use of corporate assets.

Year after year, on this combined scorecard, one company used to come out triumphantly on top: IBM. Did this amount to more than admiration breeding admiration—and self-admiration? In 1984, chairman John R. Opel commented on his top ranking: "I think this is the finest industrial enterprise in the world." This self-satisfaction was marred by only one blemish: IBM wasn't placed top for innovation. Opel didn't "really understand it. We've got a portfolio that testifies to our technical innovations, and we have got a remarkably successful marketing organization that does some very creative things every day."

A year later, although IBM still came out on top overall, the innovativeness ranking was down again, this time to 31st: even in its own industry, with ten runners, IBM was only fourth. Yet another slump on this ranking, to 78th, didn't prevent the champion from keeping its overall lead in 1986. But that was the last time. On January 16, 1987, came the bombshell: "The king is dethroned; IBM, No. 1 since the survey began, drops to seventh place." The slide down *Fortune*'s league table continued: 32nd in 1988, then 34th, then 45th. The latest overall number is an awful 206th.

The judgment was not simply that of IBM's peers, but of its major customers, the bosses of America's largest corporations. The very people who should have constantly seen evidence of IBM's innovation in products and marketing, had Opel been right, had turned thumbs down—even when the company's general reputation was still riding high. These warning doubts marked the real turning point in IBM's fortunes. The world in general may give you the benefit of the doubt, but what your competitors and customers know (and do) carries the real punch.

Customer satisfaction surveys are the alpha and omega of most Total Quality programs: the beginning, in the sense that they establish the company's starting point on the road to perfection, and the end, in the sense of "objective." The whole program is directed towards raising customers' opinion of the firm, its goods, and its services. But you don't need to embrace Total Quality to see the value of customer surveys—not least because of the shock they generally apply to corporate self-esteem.

Jacques Horovitz, the service quality guru, finds that, when managements see his survey results, their attitude invariably undergoes extraordinary change. Always, before receiving the facts, there's a "perception gap" between their own (higher) and the customer's (lower) view of their performance. Simple lack of listening skills means that companies are out of touch with the reality of customer perceptions: witness Opel, above.

Like him, managers even argue against perceptions. How can the customers have got it so wrong? Whether the perception is right or wrong, in the manager's own eyes, is immaterial. A perception is a fact in itself. Perceptions can be changed, but those which lack a foundation in reality are unlikely to last. Far better to establish an excellent reality—and then bend all your efforts to getting the perception to fit.

Dancing to

Customer Tunes

4

The power of perception is infinite. That's true even in areas where pure science seems to apply. Pharmaceuticals are an excellent example. Merck, the successor to IBM as year-in, year-out Most Admired Corporation, ranked as "the most admired company by far in the most admired industry." Innovativeness is among the prime explanations for this high level of celebration. Yet drug companies spend money lavishly to create perceptions of innovation where none exists.

The product advantages (smaller, fewer doses) which Glaxo's anti-ulcer drug Zentac held over the rival Tagamet don't fully explain why the latecomer shot past the pioneer in sales. Glaxo simply outmarketed the future SmithKline Beecham. Its marketing strategy, which included charging higher prices and *raising* the promotional spend after a successful launch (the direct opposite of industry practice), was cleverly designed to enhance the perception of superiority.

People in pharmaceuticals should know more about the power of pure perception than anybody, for the placebos which they use in testing drugs achieve a significant success ratio. The sugar pills heal through the perception that they are powerful medications. In this case, perceptions are wrong, which they very often are. At the basic level of the senses, people misperceive what they see. The brain is very flexible in deciding what the retina has picked up, changing its mind (so to speak) all the time: it's far less flexible on weightier matters.

As the British scientist Richard Gregory has asked: "Why should the perceptual system be so active in seeking alternative solutions, as we see it to be in ambiguous situations? It seems more active and more intellectually honest in refusing to stick with one of many possible solutions than is the cerebral cortex as a whole—if we may judge by the tenacity of irrational belief in politics and religion." And that goes for business and management, too.

This isn't by any means exclusively a matter of external perceptions. They are vital. But so are managers' internal perceptions of their companies and their capabilities in the market. How much earlier might IBM have changed its wrong-headed ways if top management had put external perceptions before the internal view? The smartest moves a company can make include finding out how its core activities are viewed by the management itself: researching to check these basic perceptions against ascertainable truth, and then acting on reality, instead of inner-perceived reality.

Outside perceptions will then be calling the tune. In his book *Relationships Marketing,* Regis McKenna stresses the crucial importance of "dynamic positioning," which has three aspects, all of them concerned with the outside view:

1. *Product positioning.* How does your product fit into the competitive marketplace? What's its selling proposition—low cost, high quality, advanced technology? How should you segment your markets? Who are the target customers?
2. *Market positioning.* How is the company *perceived* by customers and by the "industry infrastructure": retailers, distributors, suppliers, analysts, journalists and other opinion-makers?
3. *Corporate positioning:* What do people *think,* not about your products or services, but the company itself?

As the italicized words above indicate, perception is central to the positioning—and it's seldom a clear-cut issue. Take product quality, which is especially important today. *Perceptions* of quality are influenced by many items: not only performance, reliability, and durability, but "knobs, bells, and whistles," aesthetics, status enhancement, availability, service, and reputation.

You dare not leave the perception to fate. Management must focus on one or two elements: and the choice must be very deliberately made and implemented and communicated to customers. The object is to persuade them to prefer your product or service. Change of preference (that is, change in perceptions) is what the astute marketer of fast-moving consumer goods seeks to achieve: it's the most meaningful test of an advertising campaign's success or failure—far more meaningful than spontaneous or prompted "recall" of the ads.

It may seem ridiculous that mere words can create commercial success, until you remember the Chinese gooseberry. That was the name of a product, grown in New Zealand, which was all but unsalable until some genius renamed it the Kiwi fruit. The rest is world market history. At one time or another it was impossible to market ballpoint pens, vacuum cleaners, Post-it notes, liquid soap, Vicks VapoRub, or Vaseline: not because of any disadvantages in these splendid products, but because critical links in the market chain had negative perceptions.

One of those links, again, is the company itself. Market leaders tend to the pre-conception that they excel the competition at every point. The competition tends to believe the same thing, and the smaller the market share, the greater the negative conviction. That's why industries so often play follow-the-leader. If McDonald's starts building bigger and fancier restaurants, with larger and fancier menus, so does every other fast-food company.

That flies in the face of the Unique Selling Proposition. If you're not perceived as different, why should anybody buy from you, and not somebody else? In fact, some people will always buy from you—but not enough to reverse the depredations of a poor relative market share. The perception that a competitor's larger share is the decisive advantage, however, is likely to be false. In fact, many market leaders by size have small returns: the reasons include inept marketing.

One study found, for example, that some 51 percent of a group of low-return leaders shared more than 80 percent of marketing programs with other lines. That compared with only 39 percent of the leaders with high returns. Leaders may also lag seriously on two of the most important aspects of perception: relative *perceived* quality and relative *perceived* service. High scores on these dimensions can help to substitute for a lower market share.

That's why Jacques Horovitz, founder of the consultancy network MSR (Management of Strategic Resources), warns against relying on a single overall measure of customer satisfaction. That doesn't give you any guidance on the most important aspect of all: how to close the gap. The MSR breakdown gives a total of forty measured variables, reporting the reactions of anything from one thousand to five thousand customers—far more than you need just to measure overall satisfaction.

You can't know too much about your customers, or how they perceive your competitors. If you proceed on your pre-conceptions, and not customer perceptions, you are certain to make mistakes. The object is rather to correct *their* mistakes, by aligning their perceptions with yours. Many cases show how, when perceptions were changed by abandoning the entrepreneurs' own false pre-conceptions, product failures were turned into historic successes. In *Getting It Right the Second Time,* author Michael Gershman offers a dozen telling *P*'s for those who want to emulate such triumphs:

1. *P*itch it in the right way.
2. Look for a *P*iggyback ride.
3. Have faith in public *P*erception.
4. Correctly *P*osition the product.
5. Don't overlook the *P*ackage.
6. Sell in the right *P*lace.
7. Set the right *P*rice.
8. Consider a *P*remium.
9. Don't skimp on *P*romotion.
10. Use the full power of *P*ublicity.
11. Add a *P*romise to the product.
12. . . . and at all times *P*ersevere.

Gershman's examples for Pitch include the shift of Kleenex from beauty aid to simple nose-blowing. The Zantac success mentioned above was initiated by a Piggyback: Glaxo used the much larger Hoffman–La Roche sales force in the United States. The change in Perception achieved with Green Giant was overcoming the prejudice in favor of small peas, and against larger ones. The Position switch of Marlboro from ladies' cigarette to the outdoor man image is a classic of the culture.

In pharmaceuticals, which traditionally turns a blind eye to the Package, the British brand of analgesic Nurofen (ibuprofen), radically different from either aspirin or acetaminophen, was given a radically different pack. The Place chosen by Swatch to defeat the Japanese watchmakers was any place where watches had not traditionally been sold. Zantac's Price (and Promotion) gambit has already been mentioned. As for the Premium, Wrigley's didn't offer gifts to the customers who chewed its gum: but dealers who placed larger orders got free coffee grinders, cheese cutters, lamps, and ladders.

With the aid of Promotion (samples distributed to doctors) both Vaseline and VapoRub got off the ground. The Publicity strategem used by the legendary Patrick J. Frawley to save Paper Mate's day was obtaining endorsement by the ballpoint pen's severest critics, educators and bankers. The best kind of Promise is the service or product guarantee—like the long-standing Marks & Spencer promise to replace any product for any reason, or none at all.

As for Perseverance, Procter and Gamble stuck with Pampers through production problems, high prices, and buyer resistance. The manufacturer finally outdid cloth diapers by using the customer's point of view (i.e., perception). The crucial customer turned out to be the baby. In all these examples, money was involved, but rarely much of it, and never as the crucial factor. The key to changing perceptions, which are other people's thoughts, is *thinking*—your own thought.

If you don't think, you won't change anything. But it's easy to stop thinking altogether as mental rigidity takes command. A simple example lies in a statistic which all good retailers should know: what proportion of customers intending to buy enter the store, but leave without purchasing? In fact, many retailers have no idea of a figure which, in one Horovitz case, was as high as 40 percent.

It doesn't take a genius to work out the increase in sales and profit available from reducing that 40 percent number. But even genius won't help unless you analyze the global result. *Why* didn't 40 percent of them buy? Was it a poor salesperson? Lack of sales staff? Out of stock? These questions have their equivalents in any business. What proportion of proposals/bids/sales calls, and so forth fail? Why? And then, what can—and must—be done to raise the success ratio?

That comes back to the essential point made by IBM's fall from universal admiration: the eventually decisive slippage on only one count among eight. Overall figures don't give you an operational tool. Specifics do. The knowledge that you're slipping in the estimation of your peers, or the public, on any single important count should ring alarm bells. The *Fortune* criteria for selecting the Most Admired Corporation are themselves admirable, a guide to urgent action which covers the key elements of performance and perception:

1. On a scale of 1 to 10, how is your "quality of management" rated *(a)* internally, *(b)* by customers, *(c)* by competitors, *(d)* by opinion-makers?
2. How is the quality of your products and services rated by the same four groups?
3. And your innovativeness?
4. How do your key financial ratios rank against *(a)* competitors, *(b)* the best comparable statistics anywhere?
5. How does your use of assets rate on the same comparisons?
6. How has the business performed as a long-term investment—very good, good, average, poor, or very poor?
7. Do you have reason to be proud of your policies towards the community and the environment?
8. Do you attract, develop, and retain talented people?

It's pointless asking these questions, though, unless you're prepared to believe the answers, however unpalatable, and to respond to the message from the all-powerful market. Looking at the top ten companies in the *Fortune* list, the unifying theme is less their high financial performance than the marketplace strength from which the money derives. Note the power of their customer franchises: Merck, Rubbermaid, Wal-Mart, 3M, Coca-Cola, Procter & Gamble, Levi Strauss, Liz Claiborne, J. P. Morgan, and Boeing.

Customer power thus rules from stores to jets, frocks to finance, low technology to high. In electronics, George Fisher applied that lesson during his successful tenure at Motorola: so successful that his head was expensively hunted for Eastman Kodak. Interviewed after his appointment, Fisher was quick to include, among the fundamentals for such success, "first and foremost, a focus on the customers, because they are the people who pay the bills. . . . If you get that right, almost everything follows."

Fisher's statement will attract enthusiastic echoes from managers worldwide, including some who haven't satisfied, delighted, considered, or possibly even seen a customer for years. But Fisher's words are defective: what does "getting it right" mean? Without a clear focus of the kind a Horovitz-type inquiry seeks, nobody can judge whether "almost everything" truly does follow. And what about "getting it wrong"? Does everything else collapse?

If so, all companies are in deep trouble, for nobody gets it right, not if the definition is 100 percent customer satisfaction. For instance, corporate users of PCs register only 65 percent satisfaction with the service they receive—and 70 percent counts as only satisfactory. Yet these are among the most reliable, best-produced, and most productive devices ever made by man. Along with other high-tech products, mostly Japanese, they have raised the whole level of customer expectations.

Even relatively low-tech manufactures like cars have climbed into a new zone. As Mercedes-Benz has found, to its acute pain, today's buyers won't pay a premium for quality alone. In many markets, for consumer and industrial goods alike, quality, however defined, has become a sine qua non. Nor is the customer the only party to benefit as a result. The highest price for poor quality is paid, not by customers, but providers, in the costly shape of *R*ework, *R*ecalls, *R*eplacements, and poor customer *R*etention.

The last of these four *R*'s is the crux of the issue. As noted, polling customers to learn their opinions can (and usually does) deal a devastating blow to corporate complacency. Those managements prepared to correct the revealed defects by systematic improvement will indeed, as Fisher says, find that much else inevitably comes right—though not "almost everything." For that to happen, improvement must take place within the context of an organization rethought from top to bottom. You can't say "from start to finish," though, because there is no finish: the process of customer satisfaction is continuous and never-ending.

Retention provides its vital proof. Measuring customer satisfaction will show companies where they stand (or run) on the upward-moving staircase of expectations. But the votes that count are recorded with the feet, or rather the checks. How many businesses know the scale and cause of customer loss, or have ever costed the profit lost through customer turnover? Typically, 90 percent of the gross margin on an existing customer is dissipated in the effort to obtain a new buyer.

To put that more positively, as little as a 5 percent rise in customer retention can increase profits by between 20 and 50 percent. Horovitz developed his ideas and techniques through long-term work at Club Méditerranée, work which sprang from a disturbing discovery: vacationers, expensively won by advertising, were not returning in large enough numbers. Club Med has made mighty strides since then. It epitomizes the customer-led business of Fisher's ideal: but, then, it does have an advantage: living, breathing customer contact, day-in, night-out.

The ultimate logic of Fisherism is that all companies should try to replicate that environment. The ultimate reality, though, is that people inside companies don't only face outwards, and can't. The customer pays the bills, but not the wages: that is, decisions on promotions, powers, positions, perks, punishments (and all the other P's) are made internally. The practice of internal politics, in most companies, heavily outweighs the theory of putting customers first and foremost.

Merely look at today's endless spate of corporate commotions. Where (if anywhere) did the customer figure in the battle for Paramount, or the wave of megabuck mergers in communications? The usual answer won't wash: that if the upheavals result in greater efficiency and lower costs, the customer cannot *but* benefit. True, but that's a million miles away from customer focus that runs throughout the organization in a never-ending circuit. That demands commitment to constant change as the customer—rarely satisfied for long, endlessly wooed by others, periodically shifting in requirements—calls the corporate tune.

Commitment to customer-led change comes easier in greenfield organizations such as the high-tech newcomers of Silicon Valley. What can be done on a virgin battlefield, with an army composed entirely of volunteers, far outranges the immediate possibilities of long-established organizations. Their armies have old lags, conscripts, and some soldiers who, maybe for the highest-minded of reasons, are conscientious objectors. For the established, the problem is that Fisher's dictum needs reversal: "Once you focus on the customer, almost everything looks wrong."

It takes a brave, rare top management to vacate its throne, and set about changing everything, with the willing help of all its colleagues (the people who Sam Walton of Wal-Mart called "associates"), so that the customer can rise to true kingship. Significantly, those managements that come nearest to the ideal, such as Wal-Mart and Levi Strauss, have been at the forefront of the drive to "empower" employees: to drive decisions down the organization and hand them over to people who are encouraged to use their own initiative.

The customer-first proposition has become a cliché. So be it. The customers and their perceptions really are decisive. To win, deserve, and retain their admiration, managers must endure the destruction of their own comfortable illusions. That beginning is bound to be uncomfortable. But it leads to very comforting success.

The Strategy
of Alliances

5

Technological and marketing deals now crisscross the electronics world to form a lattice that is impenetrable even to insiders. There's only one word for it: "COMPLEXITY!!!" The exclamation points and capitals are those of Michael J. Kami, a consultant of great insight who once worked at shaping the strategy of IBM and later quit to perform the same job for Xerox Corporation. One of Kami's slides is a map of computer industry alliances that resembles a subway network gone mad. It has four large hubs of which IBM is only one.

By mid-1992, though, IBM had more than twenty thousand business alliances worldwide, including almost four hundred equity investments and joint ventures, and more were being created almost weekly. The task of keeping tabs on the equity deals, let alone the alliances, must stretch even IBM's bureaucracy to the limits. The strategy could easily make managerial nonsense—as shown by the strange story of IBM's alliance with NeXT, the Apple rival created by its ousted founder, Steven Jobs.

According to Jobs, talking to none other than Microsoft's Bill Gates for the benefit of *Fortune,* "Somebody at IBM a few years ago saw our NeXTStep operating system as a potential diamond to solve their biggest and most profound problem, that of adding value to their computers with unique software"—hence the deal: price tag, $50 million. Unfortunately, IBM didn't prove to be the cohesive monolith which Jobs (and the world) imagined: "It is a very large place with lots of faces, and they all play musical chairs. Somewhere along the line this diamond got dropped in the mud, and now it's sitting on somebody else's desk who thinks it's a dirt clod. Inside that dirt clod is still a diamond, but they don't see it."

Undeterred, IBM went on to make a far-reaching deal with Apple itself. The objective was nothing less than the entire future of PC technology. The alliance would be the gateway to another stupendous revolution, in which microelectronics would infiltrate, even take over, activities across the entire spectrum of human life.

The new explosion of technology is reminiscent of the Big Bang that is thought to have created the universe. The discoveries are creating wider and wider bands of new materials from which new products and classes of product are emerging. If the Apple forecasters are right (which is arguable), the universe of the electronics companies will reach $3 trillion of sales by 2002: that's $3,000,000 million, or the equivalent of forty-six IBMs.

The vision, as Andrew Kupfer has written, is of an age in which "the borders dissolve between telecommunications, office equipment, computers, consumer electronics, and media and publishing." The "digital technology gadgets focused on the intersections of those industries," which Apple has started to produce, will become an awesome flood of things like "electronic books, electronic organizers, electronic note takers, display telephones, [and] personal communicators."

Nobody, though, will be producing these small marvels on their own. Once, companies could afford and achieve product exclusivity. A product was made entirely by the producer, from its own designs, in its own plants, with its own components, often on its own equipment—and none of these were available to outside companies. Outsiders were allowed in only as suppliers of those necessities which such companies chose not to manufacture themselves: few outside products reached the final assembly lines.

In Henry Ford's prime, iron ore went in at one end and finished cars came out the other. Today Ford and all other car makers are very substantial consumers of outside components and complete assemblies. The bought-in proportion, once a sign of weakness, is now an indicator of strength: as noted earlier, GM's excessive, 70 percent reliance on its own factories is among the factors that have crippled its comeback struggle. In all industries, Kami's complexity is evident. Other networks may crisscross less than those in high technology, but the same pressures are in play.

By the early nineties hardly a week passed without some major new alliance being announced. Usually, no financial terms were disclosed. Often, contradictions abounded. Some European company, for example, would join a partnership to wrest market share from American manufacturers. Simultaneously, the same company's deal in another technology would be pulling Americans into Europe. The sheer profusion of these cross-border deals, however, is making the old issues of economic sovereignty increasingly academic.

The biggest issue in all alliances is far simpler: whether or not the project will work out, commercially or technologically. High-flying joint ventures have a bad habit of aborting, partly for inherent, internal reasons, partly because of unpredictable results in the outside market. But the risks of failure seem much less alarming than those of being left on the outside looking in. In making as many linkups as possible, companies are seeking to bargain their own technological competencies and marketing reach against an assured position in the future.

They may be overdoing it. Back every horse in the race and you must win, but you make no money. Since all those alliances, with their usually unknown financial commitments, involve sharing profits, they must reduce the potential for all partners. In any event, nobody can back all the horses—for their number is increasing all the time. Yet the choices of partner still have to be made. Size, strength, and status can no longer be preserved by market domination, price leadership, technological supremacy, or any other traditional means.

The best of enemies in one area will be the best of friends in another—and alliance skills will be fundamental. Every company is becoming more and more "virtual," part of business system composed of strategic partners whose core competencies complement each other. Partnering sounds simple enough, put that way. Maintaining market strength through an interlocking network of alliances, on the other hand, sounds complex. But tomorrow's leaders are mastering the direct routes to the center of the web. They have no choice.

Partnering
for Profit

6

Companies that are still vertically integrated in a vertical industry—the conventional model—are in trouble. The new age is horizontal, in organization, management, and markets alike. And that produces some fascinating, unseen results in global business. As companies cease to make everything they need, to concentrate instead on those "core competencies," a new breed of businesses is emerging into the limelight: multinationals with enormous shares of invisible markets.

Some of these world-leading players are well-known, like Philips, which is a dominant supplier of color TV tubes, or Sony, which has three-fifths or more of three key component markets. But how many people have heard of Murata, Nideq, TDK, Futaba, Mabuchi, and Kyocera? Nideq has 85 percent of the world market for spindle motors for Winchester drives; TDK possesses 60 percent of world sales of printer heads; the others all have similar strengths in various key electronic industry components.

The attraction of their markets lies in the power of horizontal strength, which is inherently difficult to dislodge. These operations lie at the center of the networks of complexity. Willy-nilly, their competing customers are all in partnership with the same suppliers. The companies in these driving seats possess the core technologies. Those hold the key to the core competencies, which result in core products in two senses: the competencies are the core of the supplier, and the core of other people's products—which, being end-products, are more vulnerable.

The vulnerability lies in the rapidly fluctuating nature of end-product markets. In the early nineties, large PC companies suddenly found themselves losing money, while their suppliers, led by Intel and Microsoft, were coining cash. The partnerships with these horizontal businesses, alliances which had been the key to fabulous growth and profits, were now sources of profound irritation. At IBM, the answer appeared to lie in greater vertical integration, making its own microprocessors for PCs: but crucially, again, in partnership—with Apple and Motorola.

In markets which are so fickle, and change so fast, even fast-moving companies can be too slow. The strategic alliance aims to speed up progress by pooling existing technologies and instantly achieving combined strengths that would otherwise take years to build. When even so powerful a technological force as IBM joins with others to develop vital PC technology, it is much less a question of saving costs than saving time.

Two heads should be better than one, and two foundation users of the technology will create faster acceptance and quicker payback. It's the same principle as synchronous product development inside the firm: the savings of time are substantial. They are also essential, for research has shown that time over-runs are far more damaging to a product's economics than excess development spending.

To Peter Drucker, time is the "only one true cost" now left. Whatever the starting point of management theorists and consultants, they all end up urging speed from their different perspectives. It must be true that the less time your processes consume, the lower your true costs, and the more competitive and profitable your business. To Mike Kami, it's an "or else," urgent, urging issue: "Act faster or perish!"

Good management demands a sense of urgency. To put that the other way around, nothing creates mismanagement more surely than complacency. These two observations have always been true. But to-day the pressures have intensified. You don't have time to be compla-cent. The competition and the future simply move in too fast. The need for speed is, or should be, a built-in urgency for all businesses. Alliances, given the urgent motives behind their formation, can hardly be exempt.

It's hard enough to generate a sense of continuous urgency in a company with a defined culture and history. So how can the neces-sary impetus be achieved in an ad hoc partnership, or a joint venture that exists in the no-man's-land between two companies? Making al-liances per se isn't the answer: it's the ability of the allies to achieve joint, decisive advantages that counts.

When Steelcase, to return to an earlier example, decided to launch the new low-priced Turnstone line that was aimed at the small business and home office furniture market, speed was its fulcrum. That meant speed of distribution, which in turn involved a relation-ship with three transport and logistics companies, all owned by the British group NFC. The trio (themselves forming a partnership within NFC) took over the entire operation from completion of man-ufacture. Without the partnership, Turnstone couldn't meet its prom-ise to customers: delivery on telephone order within five days.

That's a massive reduction from the norm and the key to the success of the venture. According to Kami, massive improvement is a must: a 20 percent gain isn't even worth considering in most cases. Delivery time (see Turnstone) should be cut by 50 to 70 percent, de-velopment time by 50 to 60 percent, inventories by 50 to 80 percent. Available efficiencies on the plus side include a rise in "first pass yield" by 60 to 80 percent, and gains in productivity by from 20 per-cent (if you're very, very good already) to 80 percent. Return on cap-ital employed, again, should rise for the already good leaders by at least a fifth, and by 80 percent for the laggards.

The greatest gains won't be won from existing processes and strat-egies. That holds the clue to the first principle of alliance management. The fact that new partnerships travel without luggage facilitates a famil-iar but revolutionary type of management: greenfielding. Allies and partners can start from scratch, just like a new factory. C. K. Prahalad strikes to the heart of the greenfielding philosophy with a simple ques-tion. Which of these two situations would you prefer?

A. Low resources and high aspirations
B. High resources and low aspirations

It takes a smidgen of soul-searching to arrive at the right answer. Every manager would prefer to work in a rich organization. But the poor company has the urgency of its poverty. As Prahalad asks, "Would you invent Just-in-Time if you were rich?" Of course not: you would afford and tolerate unnecessary inventory. Innovation is inherent in the firm which has high ambitions but lacks the means to achieve them by conventional methods. So it must break the conventions to realize its ambitions at the least possible cost.

That must mean in the fastest possible time. The low-resource company with high aspirations is the better place to be: for those lofty ambitions, if realized, produce towering payoffs—witness McCaw Communications. It was started on its cellular journey by a thirty-three-year-old with $10,000. A decade later Donald McCaw sold *a piece* of the business for $3 billion, and then all of it to AT&T for $12 billion. If your aspirations are low, whatever the amount of resources, achievement will match the low aims.

Greenfielding requires the combination of high ambition with tight targets, for both time and cost. The greenfielders' working partnership needs to be geared up in two dimensions: *(a) internal speed,* quickening all processes and developing a state of readiness which can produce crash programs at will, and *(b) external speed,* generating fast responses (which will include such programs) to the demands and the changes in the marketplace.

The need to achieve the internal-external combination punch is no different, of course, in an established organization. The difference lies in the greenfielding mentality, which is the opposite of corpocracy. But corporations are themselves under compulsion to form internal alliances as well as external—bringing groups of people together for a specific, clearly defined purpose and disbanding them once that object has been achieved. There's nothing new with this principle where projects are involved, but its use with *processes* is proving revolutionary.

For example, British Telecom, one of Europe's most profitable companies, recently found a way of cutting the costs of generating information required by the regulatory body. Inaccurate data were costing £1 million a year to collect. A small team set to work on the process. Accurate data now cost £50,000: that's an improvement of 95 percent, enough to gladden even Kami's heart.

In new-century management, new process (innovatory, challenging, continuously improved) is the core of the ability to achieve, and teamworking is the universal tool. Within teams—and within well-founded partnerships—leadership and relative contributions vary according to time and circumstance. Football provides the analogy. If the outcome of the Super Bowl hinges on a field goal attempt from forty yards, the kicker, for that brief moment, is the most important person on the team. Yet he spends most of the game off the field.

Thus, in business, the internal or external expert joins the team for a specific task, accomplishes the task, and then leaves. The results can be spectacular. At the giant Swedish food cooperative ICA Handlanars, Andersen Consulting came in to solve a bundle of problems. Three sales regions couldn't share their data. Distribution to the stores was inefficient, and marketing campaigns were sometimes in conflict. Against that backdrop, the co-op couldn't mount an effective response to the challenge of the European Single Market.

Reengineering transformed its powers. After the cure, reported *Business Week,* all 3,350 stores shared the same database. With a third of the warehousing and distribution centers shut, overall costs had halved—thanks only in part to a 30 percent cut in wholesaling labor. Since revenue has risen by over 15 percent, the payoff must have been huge. *The prize could not have been won by the use of internal skills and resources alone.*

I've emphasized that sentence because it applies powerfully and increasingly to more and more activities. The specialist needs for his speciality a range and depth of talents that are applied every day of every week of every month. For a generalist to maintain the same armory would be absurd.

It follows, however, that a new meaning has been given to Attract, Motivate, and Retain. That's the old Holy Trinity of personnel management. To win the competitive wars you need specialist allies like Turnstone's distribution and logistics partners. Attracting them is superficially no problem: they are hungry for your business. But that's no guarantee of effectiveness. You want to attract the best partners, motivate them to achieve their best work, and retain them for the desired time (which may be indefinite, even infinite) at that best level of service.

In the old days, the carrot-and-stick brutalities of Theory X applied to these outside relationships. You chose the cheapest outside supplier and motivated his performance by talking loudly and carrying a big stick: bawling him out, and threatening to take away the carrot—the profits on your business. As for retention, who cared? The common practice was encapsulated by William S. Whyte in *The Organization Man.*

He wrote of the Chrysler president who would take new managers to the Cloud Club atop the Chrysler Building and pose them a question. They had employed a loyal, efficient supplier for many years. Out of the blue, a rival undercuts the price by 10 percent. What would they do? Some would give the old supplier the chance to match the new quotation. Others would stay loyal to loyalty. The president dismissed both approaches out of hand: the new bidder gets the work—either you're a businessman, or you aren't.

That president would have been totally bemused by the present-day Chrysler in which (as reported in this book's first chapter) suppliers collaborate with the company in improving, not only their own productivity and added value, but Chrysler's. Dependence on supplier alliance has become absolute even for companies where internal collaboration is visibly lacking. In one such group, a European carmaker, an executive was asked how he could bear to depend on a single source of a single vital sub-assembly. He replied simply: "You've got to start trusting somewhere."

"Trust and teamwork" are the essence of successful partnering. That's the title of a section in *The Virtual Corporation,* by William H. Davidow and Michael S. Malone. Their ideal of a company without frontiers, which (like the self-consciously virtual Turnstone) forms a continuum with its outside relationships, can't be realized without expertise in managing those relationships. Yet the book devotes no attention to the management issue, which is of paramount importance.

After all, this isn't a question of passive, IBM-style investments, like Intel (a grand success) or the $100 million stake in Steven Chen's supercomputing venture (a flop). Most such investments will follow the pattern of the past: they will fail. That's simply because the original decision to invest is mistaken, and the investor lacks the leverage, and very possibly, the ability to correct the mistake. The wave of the future is the collaborative, jointly "managed" venture.

The "managed" is in quotes, because the management of a consultancy relationship or a supplier nexus is a different matter from that of, say, the Apple-IBM joint companies. Historically, such joint ventures have the same record as passive investment stakes: they fail (the result in 70 percent of cases, according to one study). Nobody has paid closer attention to the management issues involved than Rosabeth Moss Kanter. As she has pointed out, joint ventures need to dot six very demanding *I*'s:

1. The relationship is *I*mportant, and therefore it gets adequate resources, management attention, and time.
2. There is an agreement for longer-term *I*nvestment.
3. The partners are *I*nterdependent.
4. The organizations are *I*ntegrated.
5. Each partner is *I*nformed about the plans and directions of the other.
6. The partnership is *I*nstitutionalized—bolstered by formal mechanisms that make trust possible.

In *When Giants Learn to Dance,* the author quotes a Harvard Business School colleague on this rollcall: "The rewards of these things must be incredible to justify all the extra short-term costs that go along with them." Given the exponential increase in partnerships since the late eighties, when the book was published, that's an intimidating thought. "Incredible rewards" can scarcely be earned from everyday relationships: "these things" have become requisites for staying in business, not building blocks for bonanzas.

"Extra short-term costs" are insupportable at a time when cost disadvantages can be lethal. What's the answer? Look again at Kanter's list: it translates readily into a catechism of teamwork. Team objectives must be *important,* they will not be achieved without supporting *investment* in adequate resources, the *interdependent* roles of the team members are fundamental, their work and disciplines must be *integrated* to achieve the common purpose, everybody must be fully *informed* at all times to fulfill their roles.

Those first five principles apply to every kind of team, from the short-term project that saved British Telecom the best part of £1 million on data collection, via the medium-term consultancy exercise that reengineered ICA Handlanars, to the longer-term IBM-Apple-Motorola joint venture that created the PowerPC microprocessor. The importance of these projects varies with their scale. But one reason for disappointments in reengineering and total quality is the choice of projects that are too limited in scope.

Another road to regret is failure to back the team with the needed resources. When BA Engineering faced a typically knotty management problem—the need to open a second, separate engineering workshop for the same Heathrow Airport terminal—the task was delegated to a foreman and two co-workers. This small team came up with the solution and sold it successfully to the labor force, but *after* management had agreed to the necessary enabling investment. As a result, reported the managing director, what could have been a nightmare was "a dream beginning to come true."

Interdependence, integration, and information are the standard tool kit of teamworking's ability to realize dreams. Turf wars are abolished, differing agendas are harmonized, unnecessary secrets are no longer hugged to jealous bosoms. Horizontal management based on project and process thus eliminates vices that bedevil established organizations. But what about Kanter's sixth principle: institutionalization?

The word has become as ugly in reputation as in sound. The principle, though, can't be gainsaid: unless the institutional setup of the partnership, as of any team, matches the mission, the latter will fail. The author writes of "a framework of supporting mechanisms, from legal requirements to social ties to shared values." What's happening today is the downgrading of mechanisms and legalisms and the upgrading of a seventh *I*: the *informality* which is a social bond, a value in itself, the underpining of other necessary values, and the way to save partnering from extra costs.

The password is not "institutionalized," but "instituted": that is, "put in place," preferably by the partnering people themselves, and in a form which, like the workings of the partnership, is flexible and continuously developing. Whether tasks are executed wholly within the organization or wholly without, partnerships and alliances are basic to the new verities of horizontal, greenfielding management. They only involve doing naturally what has been done sinfully. The results should only be virtuous.

SEVEN

The Shock of the New:
How to Renew
Constantly

The

Perfectionism of Intel

1

A multitude of companies created the electronics revolution. Among them, Intel has five-star ranking. It brought together scientists and engineers without whose achievements the revolution couldn't have happened. True, so did Xerox at its Palo Alto Research Center. The difference (shaming for Xerox) was that PARC's team broke up without achieving business results. Intel kept its team together and developed their creations into lasting commercial successes.

In 1991 Intel had $4.8 billion of sales and $819 million of profits. Double Microsoft on the first count, it was 40 percent higher on the second. Yet the software company was the more acclaimed: far more talked about and talked-up than the world's largest maker of microprocessors, the core products of the revolution. In the publicity concert, Intel played second fiddle. In the real world, it led the orchestra.

Over an amazing decade from 1982 to 1992, Intel achieved a 21 percent annual increase in total return to shareholders. Those riches were founded on a 36.8 percent gain in earnings per share, the fourth fastest in the *Fortune* 500. That must have placed Intel among the best investments IBM ever made—although it gave the lie to a proud boast: "IBM takes a back seat to no one in technology, and that technology lead is growing, not shrinking."

The hubris of Jack D. Kuchler, then IBM's technology czar, contrasts oddly with his company's key decision of 1982. It then purchased a 12 percent interest in Intel for $250 million precisely because of its lead in a technology vital to the development of IBM, the whole computer industry, and the American economy. Indeed, thanks largely to Intel, in this crucial sector of the electronics revolution, U.S. supremacy is unchallenged.

Intel's challengers are strictly home-grown: Advanced Micro Devices, Texas Instruments, MIPS Computer Systems, Cypress, Cyrix, Sun Microsystems, Motorola, Hewlett-Packard—and IBM. The giant has been biting the hands that it has fed. IBM hasn't turned on Intel with the same ferocity brought to bear on Microsoft. But by teaming up with Apple Corporation and Motorola to launch the new and competitive PowerPC microprocessor, IBM in 1993 confronted Intel with its most significant challenge.

Part of the significance is that Apple, using Motorola chips, is the only sizable standout in a PC world dominated by Intel and that IBM is an unquestioned leader in the PowerPC's RISC (reduced instruction set computing) technology. That constitutes one of several strong threats to Intel's pre-eminence. The challengers started from so far behind, though, as to be almost out of the race. Intel's products were the heart of well over 100 million IBM and IBM-compatible computers worldwide.

In 1991, five years after RISC chips first arrived, Intel beat them by a mighty margin: 20.4 million to 308,000. "We have won the RISC battle," crowded Intel CEO Andrew S. Grove—maybe prematurely. The competition from all sides is real and rugged. Intel faces energetic cloners (though cloning an advanced microprocessor is one of the most intellectually taxing tasks), plus leapfrogging innovators. The many-sided, intense competition in this sector is a national plus: a vital factor in America's continued and colossal superiority.

It stems back to the late Robert Norton Noyce's historic patent, filed on July 30, 1959. The patent covered an integrated circuit that used the "planar" process. By spreading a flat plane of oxide over silicon, wireless connections could be made between two transistors and other components on the chip. Noyce was then working as general manager for Fairchild Semiconductor, which he left in 1968 to establish Intel.

With Gordon Moore (also from the Shockley Laboratories, founded by the inventor of the transistor), Noyce got $30,000 of venture capital from the farsighted financier Arthur Rock. The partners started making memory chips in Santa Clara. The DRAM, or dynamic random access memory, Intel's first smash hit, is one market where Japanese competitors have since seized the lead. But the 1971 invention of the microprocessor by Ted Hoff took Intel into regions where no man had trod before.

Ironically, given Japanese failure to follow, the invention was spurred by a customer from Japan. Called Busacom, this firm made complex scientific calculators. Ted Hoff was given the task (one of his first jobs at Intel) of designing a set of a dozen integrated circuit chips. His inspired response was to wonder why such work had to be constantly repeated: "Why design 12 special purpose ICs for the Japanese calculator this time, another set for a missile guidance system and yet more for a music synthesizer? Why not put all the circuitry on a single integrated circuit and then, like a normal computer, program it to do whatever you want?"

Hoff's insight was that integrated circuits are proto-computers which, if made programmable, will work like computers—hence the "computer on a chip" sobriquet for his "microprocessor." Even though the Japanese customer had no interest in Hoff's idea, Noyce did: he saw that this masterstroke of genius would revolutionize the industry.

For a long time, though, Intel's customers couldn't see the power or the value. In 1966, when I started the magazine *Management Today,* I rejoiced in the satirical contributions of Ivor Williams, who concealed his bumbling employer behind a mythical name, Minipute, and mythical product—the expendable computer. Now Hoff was making myth into reality: "It's like a light bulb. When it burns out you unplug it and throw it in the garbage and plug in a new one."

Until the personal computer was born, Hoff's invention couldn't come into its full glory; but without the microprocessor the PC couldn't be given life. What one book calls "the hobbyists, the hackers and the nerds—highly technical people at the margins of society" were to break the vicious circle, seeing and seizing the opportunity. Both IBM and Digital Equipment considered the prospects, but at first "they could not imagine why anyone would need or want a small computer."

Intel had that imagination and turned its vision into a saga of technological and economic achievement that surpassed its great patron. By late 1994 that saga had plainly entered its most testing period yet. Intensified competition had forced Intel to cut prices by up to 40 percent, while Compaq CEO Eckhard Pfeiffer, a key customer, threw a bombshell into a Barcelona conference in September by attacking Intel's policies—including heavily advertising the innards of the computer at the expense of its customers' brands.

A couple of days later, Cyrix announced a new chip to rival and maybe outperform the new Pentium. The technological onslaught will continue—Compaq is now buying heavily from rival AMD. Intel's success, though, was never a testament to leading-edge technology alone. The key was the leading-edge management that kept Intel thrusting forward past its own best standards toward perfection. That's the pursuit of the unattainable. But in the nineties and beyond it's the only chase in town.

Continuities of

Improvement

2

Why do innovative companies backslide into conservatism? Manfred Perlitz of the University of Mannheim traces a kind of managerial rake's progress, in which the risk-taking start-up develops through successive stages of maturity until it reaches the ossification from which dwindling performance and eventual crisis result. Xerox Corporation's progress from Great Innovator to Japanese victim perfectly illustrates the cycle, but doesn't explain it.

Research cited by Perlitz suggests a potent explanation, however. It lies in the risk-to-reward ratio. In academic theory, he points out, managers confronted with a choice of investments will select the alternative with the highest probable rate of return. Thus, a straight financial investment yielding 10 percent will not be chosen if a riskier option has a 25 percent chance of yielding nothing, but a 75 percent chance of returning 15 percent.

The calculations are simple. Multiply the odds by the return, and you get $0.75 \times 0.15 = 0.1125 = 11.25$ percent. So the safe 10 percent choice should lose out. When tested against the reality of real-life managers, however, the theory collapsed. Offered a choice between a safe 10 percent return on a financial investment, and a higher but riskier yield on a new product or new process, managers questioned in a sizable survey plumped overwhelmingly for safety. The risk they are dodging is that to their own careers. The risk they unwittingly run is to the future of their company.

What happens when that unacceptable risk has had unacceptable results? Now, the business is in trouble: continuing with present policies means losing 10 percent on investment. In the worsened climate, however, a new product, if you're lucky, will yield a zero return: that's a 25 percent chance. The odds are 75 percent that it will lose 15 percent. The simple calculation now shows that the certainty, a 10 percent loss, is worth more than the risky option: $-0.75 \times 0.15 = -0.1125$. The probable outcome is an 11.25 percent loss. Yet the surveyed managers now overturn theory in the opposite direction: less than a third will select the certain loss: all the rest go for risk.

With new processes, the disproportion is extreme. Nearly six times as many managers will take the risk. The worries about their careers have been swamped by their anxieties over the crisis of the company. In crisis, a break-even risk investment seems a better choice than a certain slide into further losses. As Perlitz argues, the better course is to create crisis conditions when no crisis exists. Alter the target-reward system in favor of taking innovatory risks, and more innovation will follow.

Better still, thrust the company into a furnace of technological change in product and process, fanned by intense competition, and fueled by compulsory billion-dollar risk investments. Intel is driven by incipient crisis that demands continuous innovation. Its previous pattern was demanding enough: each year, one or two new-generation chips, and every three or four years, a whole new micro-processor family. Today's profusion of variants (thirty for the 486 in 1992 alone) is accompanied by a mere two-year gap between new families.

The management lessons of Intel, like its microprocessors, have developed increasing power over a shortening time-scale. Its strate-gies have been annealed in the furnace. The fires have propelled the company towards achieving the highest technological and commer-cial standards it can reach—and then beyond them. The wonderful soprano Amelita Galli-Curci observed that, when she listened to her recordings, and recalled her musical aspirations, she was "very humble." But when she listened to other sopranos, she was "very proud."

In lesser people (and organizations) justifiable pride in outdistancing the competition overtakes the drive to outdistance your own previous achievements. At Intel, the growing lead in cumulative sales didn't have that effect—even though its microprocessors took 80 percent of the world's fastest-growing electronics market. Even in 1991, its share was estimated at two-thirds, dwarfing everybody from Motorola (13 percent) downwards. By 1993, it had overtaken the Japanese giants, by then over-dependent upon memory chips, to lead as the largest supplier of semiconductors.

Symbolically, America was back on top. Intel's domination in microprocessors is reminiscent of IBM at its peak. As its backer, IBM deserves much credit. Headlong growth often stretched Intel's management and financial resources—hence the IBM stake. As a commentator noted, the original 1982 deal "basically solves a financing problem at a price somewhat above the market." Intel was to need further help in the continuing struggle with immense and mounting development and capital costs.

It's no tribute to the shrewdness of IBM's executives that Intel could still supply the clones without let or hindrance. The supplier took fabulously better advantage of its even-handed deal with IBM: but that reflected its customer's inhibitions as. much as Intel's own shrewdness. The RISC technology which may now threaten Intel was devised by IBM, not the other day, but in the seventies. No IBM product appeared, though, until 1990—which infuriated new CEO Louis V. Gerstner: "We should have dominated. Where have we been?"

That place is easily identified: the status quo. All market leaders are reluctant to cannibalize existing technology and disturb existing markets by introducing new technology products with superior characteristics. The Perlitz Syndrome applies. The bird in the hand looks far more attractive—in career and corporate terms—than the two or more birds in the bush. Without innovative policies today, however, tomorrow's bush may well be birdless.

Hold back today and you'll be cannibalized or leapfrogged by somebody else. In more leisurely eras, back-markers could get away with technological lags. But an age of six-month product cycles leaves no room for creative delay. The changes in markets have happened at a speed which would have been unthinkable in the days when the vertically integrated giants ruled the earth. Miss what C. K. Prahalad of the University of Michigan calls "industry transformation," and companies get thrown into the vortex of corporate reconstruction, often too late to save the day.

Perlitz offers an interesting cure for the innovation syndrome. The onrush of the new imposes mathematical obligations on managers. For example, the giant German electronics group Siemens claims that half its revenue derives from products introduced in the last five years. The huge turnover represented by those new products is equivalent to the ninth largest company in Germany. It follows that, simply to maintain this ratio, Siemens must add 10 percent of turnover every year in new-product sales.

In this way, and in every product line, argues Perlitz, life-cycles determine innovation targets. With industrial robots, whose average life is 2.5 years, nothing in the product portfolio of 1994 will be marketable after about mid-1997. Microprocessors are on a similar turbocharged treadmill. Intel's Pentium superchip features three million transistors and can process 100 million instructions per second. It has *double* the capability of the 486.

That's only the present. The future offers the prospect—rather, the certainty—of giant leaps forward. The three million transistors of 1992, seven million a year later, should be twenty million on the microprocessor family due in 1995. Those chips should have two and a half times the speed of the Pentium while proceeding en route for a 100-million-transistor chip by the year 2000. By then two bIPS (billion instructions per second) should be achievable.

The technological targets inevitably impose managerial ones. Accelerating the creative process means climbing progressively higher mountains, both technically and financially. The 486 chip cost over $250 million and 450 work-years: before it was announced, in 1989, the Pentium team was already sketching in their new design. As that proceeded toward the market, work on the next miracle was in hand.

Plainly, the company doesn't (because it can't afford to) suffer from what Perlitz sees in many cases: corporate constipation. Top management complains that nothing new is coming up: the innovators moan that none of their bright ideas are being taken up. There's a blockage in the middle. Perlitz's approach of setting specific innovation targets looks highly promising, to judge not only by the first results in the field, but by its psychological validity. Shifting people's focus alters what they see—and therefore what you get.

Refocusing is one prominent feature of the "reconfiguration" of Britain's ICL. As a relatively small manufacturer of mainframes, it was seemingly doomed by inadequate market share and uninspiring technology. CEO Peter Bonfield saw the industrial transformation in progress as the microprocessor advanced and proprietary systems lost their hold over the customer. He realized (while his less enlightened and large competitors were sliding towards mega-losses) that the company had to be turned upside down. The result of the inversion was rapid payoff.

It flowed from changing not only the strategy but (far more difficult) the attitudes as well. Target those, just as Perlitz targets innovation, and change will follow. Thus, Bonfield doesn't just use the bonus system to reward managers for a job well done; it becomes a deliberate lever, applied to alter behavior on specific issues. It's a marvelous way of overcoming the "He Goeth Not" Syndrome, in which the boss says, "Go thou, my good and faithful servant, and do such-and-such" (say, complete the appraisals of your subordinates) and nothing happens.

When Bonfield decreed, no appraisals, no bonus (no matter how wonderful the performance on other measures), the completions rate climbed magically. This sensibly mercenary stratagem has been used by ICL many times with many managers to achieve specific ends during "reconfiguration." Targeting behavior, not just numbers, is an indispensable rapid-response tool. It gives concrete and easily grasped expression to the aims of the corporation, so that people know what's expected, and it provides a mechanism for achieving those aims.

For similar reasons, I'm fond of the formula known as "Halfway to the wall." Taking this year's mark in costs or time, you fix zero as the wall. Of course, the wall can never be reached: but each year, another 50 percent gets chopped off the distance to zero. The virtue of this simplistic approach is not only that achieving the results will cut costs, shorten process time, and so forth. It also inculcates the philosophy of continuous improvement, and, if linked to reward, turns that philosophy into practical outcomes for both the individual and the business.

Companies that don't keep on going halfway to the wall risk going to the wall in the other sense: destruction. Even supremacy as great as Intel's is "under attack," as CEO Grove has admitted. Targeting and achieving innovation, while fundamental, is not enough to repel boarders. Intel has been compelled into unprecedented price-cutting and (also unprecedented) heavy advertising. By stressing "Intel Inside," the ads aim to build brand recognition. That's not easy when the ultimate customer never sees the product, but it's essential for true leadership.

Market leaders must lead on every criterion that matters to the market, including marketing itself. The traditional, quantitative measure of market leadership (share) is an outcome, not the prime objective. Lead in quality, innovation, cost-effectiveness, service, reliability, reputation, distribution, marketing, and so forth, and share will ineluctably follow. Miss any of those boats, and you may founder. You dare not persist, for example, with the arrogance towards customers that used to characterize Intel.

Here, too, Grove's management has reconfigured itself. Now, as a collaborative ally engaged in "concurrent engineering," Intel works closely with customers from early in the project. Before the Pentium got under way, Intel people visited all major customers and key software producers: the result was a list of 147 specific features. As usual in these surveys, what customers wanted differed markedly from the supplier's expectations. That alone would be enough to justify a management practice of fundamental value—make the customer a partner, listen to what he says, act on what you hear.

By spring 1992 the Pentium customers could start engineering their new computers: the software writers already had "compilers," new software tools to enable a similarly fast start on new programs. By benefiting your customers, you benefit yourself. As *Business Week* pointed out, "The lack of compilers is one reason that software has lagged at least a generation behind Intel's silicon." Six years after the 386's birth, "only a smattering of programs" was taking full advantage of its power.

The article, by Robert C. Hof, described how Intel was leading the industry into the next phase—Intel, not IBM. In a long text,

Intel's biggest customer (and competitor) didn't appear at all. That may be premature. In 1994, IBM, once so averse to cannibalization, started to compete with itself in a highly specific sense. A start-up readied itself to launch new PCs, built around the PowerPC chip, that will compete directly with its own Intel-based PC operation.

But the latter's then leader, Bob Corrigan, paid unconditional tribute to his supplier: "I've got a great partner in Intel. . . . If the Power architecture is very much of a threat . . . Intel will make substantial improvements in its own chip. . . . For us, it would be crazy to abandon the Intel architecture. . . ." That's because of the billions invested in those 100 million and more Intel-based PCs. This gigantic installed base is the foundation of Intel's financial strength and of its ability to spend 16.7 percent of revenue on R&D.

The Pentium, the latest product of that spend, is "a *veritable one-chip mainframe,*" according to one description. These designs are not just components, and not just computers. When strung together, they are even supercomputers, capable of massive feats. In this field, the technology, named "massively parallel processing" (MPP), is expected to own the future. Winning a third of MPP sales, Intel's supercomputer systems swiftly became market leaders.

The Pentium aims at computers which span the entire IBM range. At the bottom of that range, Intel also competes directly as supplier of complete PCs to Digital, Unisys, and others. In areas like interactive digital video and flash memory (storing data on semiconductors rather than magnetic disks), Intel's R&D teams again tread on its customers' ground, if not on their toes. The old adage—never compete with customers—has become another piece of ancient history, and not only in high tech.

In the old order, when suppliers never competed with customers, the latter never competed with suppliers, either. Until very recent times, IBM's impressive chip operation at East Fishkill, New York, thus supplied only its parent. While this protected the business from the fluctuations which Intel suffered, it also removed the urgency of staying at the cutting edge, in converting technology into commercial products—hence the RISC lag that so infuriated Gerstner.

Once again, old logic has been inverted by new circumstances: the Perlitz Syndrome has become untenable. Protection has become dangerous. Risk-taking has become the essential defense, and far more profitable than caution. Intel, valued at $2 billion in 1982 by IBM's purchase of 12 percent, was worth $24 billion a decade later. That figure was four times its turnover, and three-quarters of the value of the eleven-times-larger IBM. Intel had a billion dollars of profits, whereas, that year, IBM was deep in a $5 billion loss.

How many of IBM's businesses matched the fivefold rise in Intel's turnover over the decade to 1992, or the profitability (18 percent on sales that year)? How many achieved the same market results and technological advance in the face of genuinely rough competition? But then, how many IBM businesses had Intel's freedoms? Announcing the 1982 deal, CEO John R. Opel emphasized that "This is an investment and we will not participate in the day-to-day operations of Intel." That promise was kept.

Far from playing no part in the day-to-day operations of businesses that IBM owned wholly, however, top management intervened and interfered constantly. Written and unwritten rules and restrictions had the same deadening effect. It's unfair, true, to compare a start-up launched by owner-managers with the captive divisions of a vast multinational. But the unfairness makes a fair point. In many types of business, captive divisions of huge organizations are inappropriate life-forms. Speed, intensity, and innovation are inexorable necessities. Intel needed capital from IBM: but the latter needed attitudinal lessons from Intel.

The gulf in cultures between Intel and IBM is illustrated by a contrast between two apparently similar people programs. IBM has long prided itself on "Open Door," which lets employees take issues up the organization, to the very top, if need be. Few IBMers use the doorway. In 1992 the general manager of a fifteen-thousand-strong business had received five Open Doors in a year; that's 0.033 percent of his working population.

Doubtless, fear of personal repercussions slams the open door. The door openers, morever, get no guarantees. Intel's comparable program also allows employees access to any higher executive on any issue. The key phrase, though, is "AR"—"action required." The executive mustn't merely answer, but *act*. There you have the essential. Leading-edge management never lets you relax, because it always leads up to that imperative: *action required.*

The Drawbacks at Du Pont

3

Too often, research and development is thought of almost as a financial activity: throw a certain amount of money at the company's technology spectrum and results will certainly follow. That didn't happen at Du Pont, if you believe its current chief executive, Edgar S. Woolard, Jr. He complained that the company had taken too long to "convert research into products that can benefit our customers." The *Wall Street Journal* put matters more bluntly: the R&D spending of a decade had come to $13 billion—poured into "a technological black hole."

According to this report, company officials conceded that the spending "didn't turn out a single all-new blockbuster product or even any major innovations." And this is the very same company that invented nylon and a host of other petrochemical breakthroughs. That may be part of the trouble. Du Pont has continued to seek new nylons, which will always be few and far between. Costly failures along this unpromising route include Corfam synthetic leather (cows, with a helping hand from technology, turned out to produce cheaper and better shoe material), Qiana synthetic silk, and electronic imaging.

The *Wall Street Journal* goes on to observe that with "new product development faltering," Du Pont has relied on *"tweaking existing products into slightly improved versions."* Such *"slight"* improvements have enabled the thirty-year-old Lycra spandex fiber "to dominate the active-wear market." The italics are mine; anything that creates or perpetuates market dominance is by no means "slight." Just as all management and administrative processes in a company should be subject to continual review and improving revision, so should all manufacturing processes and all products and/or services.

The results may not rank high on the scale of pathfinding innovation, but the return in savings and profits may represent a recurring bonanza. Du Pont's newest efforts to improve its R&D performance seem to recognize these truths. To quote one of its own experts, the need is "to shift the emphasis in product development to improving our understanding of the processes used to manufacture our products."

Thus, more than five decades after nylon's discovery, Du Pont finally discovered enough about the fiber to make possible its breakdown and recycling, a non-product innovation that offers ripe financial (and environmental) gains. In addition to pushing more of its R&D budget into processes, the company is spending more on accelerating its response to customer demands for product variations. The same emphasis on speedup applies from the very beginning: here Du Pont adopted small, multidisciplinary teams to vet all new product ideas.

Teams of research, manufacturing, and sales people had to decide yea or nay within two weeks. They got the same time to staff a new team to carry the project forward. That recognizes the fundamental economic law that I've previously mentioned—that speed is more important than cost. That's to say, cost over-runs damage the economics of a new product less than do time lags. It's better to get the innovation to market on time than to hit the budget on the nail.

Better still, do both. The pivotal importance of time, however, is demonstrated by a global innovation survey produced in August 1992 by CHI Research. It ranked nearly two hundred top companies on three counts: the number of U. S. patents awarded in 1991; "current impact" (the relative frequency with which a company's patents get cited); and the median age of its patents. The top twenty-five consisted of eleven Japanese (taking the first four places), eleven Americans, and only three Europeans: Philips, Siemens, and Hoechst, all in the bottom half.

A weighty factor here is probably sheer weight. The much-lamented fragmentation of European industries means that innovation is spread over more companies. Yet these excuses won't wash away the hard reality. Take cars as a vivid example. Europe's motor industry is no more fragmented than Japan's: each has a full hand of world-class competitors. But Japan has three car firms (Nissan, Mazda, and Mitsubishi Motors) among the fifteen with the highest-impact patents. Europe has none.

Detroit also scores zero. There's a glaringly obvious connection between this innovatory lag and Japanese penetration of Western car markets (which would be far deeper in Europe but for artificial restrictions). As for size, neither Mazda nor Mitsubishi is large by European standards—and all three Japanese rank among the fifteen companies which, to quote *Business Week,* are "closest to the cutting edge." That is, their "technology cycle time" is shorter.

The three average about four and a half years, against nearly eight for General Motors. The latter company symbolizes another aspect of Europe's lag: that many of its key markets have a heavy non-European presence. In consequence, American technology took the European lead; the Japanese have followed suit. Countries with no camera or copier industries aren't going to generate much innovation in copying or photography. In industry after industry, market after market, Europe had abdicated what were once tenable positions. Exactly the same surrender has happened in the United States.

Defenders of the faith could argue that sheer number of patents means little: look only at IBM. It ranks seventh in "technological strength" (measured by combining the number of patents with "current impact"). Yet the giant has suffered calamitous losses of share in all key markets after disastrous lags in market entry. In computer innovation, as it happens, Europe's technologists were much quicker off the mark than IBM. It did them little good.

The explanation is that Europe's managements were much slower than the technologists. Company after company fell into one of two traps, being either too small and disorganized (Sinclair) or too large and bureaucratic (Philips). The innovation gap is one of management, not technology. The missing link must be focus—and more. Rosabeth Moss Kanter's famous Four *F*'s apply generally to management. But as Du Pont found to its $10 billion cost, the quartet are utterly indispensable in R&D. That effort has to be *F*riendly (that is, cooperative and collaborative), *F*ocused, *F*lexible—and very *F*ast.

Developing
Prime Products

4

For several years I have talked to students at an excellent course on new-product development organized at Templeton College, Oxford, by Bill Ramsay, formerly of General Foods. Looking at those mostly eager faces, mostly also young, it's easy to understand why product innovation, spiritually as well as commercially, is the renewing force of any business.

One of Japan's greatest but least celebrated managers, Ryazuburo Kaku, the builder of the modern Canon, used to stress this truth in an unforgettable way. Late in his brilliant career, he still carried in his pocket a graph charting Canon's profits over his decades of service. Against the largely upward curve, Kaku had plotted Canon's new-product introductions. As a junior employee in the finance function, Kaku had spotted that every burst of innovation had coincided with, and undoubtedly caused, a surge in profits.

He concluded that, to achieve sustained advance, new products had to flow, not in the previous fits and starts, but in a steady, enriching stream. The logic is inescapable, and Kaku's exploitation of the logic at Canon had exactly the results he foresaw. But translating the theory into practice has some inherent difficulties for most managements.

1. Outside FMHT (fast-moving high-technology) markets, neither markets nor technology are changing fast enough to engender powerful new products on a regular, rapid basis.
2. Even the best of innovators has a high rate of failure. As Ramsay has pointed out in a paper, the miss ratio is three out of ten and not the 90 percent of mythology; but those failures still represent much wasted effort.
3. In most companies the needs of innovation, with its uncertain results, unpredictable time-scales, and spiraling costs, are in conflict with the orderly processes of "ordinary" management, and possibly with financial necessities as well.
4. Kaku's Law hinges on new products achieving high profitability. In many cases, the handsome returns either never come at all, or appear only after an unconscionable delay.

The usual response to these realities is to try to improve the innovatory process: to raise its fertility, elevate the success ratio, erect higher thresholds to ensure better returns on investment, and so on. Above all, companies seek to create a superior innovatory climate, to remove the barriers which hamstring the efforts of those eager young people in new-product development. That's not enough: genuine reform should end by terminating new-product development as a separate activity.

Instead, innovation should be integrated into the company's day-to-day, month-to-month, and year-to-year management. And the operative word is "management." The ultimate answer can only lie in reorienting the management ethos of the firm away from the tried, trusted, and obsolescent and towards the continuous evolution of the new, thrusting, and competitive—competitive not only in patents, but in applications, scale, and profitable growth.

There's an essential parallel with the current revolution in management itself. The changes are directed at replacing obsolescent hierarchy with new, thrusting, competitive modes. Fully decentralized operations, working in flexible teams to pursue self-defined objectives, are inherently more creative. The Japanese, generally right in these matters, believe that, in the next industrial wave, creativity will be decisive. They are striving to develop further the kind of "creagement" (their word) that was a feature of Kaku's reign at Canon.

It has to be based on coordinated, strategically sound R&D planning. Kaku deliberately set out to create major positions in ten distinct technologies that he thought would prove valuable, not only to Canon, but to many other companies. His reasoning was that no company could hope to anticipate or afford all the technologies it would need. So he built bargaining chips, technologies that he could trade for the missing pieces in the jigsaw.

But if Kaku's correlation of new-product introduction and profitability still holds true (and it surely does), Japanese industry's leaner times of the early nineties are set to continue. Up to now, Japan's generation of new products has been profuse to the point of profligacy: 227 different Walkmans, or one every three weeks, since Sony introduced the product; six dozen distinct Toyota cars since 1979, which equals one every ten weeks. And 2,000 new products have sprung from the Seiko watch company every year, or one per designer every four weeks.

The declining profits of the early nineties have forced Japan's leading companies to lengthen product life-cycles and reduce variants: thus Toyota had only six mutants on a new Corona model, against eleven previously. Similarly, consumer electronics firms have cut down product ranges by 20 to 30 percent and also extended life-cycles. The car companies are talking of adding an extra year to the current four-year cycle, hoping to get the "third year" profit twice.

Under the old dispensation, profits peaked in year three after amortization, and then customarily dipped in year four. Whether the new philosophy succeeds depends partly on the causes of the fourth-year dip; how far was it determined by expectation of the model change among the customers and inside the company itself? Moreover, will all competitors come into line? If not, the standouts must win.

Whatever the answer, nobody doubts that new model proliferation in Japan passed the point of sanity long before 1990. Matsushita's score of vacuum cleaners in the home market compared to just three overseas. And a mere ten of its five dozen TVs account for most of its domestic sales. The relevant point about the latter statistic isn't the dependency ratio; Pareto's 80-20 Law of the significant few and the insignificant many would produce much the same result with any product range.

The point is rather that sixty TVs must mean excessive costs, a great deal of overlapping, customer confusion, and dilution of the brand over too many very similar products. Sure, the Japanese have brought down the time and cost involved in development in brilliant fashion. But excellent execution of something better not attempted is still sheer waste.

The Japanese philosophy is heavily product- and production-led. If a new feature can be economically incorporated, change the product, and its enhanced technical excellence will sell the new offering. The beneficent process was clearly at work in 35-millimeter cameras, where the boom induced by the single lens reflex was uplifted first by the compact and next the autofocus SLR. But these were significant advances, and note that the overall market subsided into relative stagnation once the boost had been exhausted.

A spate of innovations hasn't saved the personal computer market from slowdowns and over-supply. The Japanese quick-to-market philosophy has won would-be emulators worldwide. But speed and costs aren't the only factors in the final equation. A third factor outweighs either: the broadly defined quality of the new product plainly matters more than the quantitative speed of its appearance.

It wasn't Mazda's ability to produce its little two-seater sports car so fast, and to amortize it on a small production run, that was decisive: it was the imaginative daring of reviving a dead market segment. The technical development and production abilities were admirable allies for that act of the imagination. A product-driven philosophy is out of place when there's no such thing as a product anymore. As Rosabeth Moss Kanter stresses, the product is only part of the delivered package of "customer value."

This stands the old marketing concept on its head. Insurance companies and banks started talking about financial services as products: now, say the gurus, you should talk about products as services. Seen in this light, innovation takes on a new aspect. Some crucial questions need asking before embarking on a new idea for a product—or a service:

1. What additional value will this innovation bring to the customer?
2. What rewards will it bring to the supplier in terms of realized price and customer loyalty?
3. How will the customer be made aware of the greater value that's being offered?

The value-led approach also assists greatly in deciding which innovatory direction to follow. Here the question becomes: What values would the customer respond to most strongly—if they can be created? This isn't a question that responds to conventional market research, for a well-known reason: you can't expect people to give meaningful opinions about something that doesn't exist. But that is, of course, the vital task of the innovator.

The innovator must focus, not on competition, but what Edward de Bono calls "sur-petition," which means creating a "value monopoly." The tiny Apple had that when it created business computing. The "sur-petitive" innovator enters a race he is certain to win, there being no other runners. In the hierarchy of sources for creating new customer value, sur-petitive monopoly comes easily top in potential power. New value has plenty of other sources, however, such as

1. Unfilled need
2. Disadvantages in existing products
3. Gaps in otherwise well-served markets
4. Extensions to, and new formats for, existing lines
5. Technological breakthroughs
6. Successful ideas transferable from other markets
7. More economic ways of satisfying expensively met needs

Any annual roster of best new products can be matched to this list: Take *Fortune*'s 1991 winners: (1) pharmaceutical innovations always rank high on meeting *unfilled need*—like Amgen's Neupogen, which helps cancer patients to cope better with chemotherapy, and reached $50 million of sales in two days; (2) conventional racket-and-ball games have the *disadvantage* that the ball can cause injury, but Super Grip Ball (4.3 million sold at $20) uses Velcro-covered rackets to which the ball will stick; (3) low-fat beef opened up a wide *market gap* for ConAgra's Healthy Choice; and (4) Reebok *ex-*

tended its sporty footwear with a shoe designed for the new exercise craze of "step jumping," and added steps as well.

(5) Also, *new technology* made the pen-driven portable computer a reality: NCR was able to charge $4,675 for its product; (6) noting the Japanese success with small sports cars, and producing them at speed and low outlay, Chrysler *"transferred"* the idea, getting the Dodge Viper out in a record-breaking thirty-six months and for only $70 million; and (7) to save you building up a massively expensive, space-filling reference library, Sony offered the far *more economic* Data Discman at $550, plus $30 to $150 for the reference books screened via CD-ROM disks.

Scanning existing product lines and markets on the seven counts will throw up many opportunities. If the search is organized both systematically and creatively, the problem isn't to generate ideas, but to choose among them. That means deciding which proposition offers the most value to the customer *and* the company. In an existing market, that doesn't necessarily mean the product or service that is both better and cheaper than the competition.

Value is a matter of perception, not numbers. Thus, round teabags, which offer no advantage over the square variety, nevertheless found a ready market. The decisive issue is increasingly quality, but not in quality's technical sense of "conformance to specification." The relevant meaning is continuous improvement, using measurable criteria, in the value created for the customer.

To make any sense, that definition plainly must include the existing as well as the brand new. "Old product development" is at least as important as new. Courses on the subject would never sell because "old" is virtually a pejorative word in marketing. My preferred term is "prime-product development," or PPD. In fact, tapping the huge potential of PPD—witness the "slight" improvements in Du Pont's Lycra, improvements that created market dominance—must be the foundation of new-product development, not just in sharpening skills and processes, but financially.

That's because PPD generally costs far less, carries significantly lower risks, and produces much higher and faster returns, from which the costlier new-product development (NPD) can be financed. PPD's better performance follows from the fact that, if a product exists at all, it must have the one essential for all success: customers. Moreover, the company has deep experience of the product, plus broad, long knowledge of the market. Provided that you don't become a prisoner of the past and its assumptions, continuous PPD offers perpetual, rich growth.

The Japanese have demonstrated this truth with overwhelming force. As Kenichi Ohmae, McKinsey's Tokyo head, pointed out in *The Borderless World,* Japanese managers can't acquire other businesses as freely as can Westerners, nor change employers so readily, so they are compelled to make the best of what they have. Hence the rapid evolution of products like the cameras mentioned above. Another of *Fortune's* best new products of 1991 was a new Minolta camera that took the SLR concept further still with "fuzzy logic," which almost thinks like a photographer.

In the United States, General Mills has made PPD the cornerstone of its strategy. The results include a staggering 36.2 percent return on equity in 1992, with most other large food companies lagging far behind. In a decade the $7 billion General Mills gave its investors a 24.3 percent annual return. The performance of the Guinness hard liquor business gave another proof of PPD. By marketing its old, prime brands with new vigor, and concentrating on prices that matched the customer value, the company achieved a 31 percent margin, and sharply increased profits, on static volume.

There's one crucial caveat. Don't be misled by "prime product" into developing only the Pareto winners, the significant few that contribute the bulk of profits. Any product that has an established position in a solid market is probably capable of yielding prime profits. That old product needs examination with the new eye of the people who created the all-new products referred to earlier. Try

1. Approaches that nobody has ever tried before
2. Analogies from other products, businesses, and markets
3. Customer value not provided by anybody else
4. Reexamining and challenging the way things have always been done
5. Looking for problems in use, and solving them
6. Finding the focus, for in R&D what you want is the surest guide to what you get

Above all, try the Aladdin's Lamp approach. The summoned genie has given you personally, and absolutely free, this product, with all its acquired brand values, its customers, its hundreds of thousands or millions of sales. There is only one condition: you are not allowed to dispose of the business. What would you do to capitalize on this gift? The right answer could open up Aladdin's cave.

The Energizing

5

# of Apple

Welcome IBM. Welcome to the most exciting and important marketplace since the computer revolution began 35
years ago. We look forward to responsible competition in
the massive effort to distribute this American technology to
the world.

When Apple Corporation ran that ad, the gesture seemed typically bouncy, maverick, and impulsive. Steve Jobs, Apple's amazingly young co-founder, had even impulsively named his company
after the half-eaten apple in his hand. But just as Jobs seized on his
apple, so he had grabbed at the vision unveiled at Xerox's Palo Alto
Research Center. "Why don't you market this?" Jobs asked. "You
could sweep the world."

"This" was the mouse-operated personal computer, with a
"graphical user interface," or GUI. Technically complex, the Alto
(PARC's prototype machine) achieved remarkable simplicity in use.
Users no longer had to master coded instructions. The computer took
its orders, and "spoke" back visually, in plain English. Jobs had seen

the future and recognized it, true, but business history is full of defunct visionaries.

The impudent ad seemed to tempt fortune: for this was the IBM of 1982, the giant (thirty times Apple's size even three years later) whose ponderous feet had crushed upstarts far more shrewdly directed than Apple. In one sense, Jobs was right to welcome IBM. Its entry widened the market far beyond its existing frontiers. With IBM's imprimatur, personal computing moved from sideshow to main event. The new PCs, using the Microsoft operating system MS/DOS, swiftly established an "industry standard" where none had operated before.

For Apple, the new standard was a disaster. Millions of programs had been sold for the Apple II, which was neither compatible with IBM technology nor capable of fighting IBM for the corporate market—of which Jobs knew little. Yet Apple didn't get eaten. Through crisis after crisis, the company prospered. Emerging from the troughs, Apple reached new peaks every time. What explained its survival?

Part of the answer lay in the new approach to computing that Jobs had discovered at PARC. This, too, was incompatible with MS/DOS. But it represented an entirely new architecture that was to revolutionize fields in which computing had made little penetration, especially graphics. WYSIWYG were magic initials: what you see is what you get. Printers and designers would be able to create on-screen, in full color, the pages and images on which they were working—and to manipulate their work at will.

But the new-technology Macintosh started slowly. The Apple II's market had slumped: the first-ever quarterly loss appeared, and the shares slumped, too. Revolutions often devour their own children, and Jobs seemed a good candidate for the role of Danton or Trotsky. Disorganized, haphazard, and inspirational, he had allowed not only overhead departments but whole factories to mushroom. Worse still, his preoccupation with the Macintosh—an operation he personally headed—weakened the company as a whole.

The hiring of John Sculley created another Apple legend—the Man from PepsiCo, whose credentials lay in neither management nor computing, but in marketing; who ousted his employer; and who, most unusually, moved on from company doctor to business creator.

The doctoring was essential to reduce Apple's bloated base: half its factories were closed, a fifth of its employees left. The product-oriented marketing of the past also disappeared as Sculley instead built the business around its three markets—education, domestic, and corporate.

For all Sculley's marketing skills, Apple might never have gotten past the hostile guardians of the corporate gate. But the new technology opened the back door: the Mac's eminent suitability for desktop publishing of all kinds delivered the market into Apple's lap as demand boomed for software like Aldus Pagemaster. When the software was coupled with the formatting and printing powers of the laser printer, all users of graphics, from great corporations to small design companies, could achieve commercial printing quality without using commercial printers.

The advance of the Mac in power and versatility was accompanied by major developments in the quantity and quality of its software. Sculley had given himself two years to prove that the Mac was a serious alternative to IBM. As it happened, Apple never truly cracked the big-business market. Yet in 1991, as the industry hit serious recession, Apple's turnover was $6.3 billion and its profit $310 million despite heavy price cuts across the range, plus the impact of a new low-priced line.

In cutting prices, Apple was a full year ahead of both IBM and Compaq. Moreover, the very factor that put Apple at risk, its lack of immediate compatibility with IBM, became a Unique Selling Proposition. The Mac was different and, in its ease of use, distinctively better. For those who didn't need compatibility, or who did need superior graphics, Apple products were first choice. Its USP wasn't endangered until advanced versions of Microsoft's Windows software arrived, imitating the Apple configuration, in the early nineties.

Apple hadn't lost its habit of laying the occasional egg, like the first Mac portable. It was too heavy and too expensive. Within a couple of years, however, Apple launched the Powerbook, much lighter, brilliantly designed, better priced, an instant best-seller. The time-lag between IBM's first portable, another costly and heavy flop, and its successful laptop in early 1992 was eight years. Not surprisingly, the IBMers who had ignored Apple and scorned the Mac now sang a different song.

Apple plainly had something IBM didn't, but which could perhaps be begged and borrowed. The alliances with Apple in microprocessing and software have already been discussed in this book. IBM's own future depends on them no less heavily than Apple's. Moreover, far from being eaten or beaten, Apple, on one criterion, was joining forces on equal terms. Its share of the PC market had been running neck and neck with IBM's and surpassed it in 1994. So what was the magic?

Sculley had created a more sensitive, responsive corporation without losing the innovative thrust of the original Jobs creation. There should be a short, sharp word to stress the need for fast, sharp response: "ert," if it existed, would be perfect, the exact opposite of "*in*ert." It also makes a useful acronym: the "ert" manager is *e*nergetic, *r*esponsive, and *t*hinking.

That ertness has been the making and the saving of Apple, from the startup's launch to its invention of business personal computing, from the Mac technology to the hiring of Sculley and the ousting of Jobs, from the graphics revolution to the latest Newton handheld devices to the ousting of Sculley in his turn in 1993—Apple had responded to the toughest challenges with energy and intelligence.

Everything now depends on the new Macs with the PowerPC chip succeeding where Apple has always failed—turning the company from a powerful niche player into a mainstream market leader. In October 1994, Apple and IBM (its PowerPC partner) were still trying to put together a convincing alliance. Their efforts looked too little too late to *Business Week,* which wrote: "They may have missed their chance to create a new standard." With the Mac technology again looking isolated and vulnerable, Apple needs its ertness more than ever. But so does every company.

.

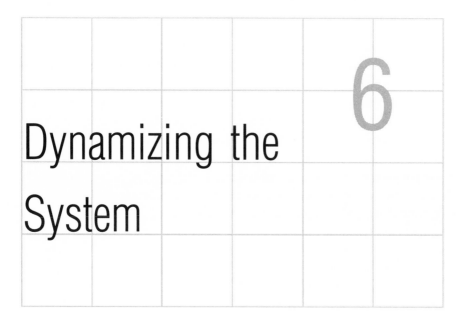

Dynamizing the System

6

Corporations rarely part company with a founding genius. It mostly happens when acute financial crisis (as at Digital Equipment) has ruled out any alternative. So Apple's removal of one genius in Steve Jobs, and then of Sculley, a virtual second founder, is a double proof of the capacity for energetic response and the need for new thinking. Like Rod Canion of Compaq (another ousted PC pioneer), Jobs and Sculley had become stuck in the patterns of past success.

That's among the most common causes of inertia, and inertia is endemic in management. The major cause of corporate failure, or lack of relative success, doesn't lie in complex problems whose solutions are unclear or uncertain. As every consultant knows, that cause lies in the refusal of managements to implement solutions that are logically and economically compelling, but which are psychologically unacceptable.

For example, Professor Jay W. Forrester, one of the original leading lights of the Sloan School of Management at MIT, cites one company in which corrective action called for reversing the much-trumpeted policies of "three generations of top management. All three . . . were alive, in town, on the board, and stockholders." And what were these sacrosanct policies? In every recession, the company was prompt to cut back ahead of falling sales. The reaction was always excessive, with the result that delivery dates lengthened, customers turned elsewhere, and market share fell.

Analysis showed that the entire long-term damage to that share had occurred during the recessions. Yet objections to changing the strategy were "almost insurmountable." The disease of inertia will infect even executives who are arguing in favor of a policy change. If that change contradicts established corporate practices, its advocates, when faced with a computer game simulating the business system, may not even try their own favored option!

That's why using the best technical means to propose improvements in the system isn't enough. That's the "hard" (i.e., objective) part of the job. But you're thrown back on the "soft" (i.e., subjective) element of human relations: how to overcome the individual and collective resistance that's also part of the system.

"System" suggests complexity. That needn't be the case. Some spectacular successes have been built on very simple formulas. The Forte hotel and catering group, for example, grew from a single "milk bar," a "fast-food" outlet before anybody had coined the phrase. Its owner, the later Lord Forte, realized that, so long as direct costs were kept at a constant ratio, he could tell, by a glance at turnover, exactly how much profit was being made.

What applied to one bar would work as effectively for several, and a multimillion-pound fortune was born. The simplicity, though, embraced a complete system. The young Charles Forte had a business model in his head. His basic equation used costs, prices, and profit. But that didn't tell him what prices to charge, or what to put on the menus. Nor could the equation decide the quantities of bought-in foodstuffs in pre-cooked items, which, if wrongly ordered, resulted in costly waste.

But Forte had strong intuition in all these other matters. The ratios provided his business sense with the necessary financial backbone, and the one-man top management made all the decisions that kept the system functioning. A modern manufacturing operation, though, has a management team instead of a single Forte. So who decides things like the production rate? In any operation, who sets the prices? If the answer is the executive in charge of production, or whoever controls sales, it's dead wrong.

Neither should be given these responsibilities, which are truly crucial. Over-produce or under-produce, and you wreck the short-term results, under-price or over-price, and you achieve the same awful effect, but with severe longer-term consequences, too. The most obvious argument against price-fixing by sales people is well-known: they will opt for the price that, in their view, maximizes turnover (and commission), and will most readily meet quotas. So long as sales are holding up, they will resist changes, up or down, for fear of rocking the boat.

Similar factors operate with production. If quotas have been set, or if pressures for delivery are intense, production rates will be upped automatically to meet any shortfall, even though the consequences may be a severe and costly cutback later on. That last sentence points to the underlying and critical truth. Neither sales nor production people are in a position to make these crucial decisions. They don't possess enough information to see the system as a whole. And the correct decision can only be made within the context of the entire system.

The object is to optimize the performance of that system, which can't be done without complete understanding of the relationship of its parts. That's exactly what the young milk bar entrepreneur possessed. The truth is stressed by that excellent book, *The Fifth Discipline,* by Peter M. Senge: as noted earlier, the Fifth Discipline is "systems thinking." The author teaches at MIT in Boston, and his views closely reflect those of the great Professor Forrester.

Forrester is the founding father of time-based competition, in which operations are analyzed to eliminate wasted time, and his thinking is basic to "systems dynamics." Take the above-mentioned prices and production rates: each fits into a system. The dynamics of pricing "interact with production rates, field service, quality, profits, and product design." Production rate "is based on backlog, inventories, production capacity, average past sales, profitability, corporate liquidity, and other considerations."

The quotations are from a compelling interview in the *McKinsey Quarterly,* which tells graphically what happens if you take fundamental decisions in isolation. Suppose sales are not being maintained, but instead are slumping. Everybody knows how salespeople will react. They will demand price cuts, not least because of the large unofficial reductions which competitors are allegedly offering. Your salespeople will, if allowed, make unofficial cuts themselves, by offering discounts. But what if the diagnosis is wrong? Sales will not improve, and the financial penalties of depressed demand will intensify.

Forrester's convincing example is the U.S. automobile industry, which kept on trying to match Japanese competition with price cuts when the real threat to Detroit's market share was quality and reliability. This mistaken approach made matters even worse. Not only did market share continue to slump, but nothing was done to correct the true causes of its decline. U.S. car makers have at last applied the necessary correctives with success: but only after losing billions of dollars and hundreds of thousands of jobs.

As for production, if you can't match output and sales day by day, the next best approach is usually to maintain a steady rate that will balance the system. At the price of an acceptable level of inventory at times of low offtake, that balance will achieve the year-round delivery performance which will delight the customer and optimize the profits. For experts like Forrester, it's a simple matter to set up the computer model that will correctly determine that steady production rate.

But there's the much more complex problem mentioned above: persuading people to obey the model's findings. The difficulty is that, while the techniques for establishing where the system needs changing, and how, are proven and highly effective, they are not matched by equal precision (or success) in getting the changes adopted. As Forrester says, "Education for implementation and getting acceptance of the required policies may be a greater challenge than the design."

Meeting that challenge for each and every change to the system is plainly exhausting and wasteful: the manager and the company have to be shifted permanently from inertia to the opposite—to ertness. Apple's saga, the information technology equivalent of the Perils of Pauline, demonstrates the resilience of the energetic, responsive, and thinking business. Ertness rests on the correct belief (an inherent part of genuine quality management) that everything can always be done differently and better. It also requires answers to some penetrating questions derived from Forrester:

1. What are the key management attitudes that account for corporate actions and reactions?
2. What are the organizational goals, and how, why, and when did they originate?
3. To what extent does past history affect current decisions?
4. What happens when people are overloaded?
5. What are the key internal financial pressures, and how are they applied?
6. What's the true nature of relationships to customers, and how are they maintained?

The thrust of all these questions is directed towards establishing how far the organization is responding to its present and future situation, and how far its behavior is conditioned by a probably irrelevant past. The past gets crystallized into procedures and manuals. These static housekeeping methods may be a more powerful, unseen influence on performance than the dynamic strategies which top management is attempting to enact.

Pricing proves the point. Many Western companies base their charges on adding standard margins to manufacturing costs. Often, these costs are grossly miscalculated (an error which applies both to direct costs and overhead allocation). But the technique is wrong in principle as well as practice, as the Japanese have demonstrated. In Japan price is determined by whatever level is thought appropriate to win the desired share of market. *That* sets the level of cost that can be afforded. Cost is thus constantly challenged.

Commenting on this difference (which has been a winning factor in far too many markets), two academics from the London School of Economics write that, in Japan, "factors such as desired market share, cycle time, reject rates and innovation are given more weight in managerial decisions, making them calculative exercises about financial viability." In other words, the Japanese manager, by instinct and training, bases decisions on the entire system, not on single issues seen in isolation.

The *thinking* part of ert hinges on selecting the interrelated factors that truly determine the success or failure of the organization. In these complex times, the factors are unlikely to be as few as Forte found for his milk bars. As a non-executive director of minicomputer maker Digital Equipment, Forrester constructed a model for his personal use. It had no less than 250 variables. The fascinating aspect, though, isn't the complexity, but the small proportion of tangible, "hard" items—a mere 5 percent.

The rest dealt with intangibles—including those covered in the six questions above. The model taught Forrester why some growth companies stagnate and others move on to greater heights. He found five key interrelated factors:

1. Prices
2. Delivery lead-times
3. Capacity expansion
4. Quality of design
5. Market reputation

The interweaving is obvious. Get any of the five wrong, and you vitiate the others. Get them all right, as the Japanese did in spectacular fashion when attacking the U.S. car market, and each factor reinforces the others. It's fascinating to speculate whether Forrester's model could (or did) foresee the crisis at Digital. The debâcle (see Part Three, Chapter 2) which forced founder Ken Olsen to retire came about because the company was over-committed to its minicomputers, whose *prices* had become too high in relation to microprocessor-based alternatives.

That produced a gross surplus of *capacity,* which compelled the company to make costly cutbacks that ran against the corporate grain: Olsen took the blame for acting too slowly. His successors are now relying on Digital's *market reputation* to support them as they seek a future built around the Alpha microprocessor, whose *quality of design* has won high praise: the key factor will be whether the Digital system, with its marvelous customer base (second only to IBM's), can achieve the *delivery lead-times* necessary in an over-supplied and fiercely demanding marketplace.

It follows that, in any organization, any strategy session worthy of the name must build on critical examination of the five italicized factors. Do they truly conform to present and future market needs? That question demands a sixth factor: ertness itself. Are you capable of *thinking* clearly, looking at the five factors with eyes that aren't misted by the past? Are you *responsive,* reacting quickly to stimulus from inside or outside the organization, and are you ready to change anything until convinced that no further improvements can be made—for the time being?

Finally, is the organization *energetic?* Will it rapidly and effectively make the essential changes that responsive thought has unveiled? Forrester is, of course, perfectly right. This is the sticking point, the indefinable quality that separates the men from the boys, the sheep from the goats, the successes from the failures. But maybe it can be defined: it's the difference between top managers who want to change their companies, and are prepared, for that purpose, to change their own behavior, and those who aren't.

Many consultants are at work in many companies to assist their clients in creating effective change in the frustrating knowledge that without changes in top management, the assignments won't succeed. The phrase "changes in top management" is deliberately ambiguous. Some managers will always find it impossible to change the set ways and thinking that cement the existing system. Sadly, there's no alternative but to replace them, at all levels, right up to the top.

Given the external pressures, it's not surprising that, in several large American companies, boards of directors have concluded that the sitting chief executives had to be changed—because *they* couldn't change. The fact that not only Olsen at Digital Equipment, but the chiefs of General Motors, American Express, IBM, Goodyear, Tenneco, Westinghouse, and Eastman Kodak have had their seats removed from beneath them is no coincidence. At other companies, including Sears and Citibank, the top chairs became very wobbly, and for the same reason.

Persistently bad results, despite repeated efforts to cut costs and improve efficiency, are always clear proof of systemic failure. The fall in IBM's employment was paralleled by a precipitate decline in the company's market value: an amazing two-thirds, from $106 billion at its 1987 peak to $30 billion in mid-1993. The fall in stock market value only reflected a fall in the "real" market.

Since 1985, IBM's share of worldwide computer revenues had dropped from 30 percent to 19 percent. Non-financial measures like market share should always be among the key system indicators: and anyone who tries to explain away non-financial deteriorations should have their arguments treated with grave suspicion. Unless management has deliberately chosen to lose share, relative decline almost always indicates relative failure in the system.

I found this true even in the magazine business, where special deals invalidate the only readily available objective count, the number of advertising pages sold. Experience showed, however, that if the share of volume was declining, even though there was every reason to suppose that share of value was rising, underlying weakness was present. And if it went uncorrected, share of value would eventually follow volume downwards.

The key words are "underlying weakness was present." The systems dynamics approach advocated by Forrester accepts that fact as given. No system can ever be equally strong at all points. But business system engineers aim to elevate the organization to much higher levels of performance by continuously raising the overall standards of effectiveness. That won't be achieved without dispelling the forces of inertia through insistence on *energetic response,* guided by the best *thinking* of which the combined minds of the organization are capable. Ertness is all.

EIGHT

Declarations of Independence: How to Fix Your Fate

The Boys from
Boca Raton

1

Three men played undoubtedly lead roles in the famous genesis of the IBM personal computer, the little machine that changed the world. The three provided, respectively, impetus, sponsorship, and execution. John R. Opel, as CEO, played sponsor. He agreed that IBM should enter the low end of the computer market. He endorsed the creation of an independent business unit, of a kind foreign to IBM, to undertake the mission. He extended indispensable protection to the unit until its mission had triumphed.

Stimulus at all points came from William C. Lowe. As manager of the Entry Level Systems Unit in Boca Raton, Florida, and then laboratory director for the site, Lowe became sure that an IBM PC had to be built. In July 1980 he made a historic proposal. At headquarters in Armonk, New York, Lowe advised the Corporate Management Committee (CMC) that IBM should enter the personal computer market. He added that, to judge by past low-end disasters, this couldn't be done within IBM's own culture.

The task would have to be executed with heavy external aid. It was Lowe, too, who conceived the general outline of an IBM personal computer; who assembled thirteen planning engineers for "Project Chess" (they entered legend as the "Dirty Dozen"); who nursed the Chessmen along as they assembled the prototype; who had it approved for further development by the CMC in August 1980; and who took it through the October 1980 "checkpoint" at which the CMC gave Project Chess the go-ahead.

It was also Lowe who, correctly anticipating his own departure for higher things in IBM, lined up Philip "Don" Estridge to take over the execution. That choice was as decisive as Lowe's other moves, for Estridge, the right man at the right time in the right place, provided the charismatic leadership that made victory possible. The irony of that smashing success is that, had top management foreseen the triumph, it might never have happened.

"The corporation had the insight to turn us loose!" said Estridge later. "They let us act like we were a venture capital investment of IBM's. This freed us from a number of time-consuming reviews and clearances so we could move at our own speed." That speed was blistering by anybody's standards, let alone those of a multibillion-dollar multinational. One year and one month after Armonk gave its go-ahead, IBM started shipping the first PCs.

The expectation was that 250,000 units would be built over the entire life of the project. That put IBM at risk for no more than $14 million, which the corporation took a mere five hours to generate, if the project where to flop completely. With so little at stake, IBM could afford to put pace before procedure. But who was responsible for this decision—fundamental, as it turned out?

All these events, including the superlative handling of the management and the technology by Estridge, have been chronicled by James Chposky and Ted Leonsis in *Blue Magic.* They tell *how* the PC got to market at such lightning speed. But *why* were impossible deadlines set? Who found this project so compellingly urgent? In retrospect, the urgency, as so often in management, created much of the excellence. Under time pressure, and because of it, the team made decisions that, in a more leisurely atmosphere, would neither have been considered nor approved.

With the program's fiendish constraints, IBM's traditional time-consuming system of approval couldn't be accommodated. For instance, the heresy of selling through non-IBM retailers couldn't have survived months of opposition from the vested sales interests in IBM. But there was no time to mount the opposition. Nor was there time to manufacture the PC, like all other IBM products, in-house. As Lowe foresaw, IBM had to go outside.

The equally heretical idea, not just for IBM, but for the entire computer industry, was to shun the proprietary route. The architecture of the system would be "open"—that is, outsiders would be able to enter the design without infringing IBM patents. Again, the time constraint was decisive: immediately available, externally written software was essential for success.

The open architecture has often been blamed for the cloning that engulfed IBM's market share. The clones would have been hamstrung, though, but for the extraordinary deal IBM struck with a twenty-five-year-old programmer from Seattle, Bill Gates. As one West Coast rival put it, Gates "worked out a deal that had Microsoft working with IBM to develop an operating system that Microsoft then turned around and sold to IBM's competitors. I can't believe it."

The unbelievable eventually created a startling fortune for Gates. Heads he won, if IBM sold its PCs, every one containing MS/DOS; tails he won, too, if an IBM-compatible vendor, also using MS/DOS, stole the sales. Urgency had become the midwife of future chaos, just as necessity became the mother of innovation—not only in the technology of the personal computer, but in the management of a business unit within IBM.

That driving urgency bears the stamp of chairman John Opel. Project Chess expressed two of his major strategies: that IBM should offer a full range of computers, catering for every need; and that the corporation would experiment with new, decentralized, liberated methods of working. Such methods, to use the metaphor of Opel's predecessor, Frank Cary, might "teach an elephant how to tapdance." For many companies, including IBM, that lesson still has to be learned.

Contradicting
the Corpocracy

2

The Boys from Boca Raton, unknowingly, prefigured many of the trends that, a decade later, were to remake what Peter Drucker called, in a famous book title, "the concept of the corporation." First, their sub-corporation was "virtual," boldly going outside for almost all components, seeking only those that were already proven. Second, it was freestanding. Internal IBM divisions that wanted to bid had to stand in line, cap in hand, and meet the team's requirements or lose the work.

The requirement included fixed prices, which was further heresy in a culture where margins were customarily added to costs. But, third, it also recognized another principle that new-century management has to embrace: you work backwards from what the traffic will bear (that is, the customer will pay). So price determines cost, not the other way around.

Fourth, in a marketplace which (like all century-end markets) presented a fragmented and fragmenting pattern, the team understood how a product must be perceived: as different and better. You achieve that by what's almost a contradiction in terms: by playing safe with great originality. Intel's 8088 chip served excellently as the core of a design that was fundamentally cautious (for instance, the Chessmen enlarged the dimensions to keep the off-the-shelf components further and more conveniently apart).

But the designers were also imaginatively original (for example, allowing for later expansion of the memory by slotting in extra boards). Working to their own architectural rules to keep the design coherent, the task force members strove through long working days and strenuous arguments to keep the design solid and simple. Almost everybody involved was an engineer, including Don Estridge, their leader, whose degree was in electrical engineering.

Estridge had worked for IBM on both the SAGE early-warning radar system and the Apollo moon mission before being moved to the opposite end of the scale: "entry-level systems." Symbolically, that title persisted deep into the microprocessor era. At IBM, PCs were for computing beginners. That was where they came in. These customers would, as their needs developed, trade up to bigger, more powerful—and more profitable—machines.

To Estridge's engineers, personal computing was an end in it-self. That's a fifth vital principle of the new management, in which ad hoc task forces are the key life-forms of shifting organizational structures. In project-based management, the clearly defined end generates the means—and the triumph. In this particular case, of course, as with all successes, hindsight casts a retroactive glow over every decision. But the team deserves its myth, as much for its management originality as its record-breaking product.

Their embrace of virtuality is all the more admirable in the context of their employer's notorious insularity. Years before the idea of customer partnerships became established, the team approached outsiders like retailers Computerland (its president, Ed Faber, was a former IBM salesman), who duly made important contributions. The people at Boca Raton had plenty to learn about PCs and everything to learn about mass merchandising.

Customer partnership was thus a sixth original principle—and a seventh followed from the group's innocence and haste. It stumbled on what in the nineties became a highly fashionable management approach: synchronicity, or executing component tasks in parallel, rather than in sequence. Not only was the software under development before the hardware was perfected, but the "communications" plan for advertising, public relations, and so forth was commissioned before vital facts about the machine and its market were confirmed.

The eighth essential is to liberate the energies and abilities which the organization will otherwise hide from itself. The man responsible for communications, Jim D'Arezzo, was an unknown, one of several administrators for IBM's advertising, operating in the Office Products Division. A few months later, he was presenting his campaign for the all-powerful Corporate Management Committee's approval. The hero of what is still computing's most famous ad campaign, Charlie Chaplin, was shrewdly slipped before the CMC almost as an afterthought.

That was how the task force worked. People plucked from other jobs seized total responsibility in their areas and exercised it with full freedom from the familiar corporate constraints. It wasn't a garden party. New-century management (Rule Nine) is fully as demanding as the most Draconian traditional regime. Anybody who couldn't keep up with Estridge's demands was rapidly removed. Nor did individualism run riot. Estridge invented democratic, informal Saturday-morning meetings so that the "inner circle" could stand clear of day-to-day pressures and pull the project together.

There was no time for slow decisions, indecision, or second-guessing. Wrong decisions were simply corrected. Estridge didn't like—or have time for—the contentious style of argument (what Edward de Bono has described as "I'm Right, You're Wrong") that dominated IBM. According to technical overlord Joe Sarubbi, his boss "would stop everyone and say, 'Wait a minute. What is it we have to do? What do we have to provide?' Then he'd make us stick to the point until we agreed on what we had to do and when. . . ."

This is another demonstration of later management fashion, and of a vital tenth principle, that of "consensus." The most effective demonstration of the group's cohesion, and of an eleventh necessity, speed of reaction, came when a too-close tolerance raised the threat of electric shock for anybody who touched the PC's casing. The launch demonstration at Sears Roebuck was only eighteen hours away, so a task force was flown to Chicago by private jet to put insulation in every machine.

Estridge was an instinctive master of a twelfth new management principle: leadership by example and encouragement. He knew how to generate the invaluable morale behind such endeavors. He gave team members a small red rosette to show they belonged to "the finest, most professional and most loyal team that's ever been assembled in the history of IBM." From time to time he staged a mass "pep rally," including one in which a thousand staff members filed into a college auditorium to the strains of rocked-up classical music.

That was in January 1983, early in a new era which saw the morale gradually ebb away. Until the launch, the project had been driven by the timetable. Now the business was being driven by demand—pent-up, bursting, insatiable demand. After its New York launch, right on deadline, complete with eight software programs, the PC took off into a sunrise of media approval.

The boys in their dingy headquarters at Boca Raton had assembled not only the wonder product of the microcomputer age, but a blueprint for the future of management. They had shown what energy and power could be let loose by "turning loose," and the publicity machine was quick to exploit the implications. The publicists had a flying start from the product itself, launched to what one business reporter styled "more hoopla and excitement over a product than I've seen in years."

The product blew up a storm. Orders outstripped trade forecasts ninefold. Boca Raton fell stupendously short of need. Production couldn't come anywhere near the demand. IBM had not so much stimulated the market as re-created the industry by providing the missing, crucial factor: a standard. There was a problem; in modern markets, there always is. Boca Raton's was the lack of fundamental technical difference between the PC and its eventual rivals.

There was a non-technical difference, though—the magic letters IBM. Now was the time for all those years of brilliant design and image-building to prove their worth and might. The host of small manufacturers seemed doomed, just like the myriad early car firms forced out by Ford and the other Detroit giants. Without the IBM sales volumes, how could the minnows compete on costs? And if they couldn't match IBM's costs, how could they cope with its prices?

Yet still the competition refused to die. It even prospered. Compaq Computer was launched in the teeth of the IBM storm. Rod

Canion, its president, warned that "you have to offer something else. Playing the price game is dangerous." Compaq's "something else" was portability (you could carry the first Compaq about, if only just). Having created an open industry standard, the giant was powerless to insist that its customers bought from IBM and nobody else.

This dilemma hardly seemed to matter in those heady days of the early eighties. It cannot detract from the triumph of the first PC: it was, without question, the best in specification and in quality on launch day and for a long time afterward. Here Estridge and his team can hardly be faulted. The task facing them, however, had wholly changed.

It was no less formidable. Then, they had been stretched to meet a near-impossible deadline. Now, they had to raise production and employment by leaps and bounds, and to extend the PC family amid all the pressures of runaway success. Many of the pressures were exerted from within the parent organization. Estridge & Co. had never been entirely free from its influence, even in the days before success, in its paradoxical way, made them more vulnerable to interference.

For instance, the team had rightly (remembering the importance of "different and better") adopted the faster and more powerful sixteen-bit architecture, leapfrogging the eight-bit used by Apple and other players. But Estridge's men balked at going beyond Intel's 8088 microprocessor to a newer chip whose power might be uncomfortably close to other IBM products. Fear of cannibalization, of robbing Peter's sales to achieve Paul's, was to bedevil the future of the IBM PC.

The devil's work, though, was mostly done by the organization men. The critical issue for an independent business unit is whether, once successful, it keeps its independence. All the tendencies inside large corporations are centripetal: the power over all significant operations gravitates towards the center, and managers who go out on a limb often get cut off. Sometimes, true, companies voluntarily subdivide, but the division is usually less voluntary than it appears.

For example, when Britain's largest manufacturer, ICI, split its chemicals empire into two in 1993 (one-half high-tech, the other low), the hope was that synergy would work in reverse: that instead of two and two making five, one divided by two would create the same magic. But that pious expectation wasn't the real cause of the

split. It was a defensive move spurred by the predatory Lord
Hanson's purchase of a potentially key stake in the undivided ICI.

Some of the most sweeping reorganizations of recent times had
no higher management logic. That old maxim—when in doubt,
restructure—hardly ever loses popularity. Nearly one in three of the
British companies subjected to some intriguing research had "been
involved in organisational changes" in the past three years. The
American ratio is unlikely to be lower.

If you accept the logic of Boca Raton, that's all to the good.
Don't the gurus bless the reorganization of businesses into smaller
sub-units, each given the fullest possible decentralized authority by a
small, strategic headquarters? Just as the gurus would specify, many
firms surveyed by Exeter University's Center for Management
Studies had indeed decentralized. Alas, an equal number had moved
in the opposite direction.

Whatever the gurus propose, those who dispose have simpler
thoughts. The decentralized business, eager for change, or forced into
changing, centralizes: the centralized outfit (like ICI) does the opposite. Top management has no trouble in making persuasive cases for
either of the contrary courses. The argument, however, is mostly
much less persuasive to the lower ranks of management, for whom
the pains of restructuring are reserved.

"De-layering" sounds wonderful, and is: provided that management processes are reorganized around the fewer layers. If processes
stay unchanged, the layers may vanish, but the duties don't. As the
Exeter report says: "The removal of a layer of management which
many companies have undertaken has meant that responsibilities
from the moved tier have been reallocated to the levels above and below. . . . The staff remaining have more responsibility, in some cases
too much, which can lead to stress and inefficiency."

Much of this "restructuring" has been done in haste to cut costs,
with little attention paid to what the company's shape should be in
two, five, or ten years' time. This was certainly true of Boca Raton.
It was taken for granted that the same divisional form which had won
all IBM's previous successes would suit this new market, that the
corpocratic formula—broken with such conspicuous success for the
PC launch—should now be reapplied.

Today it's doubtful whether the traditional layered hierarchy continues to make sense—even with fewer layers. By the mid-nineties, all managers stood agreed (in theory, anyway) on the need to break down barriers between departments. They are less eager to contemplate the radical solution of breaking down the actual departments. The concept of the decentralized sub-unit that Boca Raton exploited so brilliantly is the antithesis of departmentalized management. What explains the latter's continued strength?

Why keep large central functions, from marketing and sales to finance, if the organization is sub-divided into discrete businesses? Some sub-units, of course, are so large that they can readily breed bureaucracies of their own: the test of the sub-divided ICI will be whether either part (or both) can buck the centralizing, corpocratic tendencies. The latter are always at work, because top management loves to "manage" (or interfere)—and requires human machinery to help run the interference.

There is an extreme alternative. A few companies have developed the task force idea into an organizing principle. At Sherwood Computer Services, a relatively small British firm, each business has full powers: so that one unit, threatened with loss of its market, itself found and developed another activity to fill the gap. There's no reason why self-managed groups, each with full functional services, shouldn't be the building blocks of the organization—which gains in flexible speed and shared experience what is lost in tidiness.

The tidiness of departmentalized management can be illusory, anyway. I recently visited a great European company which is making rapid (though belated) progress in raising productivity and quality in manufacturing: but all its departmental functions remain resolutely immobile. The test of restructuring is whether the new structure goes hand in hand with new management processes that will liberate the talents of the whole organization in new ways. That test, not cost-cutting, should be the starting point of reformation for the nineties.

The principles of Boca Raton add up to twelve: the Clean Dozen of the Dirty Dozen. All are concerned with process, and all contradict corpocratic principles:

1. Look outside the company for whatever is better done outside.
2. Let freestanding units stand truly free.

3. Have prices determine costs—not vice versa.
4. Always be "different and better."
5. Concentrate on clearly defined, discrete objectives.
6. Make the customer into a partner.
7. Synchronize all activities and all functions.
8. Liberate talent at all levels.
9. Insist on excellent performance at all times.
10. Manage by true consensus—by fact-based agreement.
11. React at speed to the unexpected.
12. Lead by encouragement and example.

The compelling virtue of the management philosophy exemplified by the Clean Dozen must be as clear to managers as to theorists. It was clear even in IBM itself. Ex-chairman Frank Cary had seen his hope become reality. An independent business unit had shown the whole world that part of the elephant could indeed tapdance like Fred Astaire. Unfortunately, in 1982 the paths of the elephant and the hoofer were converging fast. The result of their collision could never be in doubt.

That provides the last sad moral of Boca Raton, and the most valuable. It isn't a question of teaching the elephant how to dance. Eliminate the elephant entirely. Then whole chorus lines of dancers, led and accompanied by brilliant soloists, can produce a corporate choreography for the new century.

The Cash-in
at NCR

3

The problem and the opportunity of the new century are highlighted by a dead plant that didn't die. It belonged to NCR—though IBM plays a pivotal role. The paths of NCR and IBM didn't cross during the first decades when Tom Watson was outshining his former company. The digital era ushered in by Watson's son brought them into collision, for NCR's powerful position in banking and retailing was threatened by the computer. So NCR joined the heavyweights who mastered its technology, but it never mustered the marketplace strength to match IBM.

The Dayton company was even thrashed by IBM on its home ground, selling automatic teller machines (ATMs) to banks. But in 1980 strange things began to happen in one of NCR's feeblest facilities. Its Dundee plant in Scotland had once supplied cash registers to the Empire. When a local manager named James Adamson took over, the Empire had long since vanished, and closure loomed, for Dundee had no profits or products of its own.

Its first ATMs, ordered by Dayton for two of Britain's Big Five banks, were sent back. Their awful standards launched Adamson on a new tack. Well ahead of most other managers—and not just in NCR—he put overwhelming stress on customer satisfaction, even customer "worship," and engineering quality. *Fortune* reported how "Adamson asked his engineers to develop a machine twice as reliable as the competition's. They laughed. He persisted."

The result? "One day the director of engineering found a way to *triple* the reliability. That became the new target. . . . The engineers redesigned virtually every element of the machines." The customers and Dundee grew closer ("The more I talked to the customers, the more rope they were willing to give me"). The closer they grew, the more ATM business was funneled from Dayton to Dundee. In 1980 the factory made only a thousand or so ATMs: by 1983, it was NCR's only source worldwide.

From ninth position behind IBM and Diebold, NCR was moving up fast. By 1984 its output had quadrupled; that year's four thousand installations took it to third place. Then IBM shot itself in the foot. The long-time philosophy of moving the customer up-market and up-price misfired. Superb specifications (a new IBM machine that could read checks and cash them) failed to impress a market that actually wanted "an incrementally better, low-cost" replacement ATM.

IBM's sales slumped by over a third in 1985, as NCR took over leadership and piled on the pressure. Given the freedom to raise their own performance, workers increased output over ten times in the decade to 1990. NCR's base of installed machines—the vital statistic—expanded to two-thirds higher than that of IBM. That was too much for the ex-champion, which promptly surrendered, forming a joint venture that left Diebold in control.

Dundee had taken charge of the industry, setting its pace and its agenda. More important, like IBM's PC team, it had pointed the way to ending the crisis of the American corporation and the threat to its equivalent, the European multinational. The corporate genus has spread right across the American sub-continent and right around the world. It has spread beyond the reach of central control. It has not outreached the intelligence, initiative, and ability of its members.

Not that far from Dundee, in Newhouse, Scotland, another of IBM's defeated opponents in mainframes (Honeywell) has similarly soared. Again, the surge has been led by customer service. Again, power has been devolved to the workforce. Again, the initiative is local. Again, difficult transitions have been accomplished with a will. Newhouse has moved to flexible manufacturing in cells (in which workers in effect run large manufacturing businesses on their own). Again, the impact on capabilities is startling.

Overheads have come down from 270 percent of direct labor cost to 100 percent: the building systems side, which used to turn its inventory over eight times a year, now does so thirty-six times; in food controls, as service improved by 30 percent, inventory came down by 80 percent. Overall, in thirty months of recession, turnover advanced 29 percent and margins doubled. Yet these advances weren't obtained by a company in crisis. The business is what managing director Dennis Kennedy calls "prime-choice supplier in our markets."

Business transformation, not only in the factory, but company-wide, was aimed at keeping Honeywell that way: prime choice. As at NCR, that could only be achieved by prime performance—and that, in turn, can only result from understanding that performance is relative. As Kennedy asks rhetorically, "What else should you be doing but improve?" Companies that turn their problems into opportunities to achieve acclaimed success have to preach and practice another principle, though: "If we're the best again, people will have to be reminded of the task that lies ahead."

Closing the
Management Gap

Managers have become very familiar with the concept of the "management gap"—meaning the distance between the actual and the ideal. In both operations and strategy, it's the gap between "where we are" and "where we want to be." There's a more important gap still: the distance between knowing what needs to be done and actually doing it. As Peter Drucker has written, the first part (knowing what to do) is relatively easy: but why is the second so hard?

Why do managers understand that strategic thinking is essential, yet fail either to *(a)* devise a strategy, or *(b)* communicate the strategy down the line, or *(c)* ensure that it is implemented? They commonly, worse still, believe they have a clear strategy, clearly grasped by everybody who needs to know, and vigorously pursued, when all three beliefs are totally unfounded. Such managers get comfort from their illusions, of course, and that may explain much of the yawning gap.

In quality drives, for instance, top management itself won't be disturbed by a program that concentrates on operational improvement lower down. But a poor-quality strategy, devised by top managers, will vitiate those operational efforts; there's no virtue in excellent performance of missions that should never have been undertaken. No doubt, the Charge of the Light Brigade was wonderfully executed. But riding into the Valley of Death doesn't win wars—or commercial prizes.

The most conspicuous valley-of-death strategies in recent years have involved mergers and acquisitions, bids and deals and diversifications. As Michael Hammer and James Champy write in *Reengineering the Corporation,* "Some people think companies could cure what ails them by changing their corporate strategies. They should sell one division to buy another, change their markets, get into different businesses. They should juggle assets or restructure with a leveraged buyout."

As the authors say, "This kind of thinking distracts companies from making basic changes in the real work they actually do. . . . If they are not succeeding in the business that they are in, it is because their people are not inventing, making, selling and servicing as well as they should." Real corporate strategy is directed at these organic activities, at pointing innovation in the right direction, at making and selling in more effective ways, at serving the customer with greater perceived success.

That's the essence of the transformation at NCR's Dundee plant. The strength of CEO James Adamson's strategy and its implementation lay not only in its particulars, but its origins. This wasn't a strategy imposed from across the Atlantic. The people concerned were seeking their own salvation. Even within the plant, nobody imposed the winning strategy from above. The entire body of employees was enlisted in the effort and that enlistment, too, was emphatically strategic.

Strategy in this sense is everybody's responsibility, not just that of top management. Its wheeling and dealing may have an ancillary role in strengthening or accomplishing the strategy. But the leadership's fundamental task goes beyond devising and revising the overall strategy. Good leadership ensures that the makers and sellers, and the innovators (ideally, everybody), are all moving forward. That means continually closing the gap between the ideal and the actual by turning radical rethinking into conspicuous achievement.

One such miracle was achieved in a British motor industry distinguished more for its failures than its successes. The Landrover Discovery required one of the world's shortest-ever development times twenty-seven months against a forty-eight-month industry norm) to create an off-road vehicle whose sales volume far exceeded expectations. It did so by forming a multidisciplinary project team, headed by a man—among the youngest involved—who had never led a team before. In fact, after initially refusing the job, he only accepted when convinced that the organization would provide full backing for radical solutions.

In the event, so much waiting time was eliminated from the processes that the team leader's own leader, deeply impressed, now has nine-hundred project teams beavering away all over his new company, Perkins Engine, to achieve similar successes. Phenomenal results can be achieved by rethinking before reworking: in Part Three, Chapter 2, I cited the Hammer-Champy account of how IBM Credit cut a seven-day turnaround to four hours, eliminating inefficiencies in the system which had accounted for a whole week's delay.

Nothing could better support the thesis of the late W. Edwards Deming that the system, rather than individual effort, determines the outcome of work. The solution—entrusting the task to one generalist, who handled the application from start to finish, instead of four specialists, one for each stage—nearly always works in such circumstances. In one Dutch bank exactly the same process defect had applied in mortgages: the five units active in this market supplied mortgages that ranged from very simple to highly complicated.

Paradoxically, the most complex took the least time (three days) and the simplest the longest (ten days). There were too many checks, for a start. After redesign, accelerated processes are being implemented in all five units—and even the quickest has learned from the others. People involved in the process told the reformers that "we could have told you that years ago."

That cry is frequently heard when archaic processes are held up to the light. It's a compelling reason for treating front-line people as front-line consultants when tackling defective process. IBM Credit's reforms were led by senior managers. But the mortgage attack was conducted by a multitalented team that consisted of a quality leader, a process designer, salesmen, product managers, and back-office people.

You don't have to be senior to have senior ideas. At Honeywell, for another proof, a group of sales engineers cracked a familiar hard nut. It arises when you're visiting a customer who expresses interest in another product made by the company, but not in your province. If you remember the inquiry at all, you don't know the right contact: even if, with difficulty, you find that contact, the inquiry disappears into what Dennis Kennedy, the U.K. managing director, calls a "black hole."

The sales engineers found the answer: link a toll-free line to a central inquiry desk. The call can be made then and there from the customer's office, the desk keeps track of the inquiry, and the messenger gets reports on his message's fate all the way to the end result: sale or no sale. Processes can also be reformed by a team of one: one customer-service man in fluid control components single-handedly pushed through a project which halved inventory, cut obsolete and obsolescent stock by 90 percent, and doubled service levels.

The power available lower down the organization was brought home to me by another manager-led Hammer-Champy example, at Ford Motor. Accounts payable employed more than five hundred people in North America. Senior management was enthusiastically pursuing a 20 percent head-count reduction when Ford made a stunning discovery—its associate in Japan, Mazda, needed only five employees for the same function. A far more radical solution was then devised: Ford reengineered its system, not around the invoice, but around the original purchasing order. Confirmation of delivery instantly triggered payment, and the accounts payable activity became redundant.

What struck me, on reading this, wasn't the brilliance of the concept, for I had encountered exactly the same revolutionary introduction of new logic, at a life insurance company, just a week before. Only this time the discovery had been made, not by senior executives, but by a quality improvement team of very junior people in the finance department. It was their own solution, reached without any knowledge of what was happening at U.S. Ford, or anywhere else. You couldn't ask for more convincing proof of the great untapped powers that reside down the line, in groups more than individuals, in all organizations.

You can't help observing, either, that IBM and Ford were stumbling into deep macroeconomic trouble at the time when these micromiracles were being achieved. That comes back to my starting point. Both gaps have to be closed: both the strategic framework *and* the operational processes have to be reengineered if either is to achieve its maximum benefit. Otherwise, it's all too easy to fall into the trap described by Gary Hamel and C. K. Prahalad in 1989 in the *Harvard Business Review:*

> Too many companies are expending enormous energy simply to reproduce the cost and quality advantages that global competitors already have. . . . Assessing the current tactical advantages of known competitors will not help you understand the resolution, stamina and inventiveness of potential competitors.

I would put that even more positively. Strategy and its implementation are the ultimate test of your own resolution, stamina and inventiveness: of how far you dare to be different, and how effectively you capitalize on that difference. To use again the concept of management thinker Robert Fritz, it's the distinction between "resolving behavior," which takes the organization from the current to the desired state, and "oscillating behavior," in which (see Ford and IBM) everybody runs very fast to stay in exactly the same space.

The Fritz formulation dovetails neatly with the ideas of Deming (to repeat, you can only raise individual performance by elevating that of the entire system) and Peter Senge (however hard you push, the system pushes back harder). You want to achieve the double whammy effect of radically and dramatically improving performance of components in a system which is itself being radically and dramatically transformed.

To express the double whammy concept at its simplest, cutting costs on falling turnover only sustains profits. But cost reduction on rising turnover must mean that profits rise faster than sales. John Martin, the chief executive of the Taco Bell fast-food business, tells of many operational gains, like the $7 million savings won by removing food preparation from the outlets. By simultaneously concentrating on a value-for-money strategy, Taco Bell boosted sales 22 percent per year. The double whammy duly translated into a 31 percent average rise in earnings.

Martin thinks that his company is a success "because we're a company that listens to our customers and are not afraid to change. . . . When the traditional thinkers tell you your goal is far-fetched, you're probably on to something big. . . . When they stop telling you it's far-fetched, you've probably already lost the war." His last two points are million-dollar truths, but the first point had three vital words missing. You need a company that "listens to our customers *and our employees*."

Read most accounts of management miracles—say, Chrysler's production of a Neon sub-compact that undercut Japanese prices—and one word dominates all others: it's team, team, team all the way. That raised a fascinating dilemma when top management at Chrysler, having devolved full authority to the "platform team" for the Neon, didn't like the front bumper design. In the old days, the bosses would have simply ordered a change. What action could, or should, they take under the new dispensation?

The team was strongly against any alteration because of the high cost: $27 million. Remember, it was their devolved responsibility to meet their targets. But their seniors continued to stress the defects of the design. The team went back to the drawing board and found a way to introduce an improved bumper at far lower cost: $7 million. This was teamwork in action in a double sense: the senior management joined the team, by in effect playing the role of the customer—which is one perfectly valid description of the relationship.

The Neon anecdote is consistent with Hammer and Champy's eminently practical guide to the tactics of strategy. An especially valuable checklist addresses the central problem, which is the failure rate (seven out of ten, they think) of organizations which try reengineering. The list of nineteen items is "a catalogue of the most common errors that lead companies to fail. . . . Avoid them, and you almost can't help but get it right." Turn the eight most important don'ts upside down, moreover, and you get the vital do's:

1. Change the process—don't just try to fix it (in other words, tackle the whole system).
2. Focus on business processes (i.e., don't have task forces on "is-

sues" like empowerment, teamwork, innovation, and customer service).

3.   Recognize that successful reform of business processes will trigger radical changes elsewhere in the business system.

4.   Involve people, their values and beliefs, and their reward and recognition in the change.

5.   Go for big prizes; it's not worth making a big effort for minor results.

6.   Keep right on to the end of the road: quit too early, and you've wasted your time.

7.   Have no constraints on the definition of the problem and the scope of the reengineering effort—you're almost certain to find problems you never knew existed.

8.   Kick existing corporate cultures and management attitudes out of the way.

The last do is the hardest. Managers resist change instinctively, because they fear their last state may be worse than their first. As Honeywell found in the United Kingdom, this resistance can be taken to the last ditch. When top management at the Newhouse factory set out to share ownership of problems and processes, some managers simply couldn't accept the change of style. They saw their power base eroded—and jobs were being eroded, too, where the traditional conduits between senior management and the shop floor were no longer needed.

Six months after the first session designed to reorient the company, five out of eleven senior managers had left. Unless the top people were marching to the same tune, its transformation couldn't be taken all the way down the company. Indeed, Hammer and Champy think you shouldn't even try to make reengineering happen from the bottom up. (That is true for an overall change like that at Honeywell, but, of course, it's untrue for departmental changes like reforming Ford's accounts payable system.)

The authors also advise against assigning someone who doesn't understand reengineering to lead the effort; skimping on the resources devoted to the latter; burying reengineering in the middle of the corporate agenda; dissipating energy across a great many projects; and dragging the process out too long. That last point sets up an obvious potential conflict with the vice of quitting too soon, but that clash can be resolved. The answer, in effect, means relaunching the change program at frequent intervals.

Honeywell, for example, started on the road to Total Quality Management with a 1988 launch under the heading "Taking First Steps." Year by year, that moved on successively from "securing management commitment" to "building the foundations," "experiencing measured improvement," "working to achieve 'right first time,' " "understanding the business quality challenge," and "responding to our customers" (in 1994). Beyond lie "seeing the difference" and "customer confirmation."

These stages emphasize that reinvention is a long-haul journey that never ends. Therefore, don't even start on the road unless you're fully committed. That commitment has to start with the CEO, but can't end there. Hammer and Champy actually advise against attempting to reengineer when the CEO is two years from retirement. I'd go further. Any change effort must go far beyond being identified with a particular CEO. "Team thinking," in the phrase of management consultant Ben Heirs, has to rule. Whatever title you use for radical and dramatic reform, it won't succeed unless a radical spirit, focused on achievement, runs throughout the company.

It's the business equivalent of the old Latin tag, *mens sana in corpore sano,* a healthy mind in a healthy body. As NCR demonstrated at Dundee, redesigned processes within a redesigned strategy will bring health to an ailing corporate body. And as Honeywell showed at Newhouse and in the whole U.K. business, they will also regenerate bodies that are already wealthy and healthy, and wise.

The Ruination
of Rolm

5

O n May 7, 1992, IBM made one of its increasingly common admissions of defeat. This was no big deal, merely the disposal of a half share in the marketing and service company that handled telecommunications equipment made by Rolm Systems in California. But thereby hung a much weightier story. The equal partner who swallowed IBM's half share was Siemens, king of European electronics: and once IBM had owned all of Rolm.

Rolm was IBM's first-ever corporate purchase, acquired in 1984 as part of a grand design. As technologies converged, computers and communications would form an indivisible whole. Private branch telephone exchanges (which Rolm made) would offer the desired entry into this new and wonderful world. The telecommunications market, dominated by monopolistic giants like AT&T and the national corporations of Europe and Japan, was temptingly, incomparably vast. It dwarfed even the computer industry ruled by IBM.

To add piquancy, a move into telecommunications would be a counterattack. AT&T had been trying, with ill-success, to find a place in computing (which wasn't finally achieved until 1992's $7.5

billion acquisition of NCR). The purchase of Rolm, while it cost $1.3 billion, wasn't in the same class; Rolm was a minor player in a major league. True, the buy was then at the crest of an outstanding climb, but the path from crests leads downwards. The Rolm founders and shareholders got out while the going, for them, was good—in money terms, superlative.

The experience recalls Xerox Corporation's disastrous buy of computer maker Scientific Data Systems, another strategic inspiration turned money-losing dog. IBM wasted a further billion on absorbing Rolm's deficits and development costs before cutting its losses in late 1988. Selling manufacture to Siemens, IBM kept only the marketing half-stake that disappeared four years later. The net loss was $1.35 billion in money. But the damage in intangible terms was far greater.

Not only had IBM lost its foothold in telecommunications, but the episode had shown its vaunted management powers, in their first real test outside the walls of the corporation, to be ineffective. The many IBM managers drafted into Rolm floundered in this unfamiliar territory. Having bought in badly, IBM couldn't manage its way out. The 1992 sale (on undisclosed terms) fitted in with a new strategy which recognized that reality.

From now on, IBM would concentrate on its areas of expertise. If it needed related technologies, they would be obtained by strategic alliances, rather than strategic takeovers—even though the original Rolm deal, the purchase of a 15 percent stake, was more in the nature of the former. For all the attempts to put a brave face on IBM's withdrawal from Rolm, this climbdown totally denied its original grand design.

That vision had equally mesmerized outsiders. "Soon IBM will become the first—and likely the only—worldwide telephone company," wrote the well-informed Richard Thomas DeLamarter. Some, he knew, might find this reading difficult to believe. "IBM the global phone company? Preposterous idea. Impossible." Not only was AT&T the "undisputed world leader" (and moving to build its international strengths), but national telecommunications companies had monopolies or quasi-monopolies in every country. "Besides, IBM makes its money processing data, not selling telephones or moving calls between them."

Rolm was only a start, though. "In late 1985 IBM dropped broad hints that it would soon enter the telephone central switch market as part of an effort to double its sales of telecommunications gear in Europe." Two further forays (both of which eventually failed) suggested the same conclusion: invested in the long-distance carrier MCI and IBM in U.S.-wide radio links (with Motorola and the Public Broadcasting System). It seemed set on building an "international telecommunications network" that would "greatly expand" its corporate power.

A former trustbuster, DeLamarter scarcely welcomed the thought of customers being dragooned into the IBM net. The giant would be able to exclude competitive products from a system built on its own standards, which could be changed at will to disadvantage the competition. Two French critics saw the threat to national communications companies in near-apocalyptic terms: IBM is "going beyond data processing. . . . IBM is entrenched . . . with such reserves of power that it cannot be seriously threatened."

Compared to this "dominant" force, the world's telephone monopolies, even AT&T, were puny, depending on over-priced services and outdated technology. Leapfrogging the latter, and undercutting the former, IBM occupied the "high ground," overlooking a battlefield on which the monopolies were being fragmented by irresistible technological, economic, and political pressures. IBM was bound to "prevail, for it held significant advantages."

DeLamarter had read IBM's psychology right, but misread its capabilities. He was by no means alone. A year after the Rolm deal, for example, *Business Week* reported on "How IBM is Getting the Most Out of Rolm" . . . "Respect for the phone switchboard maker's more casual culture has paid off." In 1992, however, the magazine reported that the sale of Rolm "will put an end to one of the most embarrassing chapters in Big Blue's history." Respect for Rolm's culture, far from paying off, had delayed and muffled IBM's reaction to its acquisition's poor performance.

Both former and current insiders thought that IBM should have taken charge as soon as the problems emerged. Instead, "IBM people kept saying: 'No, no, no!' They wanted to try . . . more entrepreneurial methods," said a former Rolm insider. Understandable doubts about this West-East marriage between Santa Clara and Armonk had surfaced at the very beginning. But two IBM dignitaries had traveled West to reassure the soon-to-be employees about their operating independence and their informal ways.

One of the potentates said graphically that "we're not here to drain your pool." That was John F. Akers, president and future chairman, showing early on the flair for the telling phrase that highlighted his troubled reign. During that reign, Rolm shrank from eight thousand employees to three thousand, lost nearly all senior managers within a year or so, and utterly failed to deliver any of IBM's objectives. Rolm's pool was drained all but dry. The only consolation for IBM is that it was not alone. In the many other cases of failed and botched acquisitions, circumstances naturally vary. But the step-by-step rake's progress is much the same—and just as readily avoidable.

Acquisitions of Advantage

Companies which long shun takeovers, then finally take the plunge, must be more than likely (witness IBM and Rolm) to bungle. But the errors won't be unique, or confined to first-time buyers. The Rolm buy failed, as most acquisitions fail, for reasons that are common to other calamitous "strategic" buys:

1. The strategic grand design becomes a "must," which by definition excludes all other possibilities.
2. The strategy is not subjected to continuous review—and plans are not promptly modified or scrapped if events contradict them.
3. The strategy plays not to the buyer's strengths, but to its weaknesses.
4. The initial risk exposure is increased by unplanned post-acquisition management initiatives.
5. External and internal approval of the strategic stroke is taken as confirming its rightness—and Cassandras, internal or external, are ignored.

6. Top-level strategies are not rigorously examined at lower levels, and top management over-commits to the deal.
7. Accepted rules and routines are applied—without being checked for relevance.
8. Messengers are discouraged from bringing bad news—and corrective reaction to bad news is dangerously delayed.
9. Failure is not admitted: rather, it is denied.

Announcing the first Rolm handover to Siemens, Akers unbelievably denied that the Germans were "taking over anything. We're forming an important partnership." The price of failure is magnified if it's not recognized. Failure to admit error and thus learn from the mistake is the unforgiveable management sin and no way to make a success of the next acquisition, if there is one. For IBM, though, Rolm was both its first significant acquisition, and (so far) its last.

Maybe that was one valuable lesson learned—the easy way to avoid the pitfalls of acquiring: don't. One breed, however, has made acquisition a way of life. The financially oriented conglomerates have a better record in general, and in making acquisitions pay in particular, than grand strategists. They start with a powerful advantage. Unlike IBM with Rolm, they don't over-pay; bargains are their meat and drink. Acquisitions work financially with the most ease if value is bought inexpensively.

That sounds just as trite as Bernard Baruch's famous stock market tip: buy cheap and sell dear. But it happens to be true. The conglomerates, however, claim to go beyond mere bargain-hunting: their buys are supposedly being transferred from weak hands to strong. To revitalize their buys they apply a management formula which sounds convincing and coherent. Their acquisition methodology is the antithesis of the strategic fumbling enumerated above. Instead of fumbling, the conglomerate goes straight to the point:

1. There is no grand design; the deal is strictly opportunistic, and disposals are briskly made.
2. The business strategy is therefore highly flexible, and, after disposals, largely left to operating management.
3. The purchaser is only interested in the buy's strengths, and acts swiftly to eradicate weaknesses and weak operations.

4. Post-acquisition management follows a highly developed model and is designed to narrow the already small risks.
5. The acquirer is only interested in external and internal approval to the extent that approval helps or hinders the capture of the target.
6. Top management is committed only to the financial success of the deal.
7. The rules and routines applied to the new situation have worked in many takeovers and situations.
8. Bad news produces immediate and effective correction.
9. Failure is not allowed; the acquisition has to meet the purchaser's simple, clear, and comprehensive purpose: to make money.

Because of that purpose, all decisions are financially based, and all managers are financially judged. If they meet or surpass targets, they are rewarded. If they fail, they are thrown overboard. Spurred by the whip and the carrot, easily monitored through financial reports, the managers seem to have the enabling conditions for super-performance: responsible independence under demanding control. In reality, they are caught in a system as rigid as any corpocracy. The regime demands certain behaviors and allows no others.

The frequent results of those behaviors are demonstrated by Hanson's experience with Ever Ready in Britain. To Hanson management, this ranks as a splendid success. The battery group cost £95 million: of that, £40 million was recouped by sell-offs that severed most of the international assets. In its last twenty-one months of ownership alone, Hanson stripped £37 million in pre-tax profit from Ever Ready: £132 million more arrived when Ralston Purina, owner of U.S. Everready, bought the British business.

What was left to buy? That's been documented by David Bowen, writing in the *Independent on Sunday*. Before Hanson took hold, in the late 1970s, Ever Ready's factory near Consett made over three million batteries a day. After treatment, Hanson handed over a plant making a mere half a million units daily, with a workforce reduced by 87 percent. The market share of a once-great brand had dropped from over 80 percent to 30 percent by value.

Before Hanson, classic mismanagement had under-invested in the technology, the brand, and the factories. The irony is that Hanson management, with its very different motives, repeated the same pattern of decline that created so cheap a takeover target. The old management had a vast sunk investment in the old zinc-carbon battery technology. The new alkaline batteries were a threat that management chose to ignore, even to wish away, because of the damage that conversion would inflict on the company's profits.

Technology won't stop for anybody. The price has to be paid—either you pay now, in lost profit on obsolescent lines, or you pay later, in lost business. The difference is lost opportunity. Diehard management simply makes a present to competitors, as Ever Ready did to Duracell. Low spending on R&D (a miserable 1 percent of sales) was a down payment on a cemetery plot. Curiously, though, a successful product emerged from this myopia.

Starting alkaline production too late to save the day, the old management sought to avert that day's evil with a technology that used the existing plant: zinc chloride. This stopgap "Silver Seal" was no answer to the basic loss of competitive power to alkaline brands; but the plant making Ever Ready's own Gold Seal alkaline batteries was much too small. Hanson faced a choice; heavy expenditure on the winning technology, or a far smaller, £4 million investment in Silver Seal to hold the fort—until the white flag went up.

The latter choice, naturally, was trumpeted forth as proof that Hanson didn't strip assets, but enhanced them. But it had, as noted, stripped Ever Ready of its international assets (save in the protected South African market). This doomed Ever Ready to a variant of the self-fulfilling prophecy. The proprietor could later conclude, sure enough, that a single-country battery maker had no future. "Efficiently managed decline" thereupon became the only option.

The books show that Hanson shareholders recouped their investment many times. But the books never show the fish that got away. Suppose that a truly restored Ever Ready had retained the old market share for Hanson. The shareholder value created would have far exceeded £132 million. Of course, Hanson-style mercenary management could never have created that value. There's nothing wrong intellectually (as opposed to morally) with being mercenary. But it doesn't build a business. That demands taking a long view, which may mean a short-term price in higher expenditure and lower profits.

The philosophy of financial orientation revolves around lower spending and higher profits. That can damage a business just as effectively as the misguided IBM strategists damaged Rolm. You can't create value by destroying it. The corollary is that the true object of acquisition isn't to add value for the acquiring shareholders, but rather to the acquired business. That's the other way around from the usual approach, which conceives the end solely in terms of the acquiring company—and can be very wrong for both parties.

You can understand why targets, threatened with being Rolmed or Ever Readied, resist takeover so desperately. But is there a middle way? Can you strike a happy medium between the strategic buy, which subjugates the acquisition to misplaced master strategy, and the rapacious deal, which robs Peter (the acquisition) to pay Paul (the acquirer)? The middle way does exist, but only if you imitate the predators' initial thrust: the price paid will determine the upside potential of the purchase. Buy too dear, and you will never see the color of your money again.

The concept of Economic Value Added (Part Five, Chapter 2) applies. Unless profit covers the cost of capital expended, the purchase must destroy value. If equity is involved, the hurdle becomes higher, not lower, because the true cost of equity capital is greater than that of debt. In theory, an acquirer can surmount the financial hurdle without clearing the cost of capital, but only if the capital value of the purchase business can be sufficiently enhanced.

Rupert Murdoch managed that after buying TV stations and Twentieth Century–Fox from two ferociously demanding sellers, respectively John Kluge and Marvin Davis. Note that a precise purpose, the creation of a fourth TV network, lay behind the purchases. The chances of success are far higher where the buyer has a defined strategy that stays close to the mainstream of the existing business. That's especially true if the purchase is of assets, rather than an entire company, like Rolm.

Purchased assets must be slotted into the existing organization; no other home is available. With whole companies, the option (taken fatally with Rolm) exists of allowing the buy to continue in its own sweet (or sour) way. The financially oriented conglomerates get this right, too. Being interested only in the assets, and never mind the culture, they stamp their brand on the acquired management from day one.

As argued above, the conglomerate stamp may well be the wrong brand for the long-term future of the herd. That doesn't diminish the power of the principle. It can, however, be applied in different and more productive ways. The principle, to begin with, needs careful definition. The object is to ensure that acquisition achieves the highly specific, clearly understood business purposes sought by the acquirer and achieves those ends as effectively and as fast as possible.

That doesn't necessitate obliteration of the acquisition's identity. That adept buyer Banc One Corporation takes special care over a bank amalgamation process that has elevated a regional institution (based in Columbus, Ohio) to America's twelfth-largest bank, with the fifth-highest profits. Its buys are expected to adopt Banc One's systems where the latter are demonstrably superior. The sword cuts both ways, however: the group adopts any demonstrably better ideas from the new affiliate.

The retail banking in which Banc One specializes is helpfully homogeneous, true. In a business the buyer doesn't know, interference is on balance likely to be harmful. Second-guessing and misunderstanding on unfamiliar ground offset the benefits of any better disciplines installed by the buyer. But being in the same business has never stopped less intelligent buyers from throwing their weight—and their acquisitions—around.

Too often, acquirers trap themselves into a baby-and-bathwater dilemma. A complete hands-off policy guarantees preservation of the acquired culture: the baby will stay in the bath. But all acquisitions can be improved, sometimes radically. So hands-off means accepting some degree of unacceptable under-performance. That may be eliminated by placing hands-on: but then, will the baby get thrown out with the dirty water?

In this dilemma, fundamentally a conflict between the parent's culture and that of the acquired business, *the parent culture always wins*. What's the solution? Don't create the dilemma in the first place. It reflects defects in the purchaser rather than the purchased. If a company already has a tolerant attitude towards variations between people and businesses, adding another culture will be equally comfortable. If that tolerance doesn't exist, the company will face problems of mounting intensity, with or without acquisitions.

The ability to embrace and encourage cultural diversity within the firm, and to combine different strengths to achieve unified progress, has become a driving force of modern success. The organizational pressures, however, work in the opposite direction, towards uniformity. Whose uniformity, though? The question arises urgently with cross-border mergers. As a breed, their previous history has been disappointing, but their future will have to be much brighter than the past. That's because transnational, global companies are an inevitable response to global markets.

Cross-frontier marriage, anyway, is workable, even with the volatile combination of French, Italian, and British components—which followed after SGS-THOMSON merged in 1987 to create a viable European contender in semiconductors. Tricky political issues arose (for instance, where to locate the group HQ). But the fundamental question was trickier still: How do you make sense of a $1.6 billion three-way merger spread across most industrialized countries? It proved easier than it sounds, thanks to the development of a common language—that of Total Quality Management (see Part Ten).

Adopting a new, sweeping corporate lifestyle that wasn't associated with any nationality greatly facilitated the evolution of a genuinely combined company. With Masaaki Imai's book *Kaizen* as its gospel and continuous improvement in performance and customer satisfaction as its goal, the group reduced defects from five hundred per million parts in 1987 to fifteen—and that's only one indicator of all-round advance. The uniformity wasn't French, Italian, or British. It was that of a new culture built by a new, unified management.

So you needn't impose one culture on another, or find a means of allowing distinct cultures to flourish independently under the same corporate umbrella—as if no combination had ever taken place. Murray Duffin, chief architect of TQM at SGS-THOMSON, says that "the idea that cultural differences create competitive advantage is absolute rubbish. Everything that works in Japan works in other countries." By the same token, everything can work across linked companies if you recognize that a new entrant changes the group, and must also influence its nature and destiny.

The combined success at SGS-THOMSON returns to the starting point of all successful acquisition: highly specific, clearly understood business purposes. The purchaser knows exactly what it's doing, why, and how. Too often, that's far from the case. Buyers invariably set about financial research with "due diligence" (but often get deceived): very few are anything like as diligent about nonfinancial researches, which are far less likely to result in deception.

The buying company can always find out the crucial nonfinancial truths by talking to customers, competitors, analysts, market researchers, former employees, journalists, and so forth. Without such research, you cannot complete the following catechism—short, simple, but rashly omitted, time after time:

1. Have you firmly established your own true strengths—and weaknesses?
2. Do you know everything possible about the target's activities and its strengths—and weaknesses?
3. Does the purchase make sense in relation to the mutual strengths and weaknesses, and in its own right?
4. Are you ready and able to take a rapid hold on the purchased business and its management?
5. Can you meld the two cultures effectively and swiftly into a new, mutual, lasting way of life?

Many companies (like the pre-Rolm IBM) have thrived without ever feeling an urge to acquire or merge. For those where combination is a viable, maybe a highly desirable, option, there's only one imperative: to answer the above catecism with yes, five times over. Do that, and you will easily out-Hanson Hanson.

NINE

Triumphs of Teamwork:
How to Mobilize Groups

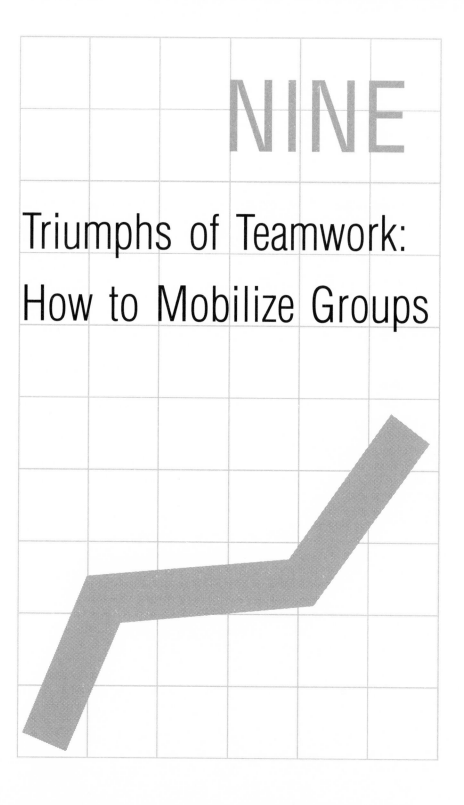

The Seminal
Thoughts of Semco

1

Very few managers have acquired guru status, and very few small companies have become widely known outside their own countries. But Ricardo Semler, owner of a small Brazilian engineering company, Semco, obeys none of the usual rules; and neither does his business. That's what has given Semler his unusual status. Semco is a laboratory for ideas that differ from traditional management mores in almost all respects—not least in its taste for radical experiment.

That's one of his ideas which deserves widespread imitation. All organizations are laboratories for management thought in action, but the testing of new concepts is seldom deliberate. Semler's book, *Maverick!,* should irresistibly stimulate managers who believe or sense that there's always a better way. It follows in the footsteps of Robert Townsend, whose *Up the Organization* also took ideas fashioned at one company (Avis) and turned a real-life attack on hierarchy into a management philosophy.

The two men share some ideas—for instance, the abolition of private secretaries—and the same overriding cause: in Semler's words, "to make people look forward to coming to work in the morning." That wasn't how the Semco saga began, however. Semler's father was a middle-aged, autocratic engineer when his son was born: so Ricardo was only twenty-four when he took over a business in deep trouble. His youth (which didn't stop him firing 60 percent of his top management at once) has an important bearing on the inventiveness which transformed both the business and its nature.

Semler went through a fairly typical period of professionalizing management and forcing a specialized manufacturer (marine pumps and centrifuges) into diversification—over-diversification, you might say, after looking at the present range. Semco still makes pumps, but also commercial dishwashers, cooling units, mixers, and whole biscuit plants. And that's after several other lines vanished as Semler adjusted to the hard, variable weather of the Brazilian economy.

He draws some important lessons from those early years. Having brought in professional management of the traditional kind, he threw himself into acquisitions and other activities with frenzy and stress (personal and organizational). The growth was sensational, doubling every year, but it "took us almost a decade to learn that our stress was internally generated, the result of an immature organization and infantile goals."

The "infantile goals" were those still pursued by adult managers in every company with any ambition: what Semler calls the "adolescent urge" for "more people, more plants, more products, more revenue." At the price of "money, time, and gastritis," Semler cured himself of the urge, and is now adamant: "To want to grow just to be big is an idea that comes from the sandbox."

The adult manager still seeks growth: to create new opportunities and wealth for people, boost motivation and productivity, and generate change. But not to please the sandbox minds on Wall Street. Sandbox management, moreover, is a prolific source of wasteful activity. In Semco's acquisitive phase, one hundred targets were studied: there were negotiations with fifteen of these; four were actually purchased.

Since "buying small family firms is a certain way to skip the ulcers and go straight to bypass surgery," the buys were discarded subsidiaries of multinationals: "the closets are typically full of skeletons," but at least the books are accurate. These subsidiaries had suffered from the same kind of matured but "immature" organization that Semler was to abandon. The mature corpocratic system achieves splendid *results*—it goes through all the right motions—but what it may not achieve is right *outcomes.*

After professional management had wrought its wonders, Semco could "track with great precision virtually every aspect of our business, from sales quotations to the maintenance records of each of our innumerable welding machines. We could generate all sorts of new reports almost instantly, with dazzling charts and graphs. . . . We thought we were more organized, more professional, more disciplined, more efficient. So, we asked ourselves with a shudder, how come we were constantly late on delivery?"

The poor outcomes, Semler came to realize, were the consequence of processes that led to other objectives which, while inner-directed, caused as much internal dissatisfaction as external. The quest for "law, order, stability, and predictability" becomes an end in itself. The corporation makes "rules for every conceivable contingency. Policy manuals are created with the idea that, if a company puts everything in writing, it will be more rational and objective."

The consequent standardization of methods and conduct, Semler writes, "works fine for an army or prison system." Actually, even that can be challenged. Armies and prisons have contemporary problems, too. But you can't challenge Semler's contention that in business corpocracy doesn't work—"certainly not for a business that wants people to think, innovate, and act as human beings."

That truth can't be denied. While "law, order, stability and predictability" are wonderful things, the world, its markets, and its individual inhabitants demonstrate the realities of chaos theory. They obey no laws (other than those of science). They are disorderly, unstable, and unpredictable. But chaos isn't anarchic. It creates simple and satisfying patterns—precisely, and rightly, what Ricardo Semler seeks to create at Semco.

Power to the Empowered

"Looking back on it, I can't remember a single decision that I made in that period. Which was just as well, for I am at my best when I am doing nothing." Ricardo Semler's new dispensation at Semco was built on a new dispensation for himself. While the company continued to revolve around him in an enabling sense, its processes stopped doing so. He lived by a new philosophy of management, a philosophy not only for himself, but for other managers.

In a dozen years, an orthodox pyramidal hierarchy was transformed into a bazaar of the unorthodox: of operatives who may set their own production quotas and have a say in product redesign and marketing; of managers who fix their own business strategies and their own salaries; of open revelation of all financial facts (including those salaries); of major decisions, including acquisitions and plant relocations, submitted to the vote of all employees; of factories moved to multidisciplinary working in groups that are free to reorganize and innovate.

Semler calls this last unorthodoxy the "amoeba" treatment. At one amoeba factory, set up to make electronic scales (which had been money losers), "The Kids" took only a few months to create such excellence that their plant became Semco's "flagship operation." Its productivity doubled that of the food service equipment plant, its inventories fell by 40 percent, its defects dropped to under 1 percent. What caused the turnaround? "The Kids innovated all over the place."

Their actions recognized an important and much-neglected management truth: that internal, non-technical innovation is fully as important as technological invention (and much cheaper). Examples from The Kids are a short start-the-day meeting for *all* employees and, instead of a time-clock, a peg on which arriving employees place a mood tag—green (Good Mood), yellow (Careful), or red (Not Today).

As Semler notes, the mood peg may be somewhat "cute," but it exemplified the new culture, in which people made their own rules, while top management abolished central ones (a particularly easy and satisfying form of innovation). After concluding that "some departments were better not created and some rules were better not written," top management wisely decided to proceed by stealth. Rule manuals were simply collected up over three or four months. People gradually found that no new manuals were forthcoming, and the rules (including control over travel expenses) came tumbling down.

Perks were abolished, too, and so was power—much to the distress of many managers: "To be the boss is what counts to most bosses. They confuse authority with authoritarianism. They don't trust their subordinates." Semler points out that in the pyramid structure, "there is always a group of supervisors, department heads, and other professionals in the middle. . . . It isn't unusual for these middle managers to be more zealous with authority . . . than those at the top."

Semler doesn't gloss over the resistance he encountered, mostly from the middle, and not least because he insisted on doing business with the unions. Nor does he minimize the problems that Semco met as it grew and became "too big for our own good"—and too complex. Attempts to combat complexity by computerization made confusion worse (Semler believes this to be a general rule). A clinching discovery was that 120 invoices were being issued monthly against

150: "Two days later the unit was off the computer and back on the primitive, manual system."

To Semler, everything now seemed clear: "either you can adopt sophisticated, complex systems, or you can simplify everything." Semler simplified. For example, the mainframe was disconnected. "Our worries about making one computer compatible with another are over. It's every microprocessor for itself and to hell with the economies of scale." Semco may well regret this as networking becomes more important. But it will never regret the introduction of manufacturing cells or its simpler "amoeba"-like division into smaller, identifiable units.

With similar simplicity, Semler cut through the Gordian knot of profit sharing. Instead of complicated schemes, each unit got a democratically agreed 23 percent of any profit and was free to allocate the money as the members decided (they mostly opted for equal amounts for everybody). This principle—letting people decide on issues that most top managements keep to their troubled bosoms—cuts out forests of complication and bureaucracy.

Semler spills out other useful hints by the score. For instance, insist on one-page memos with newspaper-style headlines. ("New Toaster Will Sell 20,000 Units for $2 Million Profit"); or set up a "Women's Program" to sweep away discrimination; or rotate managers between functions. Or subject managers to semiannual appraisal by their subordinates with "multiple choice questions designed to measure technical ability, competence, leadership and other aspects of being a boss."

There are three dozen of these questions, each with four possible answers, with a passing grade of 70 percent: below that, a manager's job is in danger. Here, doubt begins to creep in. The procedure looks somewhat cumbersome. The suspicion of overkill arises at several points in Semler's account. Originally, Semco seems to have had a dozen hierarchical stages for a hundred-odd employees: the transformed business never had more than 850 people, but the number of managers and managerial posts mentioned by name in *Maverick!* makes it sound strangely top-heavy.

Today Semco has only 300 employees, averaging $92,000 of sales each—nearly nine times the 1980 figure. That high number, however, has been achieved largely by "hollowing out" the corporation, sub-contracting everything possible, often to small workshops established by ex–Semco workers with company assistance. In this respect, as in most others, Semco does little that's unique: it's the relentless combination of many advanced management ideas that's remarkable.

Can Semco's combination transfer to other, larger firms in other countries (whose big companies, especially in America, have shown flattering interest in Semco)? Can you emulate Semler in a pyramidal organization, or do you have to demolish the pyramid and, like Semco, go "circular," with directors becoming "counselors," unit heads "partners," other managers "coordinators," and everybody else "associates"?

That's all less important than the introduction of trust and delegation, the abolition of futile restraints and complications, and the wholehearted use of modern manufacturing methods and people policies. Those principles should work anywhere. But very few other companies have followed Semler's practice and preaching. Nor does he want followers. He says there's a "fundamental difference" between himself and gurus who are wedded to particular management theories.

"What we are doing is not the solution or the model—it's one more laboratory experience of what can happen when you remove some of the strictures." For Semco, it's been a twenty- to twenty-five-year process, which is no use for people "looking for a 90-day solution." He's not even sure that "what we're doing is a finished product, or ever will be." While he's "done a lot of talking and sharing experience," he's done "little to help others follow our path"— and won't.

Indeed, when eight directors of a richly financed West Coast start-up in high technology wanted to spend a month at Semco, they were politely rebuffed. Semler's colleagues said they had nothing to sell. True, one Denver manufacturer of plastic containers and baby products, Container Industries, has emulated Semco unaided: sales have multiplied nearly eightfold in half a dozen years to $16 million. Semler points out, however, that these are "talented people: they could have gotten the same results by different means."

Nothing can demonstrate the efficacy of Semco-style management one way or the other. But Semler knows that "changes in mentality do affect the numbers," and such changes are the prime object of his philosophy. The Semco story is "not about empowerment and participation," which he dismisses as merely "topical." The experiment is "more generic and comprehensive," an effort "to shift the center of gravity towards the middle." The shift, moreover, is accompanied by the development of "the most exciting thing": the "boundary-less" company.

A BBC documentary team that filmed Semco in 1993 counted about two outsiders to every insider: the factory was filled with subcontractors and "consultants." Some of the latter were accidentally recruited when 1,430 résumés arrived for a single engineering post: Semco took on 41 of the applicants, one full-time for the actual job, 40 on a "risk basis." Experienced early retirees were given a day to find how they could help: one applicant, for example, had worked for the company that made Semco's gear-cutting machine. He reckoned he could raise its productivity, and his reward will be 20 percent of the first two years' savings.

When he returns to São Paulo, Semler is as surprised as anybody by the strange faces milling around—and the strange prototypes. Neither surprise bothers him. The new product "will fly or not fly," while the outsiders are essential to the basic organizational strategy. That strategy insists on maintaining inside Semco only the "core business: applications engineering and final assembly."

In these core activities, there's a "distinct hierarchy and leadership." On issues like what product to make, or the control of sales and distribution, the leaders have "very clear responsibilities"—even though, as noted above, "people who are subordinates have a say and the capacity to interview and assess their bosses." The capacity is used. In the marine products division, whose survival was in doubt, 120 out of 135 employees turned up to quiz its potential savior.

Despite the cumbersome appearance, Semler suspects that the recruitment cycle, from meeting potential executives to bringing them on stream, is actually shorter at Semco. "We take longer over the first decision": but the selection, by as many subordinates as care to attend the interview, is more effective—and more rigorous. The subordinates come armed with lists of tough, prepared questions. The hired managers, moreover, appear to be performing well and contendedly: in a company with a tiny labor turnover, the proportion of managers who "have left or bombed is negligible."

Their self-set salaries and their gradings by their subordinates are published for all to see, and the average grading has steadily climbed two points every year. Some Semco managers have rated 90 to 98 percent for three or four years, which sounds incredible: but, says Semler, "the trend is what matters." An uncorrected slump means that a manager is losing—or has lost—the "capacity to lead." In that case the solution is harsh, but inevitable.

Whether Semco is over-managed is hard to tell, because of the changed nomenclature. Anybody with "any kind of subordinate" is called a coordinator, which means everybody from foreman upwards. At its peak employment, Semco could have employed one manager for only nine workers: however, if their visiting cards are anything to go by, the executives are fully employed. Free to use any title they wish, 80 percent of them put only their names: because "they don't have time" for useless niceties.

The "useless niceties" goes for other items (like where to park, or company car rules) that also cause "a tremendous amount of grief" in traditional companies. In other respects, though, Semco's regime is stricter. In particular, it has a five-year plan, but only six-month budgets. The latter don't allow people to bunch "all the ugly things, or the good things, in the second half." If the orders aren't in the house, managers may include hoped-for purchases in an over-optimistic one-year forecast. But you can't get away with that inside a six-month period—not in Semco's markets.

The six-month period is by no means the only powerful financial innovation. Semler tries to make managers budget not by extrapolation from the previous period, but from a zero base (to encourage "rethinking the company"). He also insists on "big numbers" only, to the annoyance of accountants fallaciously convinced that "a budget with only the big numbers actually requires more work than one with every little detail."

Most important, Semco compares the monthly numbers with expectations: that is, each executive makes "an educated guess about the revenues, expenses, and profits for his department at the end of each month." Comparing that guess with actuals "gives everyone a sense of how much each manager actually knows about his area."

That's yet another highly inventive simplification directed towards better outcomes. But there's a paradox. The stress on simplicity appears to conflict with Semco's diversification—very high for a company of this size.

Semler explains the multiplicity of product lines partly by the imperatives imposed by the seesaw behavior of the Brazilian economy; partly by a policy of lessening dependence on any one sector in the pursuit of long-term stability; and partly by the fact that nobody lays down laws on the subject, since "the company takes its own path: it can't be held to a general strategy." Semler is iconoclastic towards missions and credos and vision statements and top managers who claim that these are "what keeps us together."

He asked top managers in one audience (he's a frequent speaker worldwide) to step forward and explain in 1993 how their corporate visions of 1983 had worked out in practice: "it will embarrass you tremendously." Nobody was prepared to accept the challenge. He's equally ready to smash the idols of topical techniques, not because they are ineffective, but because of the "Fort Apache" mentality. If the Indians are attacking on quality, managers dash to that corner of the fort. Then they charge to the other side to tackle process reengineering; and so on. They may win the fights, but they're losing the battle.

In post-Ford manufacturing, however, one technique looks unassailable: manufacturing in cells. Thanks to that, Semco was able to concentrate three factories, each occupying around eight thousand square meters, into one of similar size—and "nothing important" was lost by the contraction. As he says, in real life companies have to manage decline and advance simultaneously and with equal effectiveness. The pursuit of growth, and nothing but growth, is unrealistic. "It's just enough to be in motion."

In 1993 Semco actually moved upwards by 17 percent, but Semler has no room for the "macho culture" that sets corporate achievement on a "big scoreboard." He asks, rhetorically, "What are we increasing?" and suggests that the general answer should be "the quality of life." That's obviously a deeply felt personal view. But when it comes to the specifics of Semco, its proprietor notes that "I can't talk for myself on any of these things."

Indeed, he uses the word "we" a great deal. Who are "we"? The answer is never the same. Semco's London lawyers were baffled to find themselves dealing with a changing cast, all equally well informed about the legal issue in hand. With "the baton passing round every six months," a weekly update "on everything" is essential for the counselors. The baton won't pass to Semler, though. In 1993 he hadn't hired anybody, fired anybody, or signed a check for eight years and was planning to reduce his involvement—for good reason.

"This myth-building thing goes on." People think "I must have the Midas touch, but it's not true. But when I'm there, I have undue influence. My opinions carry excess weight." Semler wants to "remove this burden from the company so that self-confidence grows." When people are "not interested in what I think," Semler will have achieved an ultimate ambition, that of creating a "self-powered organization." Otherwise it's "just personalistic."

The personalistic elements in the Semco saga obviously can't be imitated. But others sound highly imitable:

1. Constantly experiment with better ways.
2. Tap the youthful energies inside the organization.
3. Share the power of decision—and information.
4. Rely on trust, not authority; and minimize the rules.
5. Simplify everything—all the time.
6. Make profit-sharing the pivot of the firm.
7. Make managers openly responsible to the managed.
8. Concentrate strategy on the core activities—what only you can do.
9. Give priority at all times to effective outcomes—and forget anything that doesn't contribute to them.
10. Dynamize the budget process.
11. Treat the whole company, not just its symptoms.

So which of them should you definitely imitate? The question is misplaced. The right route is to use Ricardo Semler's thinking as a stimulus and foundation for building your own Semco. For one of his ideas is mandatory. It's the twelfth principle, and must be obeyed:

12. Don't merely imitate. Find your own best way and stick to that chosen path.

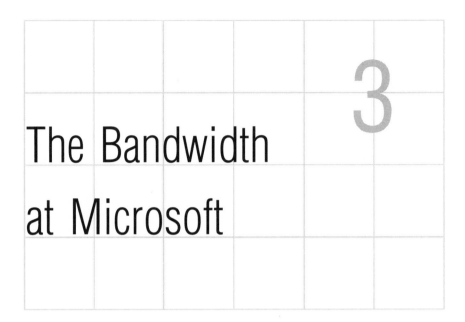

The Bandwidth
at Microsoft

3

Economic slowdowns seem to retard the development of new management notions as well. No doubt, times when orders are hard to come by and profits tough to earn are not the moments when managerial minds turn to radical experiments in running their companies. That's a luxury of boom conditions, when money rolls in so rapidly that CEOs easily believe that they walk on water.

Because of the overriding boom, any managerial experiment is likely to appear successful. The natural belief is that however a company like Microsoft, the software king, goes about its business, that way must be supremely right. You can hardly argue with a performance that, lifting sales and earnings by some 50 percent per annum to $3.8 billion and $953 million, respectively, elevated Microsoft's market value to more than that of General Motors. But it doesn't follow that there's an organizational cause and effect.

It doesn't follow, either, that none exists. The West Coast growth businesses (of which the Seattle-based Microsoft is a prime specimen) are managed as a bunch in a freer and easier style than the typical Western corporation. Their freedom and ease are visibly greater than that of high-tech businesses on the East Coast or in Europe. Yet the latter, too, have a distinctive and maybe suggestive style: for the sensible assumption is that high-tech companies, with their insatiable demands for originality and innovation, will lead the way in establishing new organizational norms.

Take Microsoft: what management style powered this middling company (sales of $3.8 billion are 10.7 percent of Sony's) to a market valuation of $24 billion? First, the style is intensely personal: founder Bill Gates owns a third of the company and dominates all aspects of its activity. Second, the driving force is recruitment: every week Microsoft hires seventy of the brightest people it can find (people with "bandwidth," in the company jargon) from campuses and competitors. Its numbers doubled in two years to June 1991, and retention is high, with labor turnover running at only 6 percent.

Third, ethos and capital gains are the retentive cement, rather than high incomes. Over two hundred Microsoft employees have become millionaires, thanks to stock options. The ethos is one of rah-rah consumer marketing, long hours (sixty- to eighty-hour weeks), youth (Gates has still to hit forty), heavy emphasis on "thinking," and extreme informality. *Business Week* quotes an executive on the minimal training: "The training we do is on-the-job. Throw them in, and good luck."

The magazine comments that in return "recruits aren't saddled with a lot of rules and bureaucracy." The main controls appear to be informal inquisitions, in which Gates sharply accentuates the negative to aim at positive results. The chief organizational cement is electronic mail, which Gates uses more intensively than anybody else ("flame mail" is Microsoft-speak for electronic mail that's "caustic or emotional"). The key organizational principle is small groups—never larger than two hundred, each divided into manageable sub-groups to maintain individuality and accountability.

With fifteen thousand employees, though, Microsoft must have several dozens of groups. Obviously, they only hold together because of the high growth (which always covers up hosts of errors) and the basic homogeneity of the business. On the bedrock of its operating system monopoly for IBM-compatible PCs, Microsoft sells only software: and only one product, Windows, is another blockbuster. Can any lessons be drawn by managers in slower-moving, multifarious trades?

Their corporate cultures were nurtured in the old mass markets created by heavily capital-intensive manufacture with long lead-times and slow replacement cycles. This norm was modified by the development of fast-moving consumer markets: but modification came to mean primarily grafting more rapidly responsive sales and marketing arms onto manufacturing functions of traditional kinds. Peter Drucker has pointed out that General Motors under Alfred P. Sloan sought to stabilize even the marketing mix.

GM was divided into three segments (Cadillac, Buick-Oldsmobile-Pontiac, and Chevrolet). The split mirrored the working-, middle-, upper-class polarization of American society. As the socioeconomic pattern fragmented, so the organization of GM became increasingly disoriented, with calamitous results for its manufacturing and marketing alike. Something similar happened to IBM, geared to a quasi-monopolistic, large-company market, and beached by its fragmentation in a multisupplier, multicustomer world.

Conventional management, too, has been left stranded. Its lead times, when it came to adopting new organizational ideas, were as painfully long as the elephantine gestation periods of new cars in Detroit. The astonishing truth is that nearly every revolutionary idea in post-war management, from quality circles to simultaneous engineering, dates back to Western innovators of the inter-war years. Today managements that move so slowly are left behind, not in decades, but in a few years: for the unluckiest, a few months.

Everybody needs originality and innovations as urgently as the high-tech newcomers. That's not because everybody has to keep up with an equally rapid pace of change. Rather, it's because the old ways in production and process are so out of sync with changing times that only radical new patterns can restore old glories. Microsoft is indisputably far better adapted to the new conditions. Its modes are thus of great potential significance to managers organizing and thinking for the new century.

But samples of one are always insufficient. Does a sample of two offer any better evidence? How does Microsoft's management compare with Sony's, for example? As noted, the Japanese group is enormously larger. Its product range is also vast, and the current overlap with Microsoft is ostensibly minute. There's much more to Sony's involvement in computers than meets the eye, however. For one example, it shared, as their manufacturer, in Apple's huge success with Powerbook laptops.

The Japanese group is also among the key world suppliers of hardware components. But Sony is coming even closer to Microsoft's territory through its profound involvement in consumer and media electronics, which are converging rapidly on computing. These unstoppable developments place Sony firmly in the game as Microsoft—and the ways of winning that game will surely set the pace for the new century.

Managing the
Creators

4

The clear fact that conventional approaches can't meet present needs places unprecedented pressures on management. The pressures aren't confined to those corporations that are actually in crisis. Their critical problems are shared by businesses far removed from present trouble. The ground is shifting beneath managers' feet as markets and methods change, and as the emphasis shifts from sustaining established positions to winning new growth by seizing organic opportunities.

The ability to grow organically, by grabbing one chance after another, is one evident similarity between Sony and Microsoft. They are similar, too, in the prevalence of the founding spirit right into the nineties. Not only was co-founder Akio Morita still chairman in 1993; but his partner, Masaru Ibuka, played a grandfather's role in technology in his and the century's eighties. It was the "retired" Ibuka who made the mental leap that created the Walkman— marrying a marketless pocket cassette-player, discovered in one part of Sony, to some lightweight headphones he had spotted in another.

That is an extreme example of a basic principle at Sony—

technological interchange, which in most companies gets only lip service. At Sony, interchange applies to (and indeed is achieved by) people themselves. Under a policy which *Fortune* describes as "self-promotion," anybody can look for a project anywhere in Sony without even telling his supervisor. The PalmTop notepad computer was thus created by a programmer in home computers. His venture sprang out of two years spent (at his own request) in technical support in Britain.

The Data Discman electronic book was invented by ten men whose boss kept both the research work and its costs (simply charged to other projects) secret from his own superior. Ethos is thus more important than discipline. Like Microsoft, Sony relies on intensive recruitment of young technical talents whose mental patterns fit the corporate environment. But in the Japanese context income rather than capital gain is the monetary incentive. One Western executive notes that many Sony project leaders "make significantly less money than some of their team members. I don't sense much friction, though."

Friction is not part of the ethos. All final design is in the hands of a centralized center, while "Corporate Research" coordinates the work in the twenty-three business groups. The idea is to avoid relying on accident—like Ibuka's Walkman wanderings. The truly original idea, though, is the annual internal trade show. Only Sony people can attend: the engineers on the stands show off and "sell" their research wares, not only to the top executives, but to their peers.

The system is far from perfect, naturally enough: the Palmtop and the Data Discman are incompatible as a result of following different development paths. Sony has been reorganizing to reduce overlaps as it becomes more and more involved in computers. There's a link with Microsoft here. The phenomenal success of Windows stems from the greater ease of use that it confers on PCs. Sony rightly believes that the latter and their programs remain user-hostile—a market opportunity which the Japanese company is determined to exploit.

Do these two companies, one West Coast, one Japanese, have a link in management as well? The emphasis on individuality and originality is very similar, obtained in both cases by like stress on youth, recruitment, technical challenge, and initiative. Communication and

results are far more important than lines of command and bureaucracy. Likewise, monetary reward is not used systematically to
achieve corporate ends, but flows irregularly from the achievement.

In both cases, personal identification is very strong—with the
organization's leadership, with the individual's work, and with clearly
defined missions. Ethos is vital; not "the way we do things around
here," but "the spirit in which we do them." For all the eccentricity
(especially visible at Microsoft with its in-house jargon and high-
jinks junkets), the management forces at work in these two companies are plainly going to affect every organization. New-century
management needs all these features:

1. Defined, homogeneous missions that are known to and shared
    by all employees
2. Vigorous recruitment policies aimed at providing a steady flow
    of the brightest and best talent available
3. Rapid deployment of talented people into mission tasks that
    will stretch and develop their abilities
4. Provision of electronic communications, preferably full net-
    working of PCs, that are freely available to all
5. Deliberate opening of loopholes and bypasses so that individu-
    als are not confined within the system
6. Loose methods of payment that relate reward to results rather
    than hierarchy
7. Personalizing management—encouraging ownership of busi-
    ness groups by long-term leaders, so that they become "Mr.
    Windows" or "Mr. Data Discman," or whatever
8. Keeping such groups to controllable size
9. Becoming "customer-led"—in the sense of concentrating ef-
    forts on improving and innovating products and services that
    will increase customer satisfaction
10. Finding informal ways of ensuring that everybody, including
    top management, knows what's going on—above all, on know-
    ing what's new

The blueprint is for a *thinking* company: one that is capable of
thinking not only about its products and their purposes, but about itself. If ideas are going to make the crucial difference in new-century

markets, new-century management must be built around the generation and realization of ideas. That demands a deep understanding of the intellectual process and the rejection of elements which stultify that process.

In the conventional company, there's a fundamental conflict between "command and control" and business creativity. Time after time, the innovator only wins by fighting his own company tooth and nail. David Benjamin, who worked as a researcher on the excellent book *Breakthroughs!*, has produced some notes based on his researches. The work could just as well have been called *"Against the Organization"*: but that isn't altogether management's fault.

Benjamin decided, after sitting through a hundred-plus interviews, that innovators are iconoclastic to a "fiendish" extent, have a threatening tendency to steal resources, and live up to the conclusion of John Jewkes in the 1950s: that "innovation is an individual enterprise—egocentric, fanatic, conspiratorial." What right-minded management would knowingly saddle itself with colleagues who fit that description—people who, in a phrase, cannot be managed?

But if they can't be managed, how can you speak of "the management of innovation"? Benjamin argues that you can't manage it. The idea that you can "is a myth that has persisted in American management circles more stubbornly than almost any other harebrained business theory." In his thesis, the "cool, controlled, orderly" process of good management is inimical to the hot, undisciplined, random business of innovation, which is why "innovations consistently occur despite management efforts, and very often out of their sight."

But the stubborn fact remains that innovations do occur, even in large companies. The examples assembled by authors P. Ranganath Nayak and John M. Ketteringham in *Breakthroughs!* include Sony's own Walkman, the VHS video cassette recorders produced by JVC (part of the mighty Matsushita), the Post-it pads of 3M, SmithKline Beecham's Tagamet anti-ulcer drug, the Toyota Production System and EMI's brain-scanner. A further and equally stubborn fact is that most of these innovations magically transformed the fortunes of their corporate parents. Some, like Tagamet, Walkman, and the brain-scanner, created whole new billion-dollar markets.

Benjamin is undoubtedly right to stress the disorderly conduct of the innovation process and its agents. If you study the Sony and

Microsoft systems, and no doubt those of other unusually innovative companies, you find that the inventiveness hinges on allowing an appropriate degree of disorder within a reasonably orderly framework. The process itself can't be "managed": if you don't know exactly where you're going—often the case with innovation—you can't draw a map for getting there. But management still has a most potent role.

In the first place, it must select or approve the areas to be explored. Second, it selects the innovators—or appoints their selector. Third, it must make the go/no go decisions, and finance the "gos" adequately and effectively. Fourth, when success has been achieved, it must turn the innovation into marketable reality. That's where the "cool, controlled, orderly" process of good management comes into its full and potentially glorious own, and where the innovation battle is finally won—or lost.

In any of these four departments, fateful choices must be made. ICI blew the prospect of discovering Tagamet by deciding that the innovator, Sir James Black, had no realistic chance of creating another breakthrough as important as his beta-blockers. SmithKline decided to concentrate on ulcers, let Black pick his team, bet its all on the discovery, put a worldwide sales organization together at top speed— and then lost leadership by losing concentration just when powerful competition appeared from Glaxo.

The latter company (as noted in Part Six, Chapter 4) managed its innovation superbly by riding on the back of Hoffman–La Roche to crack the U.S. market, charging a premium for Zantac (instead of undercutting the market leader), and intensifying its marketing expenditure after breaking through (instead of following the industry norm and spending less). That stresses the basic truth: innovation isn't only a matter of products. To manage innovation to superb effect, management must be innovatory itself.

The levels of talent in management, therefore, need to equal those in the labs. But what's talent? Like quality and innovation, the word suffers from multiple meanings. At a basic level, it refers, as in "graduate talent," or "talent pool," to educated recruits who will provide future leaders. At the opposite extreme, as in "managing talent," it usually implies the handling, always tricky, of research scientists, development engineers, creative personnel—anybody whose divine spark is more valuable than their daily grind.

The dictionary definition is more helpful: "any natural or special gift." Talent is the bedrock of genius: its possessors take their innate ability to excel others (at playing the piano, drawing lines, understanding figures, striking a golf ball) to the heights of a Schnabel, Picasso, Soros, or Nicklaus. The management use of "natural and special gifts" is what distinguishes a Microsoft or a Sony from the corpocracies. Since the latter can't afford to allow that distinction to continue, they must either cease being corpocratic or fail.

Already, in many companies, people are working in far more creative patterns, coming together in freestanding groups outside formal, fixed hierarchies; being rewarded for strategic and innovative contributions, not just for coming to work; using computerized networks to exchange data and ideas and create effective, achievable, consensus-driven plans. The Microsofts and the Sonys prove that creation is as susceptible to organized thought as any other work: the paradox being that managing creativity requires creative management.

Irreversible global changes put a premium on creative brainpower, on the acquisition and use of knowledge: and on its management. Success may well depend on the degree to which organizations become "talent-intensive," on their ability, first, to find people with the desirable attributes in which talent-hunting human resources directors rejoice ... "is extremely good at communication; has a 'winner's mentality'; has drive; is able to operate in an ambiguous environment; has not just intelligence, but social intelligence ... can take initiative and sensible risks."

The quotation comes from *Managing Talent,* by Philip Sadler (published by The Economist Books in England), who derived several such lists from his researches into the world of talent-spotting. There, two quite different problems arise. One is making the most of people's ability in an environment that encourages natural talents and, most important, develops others which are unnatural—as in the ever-popular courses on "finance for the non-financial manager." The second problem has already been mentioned: employing successfully the mavericks, the one-offs, the iconoclasts, and the creators.

These laws unto themselves can unleash uncovenanted success. But their employment does carry risks. Just like David Benjamin, but in his own inimitable way, Michael J. Kami warns his audiences about talented and creative people: they are "9D." That stands for "difficult, demanding, disagreeable, disobedient, dislikable, disorganized, disputing, disrespectful, discordant." He advises that you shouldn't expect anything original from an echo, but should "tolerate talented gorillas" and reward them in any way they want and you can afford.

There's obviously much truth in what Kami says: easygoing, undemanding, obedient, cooperative, and charming bundles of creative talent do exist—but don't count on finding them. Often great talents either can't be "managed," or aren't. In the transformation of SmithKline Beecham by Tagamet, James Black did and spent more or less as he pleased outside the control of his American paymasters. However, they totally shared his objective: to find a new wonder drug that would successfully treat stomach ulcers.

That's the crucial point. Talent is without value unless it delivers—and delivers something that's wanted. Superbly talented individuals who won't perform are worthless: average people who perform to the best of their ability are worth plenty. So are those who can lead them to that achievement. Another Sadler-quoted authority numbers no less than twenty-one "qualities or traits" associated with "the leadership of people engaged in creative activity." The list ends with "resistance to stress" and "sense of humor," after starting with "effective intelligence," defined as "ability to solve problems in a way which leads to practical action."

Solutions that don't lead to action, of course, have solved nothing. In Sony's native language, the word "creation" breaks down into two parts, meaning "first make." Creative management is about being first, not necessarily into the market or the technology, but into the latter's most successful manifestation. The crucial talent is the ability to perform—to do the right things in the right way at the right time. Helping people to rise to that achievement (above all, by the training and exercise on which even champions and maestros depend) outweighs selection every time.

The book *Strategy for Creation,* published by Nomura Research, contains the acronym FINDS for the "development of what is truly needed": it stands for "Fulfillment, Intelligence, Nourishment, Discovery and Sensibility." Without applying FINDS to creative management as a corporate priority, even inspired recruitment and good businesses (look only at IBM) will fail. Yet in all but four cases, fifty chief executives contacted by Sadler for his research referred the inquiry to human resources functions: a very bad sign.

CEOs who don't understand that their own chief job is "managing talent," in both the broad sense and narrow definitions, won't make the best use of any talents they employ, including their own. They have no role more important than that of encouraging, facilitating, and rewarding the generation of ideas. That means using all available means—very possibly including those delineated by Microsoft and Sony—of creating the thinking company. That is the reinvented life-form towards which all managements have to strive.

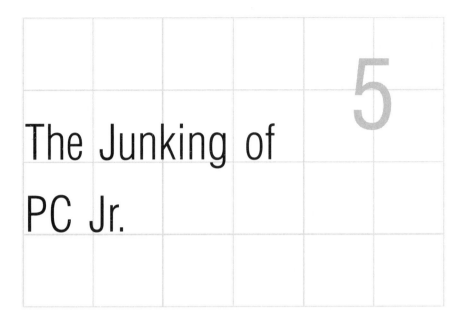

The Junking of
PC Jr.

If there's a turning point in the saga of IBM, a moment when the seeds of decay within every success visibly started to sprout, it was the launch of PC Jr.—or "Peanut." That's how it was christened by frustrated media men, hungry to know exactly what was afoot. The project didn't disappoint them: Jr. was designed to fling wide the casements to a magic world, taking IBM beyond every office, potentially into every home.

The ambitions for the original PC had been wildly understated, but those for Jr. were almost grandiloquent. It wasn't the only major project which Don Estridge and the Entry Level Systems Division at Boca Raton had on their suddenly golden plates. The Corporate Management Committee at Armonk, flushed with its Florida child's success, had approved no less than three ventures. These were a more powerful version of the existing PC, a still more advanced personal computer (using Intel's latest 286 chip), and Jr.

Add to that the burden of sustaining and exploiting the PC's breakthrough, and you have a workload heavy enough to crack most managements. If the new projects had been set wholly free, like the original PC, the task would have been easier. That had been possible within the totality of IBM, because of Estridge's direct line to the top. It wasn't possible within Boca Raton. The buck stopped at Estridge, and the project managers reported to him through IBM's conventional checkpoint system.

For Jr., the manager was engineer Bill Sydnes, a key member of the original PC team. Like that group, the Jr. people were up against an ultra-tight schedule. Sydnes was put in command in the spring of 1982 and charged with announcing his baby in July the next year. Like the Dirty Dozen of PC fame again, Sydnes started from a blank sheet of paper: no staff, no product plan, nothing. Unlike them, however, he faced some powerful constraints.

What was Jr.'s relationship to its PC parent? The more capable the machine, the more easily upgraded to work like the PC, the more it would "cannibalize" PC sales. Then, where would a "home" computer be sold? If it went through the specialist computer outlets that carried the PC, that would restrict sales. That was likely even if the dealers didn't (as they most certainly would) steer buyers towards the costlier and more profitable senior PCs.

On both these central issues, hindsight proves Sydnes right. Opposition to the very first PC itself was ultimately founded on fear that the microprocessor would cannibalize sales of larger computers. This fear was probably never articulated: nor, probably, was the riposte—that if IBM didn't cannibalize itself, others would. In the end, years down the line, IBM found itself following a Sydnes strategy; selling fully fledged PCs in electrical stores and discounters, and introducing fully compatible, low-priced machines at the bottom of its range.

That was in the nineties. In the early eighties, nobody in power at IBM would countenance such radical departures—and that included Estridge. He and his original team had been free to pursue their own strategy: their potentially vexed decision to market through non-IBM outlets had only been challenged too late, at the last moment. But the Jr. group's legs were cut from beneath them by diktat. The machine couldn't be sold through mass merchandisers: nor could Jr. be compatible with the PC. The strategy made no sense to Sydnes, who resigned before his baby went into production—to encounter a horrendous set of defects.

The ultimate tragedy is that PC Jr. was unnecessary. The vision of an IBM computer on every desk didn't require a low-priced entry model. There truly was a market for a computer that the executive could take home, but that was almost by definition a genuinely portable market—and one which IBM unaccountably missed, leaving it for Compaq and Toshiba. As for the computer in every home, that market didn't start to develop until 1993.

There was an untapped domestic demand—for a really cheap word-processor. The British entrepreneur Alan Sugar proved that with a spectacular success priced at £399. As the onetime overlord of electric typewriters, IBM might have spotted that gap. But its typewriters were *office* products, and the connection was never made. Anyway, Sugar's original market died as low-priced computers became available. Why buy a dedicated work-processor when the same money bought a genuine computer with a word-processing program—and much else besides?

The Jr. task was as formidable as the original PC project, yet it was entrusted to a notably less competent team with a much less enabling mandate. Moreover, the reliance on outside vendors had been taken too far. The entire machine was built by Teledyne at the conglomerate's Tennessee plant—and the vendor botched the job. The Teledyne disaster set the launch back by several months.

Bad projects, as every manager knows, feed on their badness. Murphy's Law ("whatever can go wrong, will") goes into overdrive. The more money that was thrown at Jr., the more it demanded. Workers in the disaster area now believe it would have been better to scrap the original project and start again. But too much publicity pressure had built up. IBM's standard safeguard (never announce a product until it's good and ready) had in effect been blown away.

Still, the machine came out. On November 1, 1983, Jr. and its specifications—impressive enough at the time—were unveiled before a generally enthusiastic press. But Murphy's Law couldn't be denied. The worst thing that could happen to Jr. (apart from not working at all) was to have a single feature so conspicuously bad that critics and customers alike would seize on the defect. And Jr. had such a feature: the infamous rubber keyboard.

That mishap was bad enough in itself. But Murphy and his law intervened yet again. Emergency action, of the kind that the original

PC team brought off in crisis, might have saved the situation, but indecision prevailed. Jr. was stuck with the hated keyboard as the first 1,700 models were rushed to the dealers. The rush was unnecessary, it turned out, because nobody would bother to demonstrate the product before Christmas. Why not? Because it wouldn't be available until the New Year.

In 1984, the Jr. duly missed its ridiculous target of 1.2 million units. At $699, the product was too expensive for the home market. A lower-priced mass-merchandised product compatible with the PC was a feasible runner: a costly, incompatible computer sold through the same outlets as the PC stood no chance. Undeterred, the marketers sought to reach virtually the entire universe of potential Jr. purchasers at least thirty times apiece in the last quarter of 1984.

Despite this ultimate in TV and media overkill, and a massive direct mail campaign, directed at 12 million households and eight million professionals and business people, sales slumped after Christmas. On March 19, 1985, the product was axed. The Boys from Boca Raton had laid a large and spectacularly addled egg. Behind the failure lay a far more serious lapse: the most successful group in the history of computing had staged a demonstration of team leadership at its worst—in an age which needs that leadership at its best.

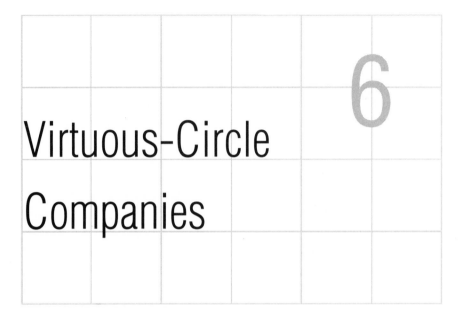

Virtuous-Circle Companies

6

Centralization has few friends in the nineties. What former U.S. Air Force general Bill Creech praises and enjoins on companies as "the power of decentralized team management" has the stage. Creech proved his point at Tactical Air Command, founding the air supremacy achieved in the Persian Gulf War on remarkable results previously won back in the States: like an 80 percent rise in productivity and a doubling of strike capability, achieved with no more money and no more men.

The Boys from Boca Raton proved Creech's point doubly. Their success was that of decentralized team management: every step towards centralizing their operation was a step backwards—and a stride towards failure. Would the retreat have been averted if Don Estridge had led the buildup team as successfully as the start-up? The question appears to invalidate the premise. If teamwork is what wins, why does the leader make so much difference?

That exposes the heart of a basic issue: the role of leadership in management, and the evident contradictions between the two nouns. They are not one and the same thing, as many managers wrongly believe. Some leaders (Churchill for one splendid example) were hardly MBA material, while many MBAs have leadership qualities in inverse ratio to their brainpower. What is this recognizable but elusive attribute, and is it truly essential in a team-based world?

The first answer is that the world of management is changing, which must mean changing requirements in leadership. Tomorrow's manager (and increasingly today's) will operate in flatter and looser structures, on a global stage, in conditions of great uncertainty, under unremitting competitive pressure. That applies at all levels and to every one of the groups or teams being led: and these groups, like it or not, are the focal points of the new leadership.

Teams, even small ones, need leaders as much as autocracies and corpocracies, but the brand is necessarily different. The new leadership demands the ability to handle complexity and multiplicity, and that includes humans as well as machines and markets. The old leadership was often called a lonely task. Walking alone is now ruled out by complexity, although too many still attempt the impossible. A common theme of recent boardroom putsches (Kodak, BP, IBM, American Express, et al.) is that the deposed boss led too prominently from the front, but with too little success.

In all these cases the deposed managers didn't obey the new messages, which come under new names like the Learning Organization, Organizational Architecture, the Virtual Corporation, and so forth. The truths are not all new, by any means: indeed, they revolve around a Holy Trinity so aged that Claus Møller, the founder of TMI, calls them "evergreens." The test of team leadership is its success on these three interrelated scores.

Productivity comes first because the difference between inputs and outputs determines the strength of the organization—any organization, public or private, small group or major company. Every operation should have a plan for reducing inputs as a proportion of outputs: which should be easier to achieve, naturally, if output is rising. But that perfect outcome of mounting productivity can't be managed (in either sense of "managed"—that is, run or achieved) unless *relationships* between people and groups of people are excellent.

Both productivity and relationships are intensely involved with *quality*. The underlying business system connects all three. Rising productivity is achieved by good working relationships that result in rising quality of products and service, which raises customer satisfaction and demand, and hence productivity, which improves relationships, which enhances quality, and so on.

You can see that virtuous circle in the introduction of the original PC. Don Estridge's unit had done everything right if you include in that definition (as you should) rapidly correcting each and every mistake as soon as it appeared. The style that had created the PC, the engine of this unprecedented growth, was charismatic, loose-limbed, improvisional, lean, concentrated. Some quotations from veterans of the Dirty Dozen days virtually define the conflict between the old management and the new:

"Don would give us an assignment," says Dan Wilkie, "or our assignments would require us to take some action and so we would just go and do it. We didn't have to wade through the layers of the corporation's bureaucracy. We knew what counted and we could see the results. . . . Before I went to work on the team, I helped deliver a printer. The printer was in development for seven years! I kept telling myself, 'It's coming . . . it's coming.' But the printer was hopelessly mired in design changes and bureaucracy."

These "layers and layers" arose "because every job at IBM is so vertical, so specialized. No individual, or any group, has a clear, visible identity—not even an opportunity to see . . . 'the whole pie' of a product, including the research and development, the marketing expenses, the direct cost, everything." At Boca Raton, seeing the whole pie for the first time, Wilkie "made more decisions in my first thirty days with that group than I made during my first fourteen years with IBM."

The old-style neglect of the "evergreens" is as striking as their interlocking success at the new-style Boca Raton. The interlocking is crucial to the system, which must be treated systematically. If you simply concentrate on one of the three areas of the system—productivity, quality, or relationships—the system will push back, with potentially disastrous results.

Push for higher productivity at all costs, and you damage quality. Concentrate on quality at all costs, and you damage productivity. Concentrate on relationships at all costs, and you damage the company's economic purpose. Negative actions have the same cumulative effect. Lay off thousands of workers to boost productivity, and you destroy relationships—and maybe quality as well. You may be applauded for the cost-cutting: but the cheers won't last.

Customers are not impressed by draconian actions taken by companies in deep financial trouble. The point is well made by Regis McKenna, the publicist who made Apple Computer famous and went on to become a Silicon Valley leader in marketing and venture capital. Part Six, Chapter 4, referred to his book *Relationship Marketing,* with its stress on the crucial importance of "dynamic positioning" and its three aspects: *product positioning, market positioning,* and *corporate positioning.*

It's the latter which leads him to point out that "when a company's profits slip, [its] position is tarnished. People are reluctant to buy from companies in financial trouble." McKenna draws product, market, and corporate positioning as three intersecting, interrelating circles, with the customer at the point where the circles intersect. That's precisely how Møller illustrates his threefold elements (productivity, relationships, and quality), with the customer replaced at the point of intersection by "employeeship."

The two diagrams should be superimposed on each other, for they cover most of the critical aspects of any organization. Team leadership is responsible in both cases for keeping the three rings revolving in a virtuous rather than a vicious circle. But the point of "employeeship," in Møller's view, is that responsible leaders can also rightly ask the employee, What about you? What's your responsibility? The exercise of good employeeship involves employees feeling responsible for the overall results of the organization—which they always are.

The essence of teamworking, by the same token, is that all members are responsible for the results of the team. The principle in no way absolves the leadership in cases like the junking of PC Jr. While a colossal disaster in its own right, that was only one calamity among many. The unit seemed to have done too many things wrong. Critical errors had been allowed to run riot. Why? The buck, at its simplest, stops at Don Estridge's door.

It's one of the oldest truisms in management. The leader who is supremely the right choice for launching a new enterprise is the wrong man to lead the business into maturity, especially if his words start parting company with his deeds. The following words of Estridge's, taken from a house magazine, have the resounding ring of the glory days: "Our management style is geared to eliminating overhead, unnecessary meetings and discussion; to operating with lower cost, fewer people and shorter development cycles."

Alas, even when Estridge wrote those words, far from operating with "lower cost, fewer people and shorter development cycles," his division was adding cost, people, and time in exponential increases: "Estridge was allowing the organization to grow far past the point of profitability," says Sydnes. "There was no earthly reason to have thousands of people working on the IBM Personal Computer. . . . My God! Look at Apple; they had more than half our revenues with about a third of the people we were carrying on our payroll."

A large contribution to the calamities came from the top management at Armonk, which wasn't inclined to let so successful an independent business unit stay independent. According to Wilkie: "The company came in and set up multiple levels of managers, multiple disciplines, new policies and procedures, and reviews upon reviews." Moreover, the problems caused by all this "protocol and discipline" multiplied because "Don was spending almost 80 percent of his time in Armonk, with just unbelievable traveling back and forth to report to all the people he now had to deal with."

Against that background, not surprisingly, the drive and sheer zing moved out of Boca Raton as the corpocrats moved in. For the residue of the Dirty Dozen and those who had joined them, it was a demotivating experience, well described by Chposky and Leonsis in *Blue Magic:* "They had been superb at what they did best, and now they had to ask to be able to do it. Instead, they were told to work on presentations, or status reports, or presentations that were like reports. Or reports on how presentations can be more like reports."

Productivity, quality, and relationships—Møller's evergreens—had thus all deteriorated profoundly in a very short time. One of the essential elements of independent group working is to cut back on "reporting to." Actually, managers can't manage even an old-fashioned operation effectively if 80 percent of their time is spent on the road: not with customers (which might well be valuable), but with explaining their actions to second-guessing superiors.

Today, fewer managers are trying the impossible. Circumstances—not least, the necessity for team leadership itself—are forcing managers to adopt the preaching of the gurus. As teamwork becomes a fact of corporate life, managers have to accept the need to change roles. They become facilitators rather than commanders, leading by encouragement and coaching, and "frequently" discussing with subordinates the way they do their jobs, and suggesting improvements.

That was the excellent practice, so they said, of three-quarters of senior managers of information technology staff surveyed by Ashridge Management Research Group. Less excellently, two-thirds of their staff reported otherwise: they had *never* discussed either issue with their bosses—let alone frequently. That survey was one of eighteen areas of management research presented by Ashridge in a fascinating day-long program entitled *2001: A Research Odyssey.*

Time and again, the researchers reported on yawning gaps between preaching and practice, on the failure of top-down initiatives on customer service, quality, and values to make any progress on any of the three counts. As one researcher noted, the top-down leaders talk about fundamental change, when they only mean *improvement.* The latter doesn't threaten their power, while the former involves its redistribution. No radical change, no real improvement. In contrast, the new leaders are concerned with potential, not power—with releasing and combining all the abilities and resources in the firm.

Group working is a potentially marvelous method for doing precisely that. But it forces many "leaders" up against a painful truth that they prefer to dodge: that their companies are not geared to accepting new ideas and initiatives from below the summit. If leadership isn't shared, it can't be exercised. That's the uncomfortable aspect of genuine group working. It faces managers with the need to change their ways. Often, they won't. That is bad leadership in the mid-nineties, and it spells disaster for 2001.

Merely look at what happened in Boca Raton. The initial profitability of the PC, which shot up as the numbers made and sold rocketed past the budgets, had been deeply eroded by the rise in overheads and the colossal, wasted expenditures on the lost cause of Jr. Yet in its brief heyday, Boca Raton had followed all the items in the following mandatory list (except for the third, for which its own technology had yet to pave the way). To achieve Bill Creech's "power of decentralized team management," you

1. Eliminate bureaucracy and hierarchy.
2. Devolve autonomy to autonomous teams.
3. Use networked PCs as the universal management tool.
4. Do all this for the sake of speed, quality, and customer satisfaction.
5. Train, develop—and learn.

The Boys from Boca Raton had unconsciously pioneered the kind of wisdom dispensed by David A. Nadler and Marc S. Gerstein in *Organizational Architecture: Designs for Changing Organizations.* They argue that an organization should be designed like a building. You decide on its purpose, consider what structural materials are available to solve the problem of achieving that purpose, create a style that marries the two, and employ collateral technology (like air-conditioning) to produce the final solution.

The metaphor is applied to a company in this way: today's *purpose* is to replace "bureaucratic control" with quality, speed, customer responsiveness, and the ability to learn; the new *structural materials* are the tools of information technology and telecommunications; these tools enable the new *style* that throws out "the traditional hierarchical organization" and substitutes "more decentralized companies where self-managed teams have end-to-end responsibility for satisfying customer requirements."

As for the *collateral technologies,* they still have to be invented: "new methods for selecting, training, evaluating and rewarding people consistent with the greater autonomy, responsibility and continuous change inherent in the new design." The pressures on organizational architecture are those of an increasingly demanding marketplace. Ignore the new management demands, and you won't be able to meet those of the customers.

The customer, as noted, is the hub of Regis McKenna's threefold circles of dynamic positioning (product, market, and corporate), all of which must revolve around the customer in the right direction—as the Møller circle of productivity, relationships, and quality must revolve around the employees and their contribution. Remember that if any one circle of the three goes wrong, it sets going a vicious circle of the whole.

It takes time and trouble to get turning, and more time and trouble to retain the forward momentum. But far more time and much worse trouble will be involved if the circles turn the wrong way—as shown by the junking of Jr. (and eventually of all that Boca Raton stood for). What you want may be called a virtual corporation. But its essence is the virtuous circle: a company composed of groupings, some temporary, others long-lasting, which practice "the power of decentralized team management," and whose virtues circle all their lives.

TEN

The True Quality:

How to Manage

Much Better

The Way to
Get It Right

1

Imagine that an unkind fate has put you in command of any or all of the following companies. Each faces tough problems, some terrible ones. But the difficulties are all quite typical of the pressures crowding in on century-end management. Tempting though it might be to run away from such situations, there's no place to hide. Here are the ten:

COMPANY A used to have a monopoly in its market, supplying office equipment. Your company's share has fallen to 17 percent in face of powerful competition, and is still falling. Your ratio of indirect costs to direct costs is double that of your toughest competitor; you use nine times as many suppliers; your rejects are ten times higher; product lead-times are twice as long; you have seven times as many defects per hundred products. What do you do?

COMPANY B has number one positions in nearly all markets, mainly for industrial products, but you are determined to stay on top—and you suspect that performance could be radically improved in the factory (where overheads are nearly three times direct labor costs) and in sales and service. What do you do?

COMPANY C is an engineering maintenance operation. After a history of strikes, constant friction, and fights over every pay deal, management has firmly asserted the right to manage: the shop floor is now under firm discipline. But the parent's profits are falling fast, and you are under pressure to cut costs. What do you do?

COMPANY D, a very large service business, has lost its monopoly. You face new regulations and regulators, new shareholders and new technology (a massive change). Also, by your own admission, you're providing some of the worst service in the Western world. What do you do?

COMPANY E runs a service business in the consumer field that has been growing rapidly, thanks to an excellent concept, backed up by heavy advertising on TV. But the feedback from customers is unsatisfactory, which is a threat to future expansion. What do you do?

COMPANY F is in high technology, but it has a difficult history of mergers, changing ownership, losses, product overlaps, and poor competitive performance in a business dominated by a single rival. Customers have a low opinion of your performance, and the market is changing radically from the tied customer relationship you have always enjoyed. What do you do?

COMPANY G is a service business that has turned itself around effectively from losses by cutting costs, raising prices, and curbing some of its services. But the customers are all unhappy. You think that you're providing 85 percent on one key dimension of performance. Your biggest customers say it's only 70 percent. What do you do?

COMPANY H will drop out of its high-tech business unless it can meet increasingly exacting demands from customers and partners. The company has only recently been created by merger. One of the pre-merger cultures is very used to meeting rigorous standards, the other less so. You have to achieve the same levels throughout—and raise them. What do you do?

COMPANY I has been given less than eighteen months to set up a major new entrant in a big, sales-driven financial services market. In that time, you must hire and train six hundred people, create an entire product line, install all the necessary systems, and convert sales agents from their traditional methods to your own philosophy and practices. What do you do?

COMPANY J is number twelve in a science-based components market where the top competition is vastly more powerful. The business is a recent cross-frontier merger, which has successfully improved its technical performance. But the business cycle turns down and catches you unprepared; you lose money and have to face major job cuts. What do you do?

The answers provided in all ten cases were exactly the same. The ten companies adopted the same philosophy, Total Quality Management, as the solution to their very different problems. Company A is Rank Xerox, which has won back market share from the Japanese while rising remarkably in customer satisfaction—from first in five markets on only nine parameters out of seventy-five (1989) to first on sixty of the counts (1992). The others all have similar tales to tell.

Honeywell (U.K.)—see Part Three, Chapter 3—cut the overhead element from 270 percent of direct labor costs to 100 percent while growing turnover and profits through severe recession. At BA Engineering (C), the *first-year* payoff was £38 million, with £50 million more targeted for year two. British Telecom (D) has surmounted enormous challenges of change and is heading towards a target of 90 percent reduction in service failures by 1995. Groupe Bull, still wrestling with a computer industry in turmoil, is another business (E) that's been remade in a rush, while achieving a marked rise (13 percent) in customer satisfaction.

Company F, Royal Mail, now delivers 93 percent of first-class letters by the next day, and ranks as the best postal service in Europe—where once it was the worst. The Italian aerospace group Alenia (G) has won the vital quality commendation of customer-partners like Boeing. The financial services start-up National Westminster Life has been spectacular: the launch of Company H was completed on time and on budget, and a business with a market value of over £1 billion has been created on total capital of £200 million.

The final company, SGS-THOMSON, has been raising productivity, crudely but meaningfully measured, by 15 percent annually for five years in the demanding global business of semiconductors. These European cases are emphatic evidence that Total Quality Management delivers. You can't seriously argue with results like those above. Yet in America, where the quality movement began years earlier than in Europe, disillusion is widely expressed. Why?

2

What
Management Quality
Means

The backlash against Total Quality Management was bound to come. No technique has ever spread so far so fast—or so wide. As the Ten Who Got It Right show, examples of Total Quality success range from great companies in high-tech industries like Xerox to start-ups in life insurance. Beyond these large firms, relatively small businesses in activities ranging from smokestacks to services have also Got It Right.

As usual, though, serious investigation of the benefits, if any, has lagged behind the adoption of the new marvel—and several of the probes, just as typically, have found performance lagging behind practice. "TQM Programs Can Be Counterproductive, Claims New Research," was the press release headline above an Economist Intelligence Unit report. The underlying research was done by Ashridge Management College: the study's leader commented that such "programs—company-wide, training-led, add-ons to existing jobs—are at best, ineffective. At worst, they inoculate the organization against real change."

Critical writers promptly seized on this critique as damning the usefulness of quality out of hand. Yet the title of the study is "Making Quality Work"—implying that it truly can be effective. This contradiction reflects confusion in the marketplace. Partly, that results from inflated claims and unrealistic explanations; partly, from fundamental misunderstanding of what Total Quality means; partly, from unsound implementation; partly, from regression. Often, all or some of these causes are present at the same time.

For instance, understanding Total Quality must embrace the knowledge that it's continuous—you never reach a pitch of such perfection that the quality drive can safely be halted. If you relax the effort, regression is inevitable; indeed, it occurs even if you *don't* relax. Both observations embody age-old management truths. The most vulnerable moment for any organization is the acme of its success. That's when the financial numbers, internal self-conceit, and outside reputation alike conspire to blind eyes to mistakes and mismanagement.

Without question, these sins are damaging the star company's performance right there and then, not to mention the failures that are jeopardizing the future. One area of error that's certain to exist is systemic degradation. In other words, systems backslide into inefficiency either through slackness or because conditions have changed and the systems haven't.

Federal Express is an example. This was the first service company to win America's Malcolm Baldrige prize for quality, that being the second most prestigious after the Deming Prizes in Japan. (The European Quality Award is only three years old.) The company's relatively poor financial performance was highlighted by the *Harvard Business Review* in another, earlier questioning of the effectiveness or otherwise of winning the Baldrige. (This critical survey was inconclusive, but grudging in tone.)

The lag in earnings growth and other measurements at Fedex implied that if its service quality was truly excellent, then its quality of management had to be inferior. That view was confirmed when the business gave a new meaning to the phrase "overnight dispatch" by abruptly firing all the people employed in its failed intra-

European services. That failure arose from poor strategy compounded by inept execution, which also explains the fate of a doubly famous company named Wallace Company.

This modest-sized Texas pipe-and-valve distributor first covered itself with glory by winning the Baldrige. Then, by failing financially, it became one of two famous "proofs" that TQM doesn't work. What actually happened? Starting very late, in early 1989, after being inspired at a quality conference, the Wallace family led the program summarized here from a report by *Business Week*. The company

1. Set up teams to analyze each department for improvements.
2. Standardized billing.
3. Identified seventy-two ways to improve delivery and invoicing.
4. Installed large numbers of computers.
5. Changed the way drivers loaded the trucks.
6. Made on-time delivery a key target—and achieved an improvement from 75 percent to 92 percent.

However, the controllable overheads went out of control, rising by $2 million. In a service business characterized by low margins, that was insupportable: convinced (wrongly) that superior customer service was the strategic lever, Wallace had bought its rise in market share (from 10.4 percent to 18 percent) at too high a cost. When management tried to recoup that cost by lifting prices, the move adversely affected sales at a time when an oil and gas slump was weakening the whole market.

The result: a $691,000 loss on sales of $88 million, unpaid creditors to the tune of $17 million, a banking crisis, the dismissal of a quarter of the workers, and entry into Chapter 11. You could argue that the quality operation was highly successful, but the patient died. The management technique was not governed by adequate business intelligence: the executives were selling the quality cause (a product from which they made no profit) all over the United States, while pipe and valve sales languished partly through this diversion of attention, which no hard-nosed businessman would have allowed for a second.

But would such a character have understood the necessity and value of a quality program in the first place? That's the point where managing and business meet, or should. The professional manager should be able to demonstrate, first, that "quality is free"—the title of Philip Crosby's famous book, and a principle roundly endorsed by eminent practitioners like Robert Galvin of Motorola. Ideally, the costs of quality programs should be absorbed (or better) by the savings from eliminating waste and rejects, with the marketing benefits flowing through as a large bonus.

To make savings permanent and continuous (which is one objective of true quality programs), the processes and behavior of the organization have to be changed from top to bottom, and back again. The emphasis on the top isn't the usual insistence on top-level "commitment." That commitment is essential. But the words must be accompanied by deeds. TQM is a practical methodology for continuously improving all business processes.

That has to include the processes which determine the future of the firm. At both Wallace and the other famous Baldrige-winning financial flop, Florida Light and Power, top management took fundamentally wrong decisions. However much every process in the business has been improved, the higher echelons can wipe out all the gains with one ill-advised "strategic" move. Some leaders have recognized this from the start, beginning with an exercise on the quality of the board and its working processes. Others have only included crucial areas, such as how they determine strategy, later in the day.

Sooner (preferably) or later, the top must improve itself, if top management genuinely want successful reform. The Ashridge-EIU study, though presented as an attack on TQM, actually argues for its adoption. Its authors warmly "acknowledge the benefits, in terms of competitive edge and profitability, that real quality improvement can bring." They recommend the following:

1. Leadership which makes quality the number one, non-negotiable priority
2. Empowering employees to experiment and make mistakes and find their own ways of improving quality
3. Building quality into the responsibilities of all managers
4. *Not* making quality the responsibility of a specific department

5. Providing training on a "just-in-time" basis, developing skills and knowledge as needed

A sixth point relates back to the hard-nosed businessman mentioned above. The whole quality effort should be dedicated to and judged by hard results. That's why there's so close a fit between TQM philosophy and what Ben Tregoe and T. Quinn Spitzer, respectively the chairman and the chief executive of the Kepner-Tregoe consultancy, call "the seven principles of cost management."

The definition of the latter sounds very much like one of Total Quality. It makes "adding value and containing costs" something "integral to everything an organization does, from setting strategy to training its people to putting the very best products and services in the hands of its customers." And, if you read "quality" for the italicized words *cost management* below, the seven principles make equal sense, as follows:

1. *Know your true cost.* Do you know the real cost in all aspects of your business, including products and services, markets and customers, suppliers, parts manufactured in-house, and inventoried items? Unless you have this information—and it's amazing how many organizations don't—you can't . . .
2. *Continuously reduce costs.* Assuming that the true costs are known, can—and do—your employees, as standard operating procedure, constantly identify opportunities for eliminating, reducing, or better managing low-value work? If people are to carry out that invaluable process, you must . . .
3. *Provide the tools to manage costs.* Are your employees being given the decision-making, team-building, problem-solving, and other thinking skills that are required to control costs, improve quality and productivity, and enhance performance? The powerfully educative nature of this training is what enables you to . . .
4. *Involve employees in decision-making.* Do you ask employees for their advice on potential *cost management* areas and thus forge commitment to *cost management* initiatives that "belong" to them? Do they understand, and have they helped to frame, the organization's objectives?
5. *Reduce complexity.* Do you constantly question why work is

done and determine if it is important? If so, do you constantly question how it can be done more efficiently? The "Rule of 50/5" is a close relative of Pareto's Law: it says that 50 percent of a company's activities produce less than 5 percent of its value added. Just as the Paretoist seeks out the 20 percent of customers who contribute 80 percent of sales, and adjusts his marketing plan accordingly, so the Fifty/Fiver relentlessly weeds out the non-contributing activities. The easiest way to improve an inessential activity is to abandon same: which, because it is inessential, can do no harm in either the long term or the short.

6. *Change the performance system.* Do your employees know that they are responsible for *cost management*? Do they have the skills to manage costs? Do they receive positive reinforcement for *cost management* activities? Do they get timely feedback on the results? While you don't reward people directly for managing costs down (because it's part of their normal work), you place every emphasis possible on encouraging and recognizing their achievements.

7. *Use your strategy.* This is the crunch item. In cost-cutting and quality alike, the actions taken must relate to the overall strategy of the company. A crucial aspect of true quality lies in developing an understood, agreed, effective, and appropriate strategy.

As Tregoe and Spitzer note, tough times create a temptation to rush into cutting costs without thinking carefully about the long-term future of the organization. Cost management *starts* with the long-term future. "The first question the true cost [quality] manager asks is: 'What does our strategy say about making the tough choices on products, markets and resources?' "

As the Wallace example shows, making improvements, continuous or otherwise, in the wrong area is a hopeless exercise. Doing the right thing right is the real game. Doing the wrong thing, rightly or wrongly, explains why only 36 percent of five hundred companies told Arthur D. Little that TQM was improving their competitive prowess. It also explains why consultants Rath & Strong found that only 26 percent of ninety-five companies rated an A or B on whether their TQM programs had increased market share, or customer satisfaction, and so forth.

These hard facts come from *Business Week.* But once again the thrust of the article isn't against quality; rather, it is strongly pro-quality. My own research into twenty organizations in Europe found example after example of brilliant, effective ideas that can't help but improve performance, provided they are applied within a context of commitment to the basic TQM philosophy:

1. Start with the customer: accurately measure current performance in serving customers—from *their* point of view—and establish the gap (generally vast) between their ideal wants and your actual work.
2. Embody those ideal wants, and plans for closing that gap, in a clear statement of policy that everybody in the organization can understand and use.
3. Expose top managers to the full disciplines of fact-based management and to the testing of their own performance, on all counts, against measurable objectives.
4. Then expose them to fellow employees at all levels to discover what obstacles prevent people from making their fullest possible contribution to meeting the policy objectives.
5. Remove the obstacles and improve the operations continuously through work by trained teams that both select and execute the improvement projects.
6. Avoid bureaucracy at all costs, but align budgeting, appraisal, and reward systems with the Total Quality objectives—and always celebrate success.
7. Never rest on your laurels. Go out and win some more prizes—every day, week, and year.

The laurels are richly green. Yet another study, by Ernst & Young and the American Quality Foundation, looked at 580 companies in North America, Germany, and Japan. This investigation concluded that huge gains in return on assets (ROA) and value added per employee (VAE) are indeed within reach—but won't be captured unless you relate the quality philosophy to your current levels of performance. That builds on the paradoxical fact that, the worse you are, the better the early gains will be.

A company with low return on assets (under 2 percent), which is adding very little value ($47,000 per employee), is forced to go back to basics. You look for the processes that add the most value, simplify them, and quicken responses to customers and the market. That should produce gains so large that they don't need to be measured (even though they should be). They'll catapult you into the next league (return on assets up to 6.9 percent, value added $73,999).

Now you meticulously document gains, and further refine practices to improve speed to market and delight the customers. All this time, you've been building up team abilities by training and by sending authority down the line. Now you're ready to benchmark: you measure everything you do against the best standards in the world (not necessarily in your own industry) and set out to match or beat them. McKinsey has calculated what this means in one area which occupies every company—buying in supplies.

The typical company spends 3.3 percent of purchase costs on the purchasing activity itself: the world-class company spends 0.8 percent. Typical supplier lead-times are 150 weeks, against a world-class 8 weeks. Late deliveries of 33 percent compare with 2 percent. And so on. Against that background, you can understand how one $115 million metallurgical company has won a forty-to-one return from its quality investments, which means $4 million a year, projected to reach $13 million by 1995. That's the reward for getting quality programs right. If they aren't right, they have nothing to do with quality.

The New Copy
of Xerox

3

Y̶ou're encountering savage competition from a new, foreign supplier who is undercutting your prices. You're especially concerned, because profits are urgently needed to finance major expansion to meet a forecast supply shortage. Moreover, you're confident that your technology is superior to this upstart rival's, and your materials cheaper. He must be selling below cost.

A researcher, dispatched to confirm the dumping, reports that the upstart's technology, far from lagging, is leagues ahead. He's almost 100 percent converted to the latest processes, compared to your 20 percent. Producing 20 percent more volume with 30 percent less people, the rival is 30 to 40 percent more efficient. He's paying no more for materials, thanks to advantageous long-term supply contracts. So the mystery of the lower prices isn't mysterious at all.

Moreover, investment strategy differs markedly. You prefer to modernize plants in stages, while the upstart redoes an entire factory from top to bottom. As for the anticipated surplus of demand, the researcher finds out that, with new competition opening all over the place, the market faces an overwhelming surplus. In this situation, your technological lag threatens disaster.

Obviously, you immediately cancel plans for expanding capacity and substitute a crash program to bring your technology level with, if not ahead of, the best in the business—don't you? Not in real life you didn't. The researcher, Ira Magaziner (now a close aide of President Clinton), had been hired by an American steel company. When it heard the above results from his trip to Japan, the employers turned ostrich. They argued that

1. Japanese steel wasn't top-quality, and never would be: the same went for the steel of developing countries.
2. The conventional wisdom in the industry agreed with that, and with every other view challenged by the research.
3. There were no significant trends towards using less steel (lighter sheet, substitution by plastics and aluminum).
4. Since the supply and demand developments unearthed by Magaziner were wrong, his foreseen glut couldn't and wouldn't happen.

The rest is history. The steel company, like its industry, sailed straight into disaster, from which recovery was impossible. Note the mental sequence:

1. The idée fixe, a preconception that can't be budged (like America's old "Red China Does Not Exist" Syndrome)
2. Appeal to false consensus ("Everybody says . . .")
3. Wishfully discounting contrary evidence ("You just don't understand this industry/company")
4. Unsupported denial of unpleasant conclusion (Lewis Carroll's Bellman Theory: "What I tell you three times is true")

No manager—no human being—is immune to the cycle of idée fixe, false consensus, wishful thinking, and unsupported denial. It's a defense mechanism. But what's under attack? The mechanism prevents users from having to change, abandoning present behavior, and moving to a new mode. Moves are inherently risky. You're moving from known ground. Even if the existing ground is slipping from under your feet, you may prefer present danger to future uncertainty.

In business, the defense mechanism is triggered by money. If your competitor appears to be stealing your markets by superior technology and more efficient plants, you have two choices: spend heavily and quickly in a catch-up operation, or bow to the inevitable. As Magaziner explains it in *The Silent War* (written with Mark Patinkin), the first course of action wasn't acceptable to the steel moguls: "In Pittsburgh, management did endless return-on-investment calculations, resisting any major modernizing. The payback, they explained, was too far away."

That irrelevant consideration also explains what happened when Magaziner, working for Volkswagen, sought to discover what Japanese car firms were planning in the United States and, contrariwise, what Detroit was planning in small cars. Talking to Detroit managers, the young consultant immediately hit the idée fixe: Red China, or rather Japan, didn't exist—the Japanese couldn't make good cars, because of inferior plant technology. Even if they discovered how, they couldn't make cars suitable for a U.S. market they could never understand.

As for small cars, enter the false consensus. These would never account for more than 10 percent of the American market, so major investment (note) wasn't justified. Magaziner easily turned up the contrary evidence. Even then, "Japanese car factories were actually more modern. . . . They'd moved to unitized body construction, for example, which the U.S. firms had dismissed." Detroit, however, was stuck in deep denial. The market trends spotted by the Japanese (higher gasoline prices, more two-car families because of working women) pointed clearly towards higher small-car demand. The signs were simply ignored.

Again, the need to report higher profits swamped reason. Revamping plants, new construction methods, and new small cars would have savaged the American bottom lines. Profits made at the cost of deferring essential expenditure, though, haven't been made at all. The account has to be settled in the end, with much greater cost and much lower chances of success—witness the later miserable experiences of Detroit.

Now imagine a similar situation. Compared to surging competition, you have an indirect cost to direct cost ratio double theirs; you use nine times as many suppliers; assembly line rejects are ten times higher; product lead-times twice as long; defects per one hundred products seven times as many. All these deficiencies mean that unit manufacturing cost equates with the Japanese *selling* price.

Do you imitate the steel companies, and keep your head in the sand? No: instead you launch a program to remake the company from top to bottom. Over nine years of continuous progress, positive figures are as striking as the old negatives. On the manufacturing side, defects per one hundred products are a tenth of what they were, as is the number of suppliers. There's been a thirteen-times improvement in the proportion of defective parts. These vastly improved figures underpin remarkable rises in the vital statistic of quality: customer satisfaction.

This is Company A from the first chapter in this section: Xerox Corporation. In the early 1980s, market share by volume had collapsed from onetime near-monopoly to around 10 percent. The numbers were shattering portents. The group was threatened by the same fate that had overtaken the consumer electronics and motorcycle industries. Japan looked as if it would rule the copier world as well. Since then, however, Xerox's headlong decline in market share has been replaced by a steady upward trend, and that reversal of the Japanese tide is an achievement in itself. But so is the way it was done.

Deploying the
Policy

4

Once upon a time, there was a highly popular nostrum called "management by objectives." It promised perfection. Top management decided on an overall target for the corporation, and each division produced its plan for helping to achieve that target. Each sub-unit in each division did likewise, and the cascade continued down to the individual managers. They all had their individual targets, agreed to with their superiors, and linked to their remuneration.

Attracted by the carrot, and driven by the stick (wielded by superiors who were defending their own interests, too), the individuals would all meet their targets. Inevitably, so would their units, and so would the divisions, and so would the entire business. MBO only had one defect: it didn't work. No matter how much care was taken in formulating the objectives, drawing up the plans, and involving all the managers, the corporate targets were invariably missed.

So the technique passed away as a fashionable management theory. More than the memory has lingered on, however. Many companies practice systems which have strong elements of MBO. But nobody now believes in, or promulgates, MBO as an entire management system. Or do they? The following definition sounds remarkably familiar:

". . . a fully integrated top-down, bottom-up management system through which the two or three critical breakthrough targets and means are identified and implemented with the full participation and alignment of all managers"—and even all staff.

This system cascades down, too: from "theme to objective, to target, to measures, to means." The definitions come from the Britain's PA Consulting and refer, not·to MBO, but PD: policy deployment. Derived from what's known in Japan as *hoshin kanri,* it's the ultimate in the process of Total Quality Management, and the most pervasive aspect of the journey on which Rank Xerox embarked to reverse the Japanese tide.

The Total Quality effort at Xerox began under the title Leadership Through Quality in 1983 and is not planned to end—ever. "Quality is not natural," says Rank Xerox chief executive Bernard Fournier. "If you stop pushing, in one year you would not recognize the company. You would lose a lot of strengths." Quality isn't a stand-alone function, either: totality demands being linked to business strategy, which at Xerox has changed significantly over the same period.

Xerox has evolved from copying to "The Document Company." Of its seven document processes, only one is copying. Eight product and service lines contributed to an $18.3 billion turnover in 1992. Worldwide, the group still lost over a billion dollars that year. However, investors have at least enjoyed a 14 percent compound return since 1982, and they must shudder at what the numbers would have been without the quality journey. It began with benchmarking of the same kind that Ira Magaziner conducted, and in the same country: Japan.

Xerox got interested in benchmarking after unearthing the distressing fact recorded in the previous chapter: that mid-market Japanese copiers were selling in the United States for less than its own production costs. Like the steel firms at the time of Magaziner's mission, Xerox immediately suspected dumping: but a team of line managers went to Japan and found truths similar to Magaziner's for themselves. "Facing up to these facts," says *Fortune,* "marked the beginning of Xerox's recovery." Note that *line managers* did the study; they wouldn't have believed anybody else.

That involvement of line managers is central to policy deployment. PD is designed to focus everybody's attention on the "business priorities"—at Xerox, customer satisfaction, market share, return on assets, and employee motivation. PD extends beyond management to every employee in Rank Xerox. Each has a personal "Blue Book" (so-called simply because the first edition had a blue cover). It sets out the company goals, records the objectives and strategy for meeting the four business priorities, and lays down the "vital few actions."

Each business unit, and each individual, has four or five vital actions supporting each of the priorities. As the set of specific aims and actions cascades down through all departments to the individual employees, they all know specifically what they are expected to achieve—and each has been involved in deciding his or her own part. Every individual Blue Book, from the CEO's downwards, has one section in common: the corporate aims. Fournier admits that the exercise "looks a little bit heavy," but says that in reality "it's not that heavy: people like to know what's expected."

That last point is definitely and importantly true. PD has clearly achieved a high level of awareness. Questioned about their knowledge of the priorities, 98 percent of the respondents were 100 percent correct. The approach differs decisively from MBO in several ways: in overall aims (with MBO concentrating on management control), objectives ("quality first" versus "cost first"), style ("flexibility" versus "political"), and focus. Getting results through tight target-setting is MBO. Getting them through improved processes is PD.

New-century management must come down heavily in favor of PD's emphasis on processes. But what the two approaches have in common is just as important as their differences. Both seek to bind together the purposes of the individual and the organization. By definition, this can't be done in a regimented manner, and it can't be dictated from the top. "In addition to being a top-down cascade," explains Fournier, "the closed loop also gives bottom-up."

Each group puts on a presentation that recounts what's stopping the achievement of targets. The quality questions then come into play (What's the problem? What are the root causes?) before the action plans are formed and followed up. In 1992 that follow-up achieved a more formal status. The idea behind "Business Excellence Certification" (BEC) is that each unit "self-assesses" its progress on action plans along a seven-stage scale, ranging from "nil-done" to "world-class."

Scoring 3, for instance, means "some work done, results not yet visible." Working out positions on this scale doesn't end at self-assessment. Then comes the certification visit when senior management examines the claims. "You say you're 4," might be asked on a particular count. "Show us the evidence." Does the unit, perhaps, think itself good in an area where actually the performance is accidental, with no foundations to sustain the improvement?

Certification intentionally relates to awards like the Baldrige and the European Quality Award (which Rank Xerox won in 1992). The EQA has nine criteria: entrants are assessed on leadership, policy and strategy, people management, use of resources, processes, customer satisfaction, people satisfaction, impact on society, and business results, with forty-two separate items. At Rank Xerox, the assessors found six which wanted a "big, big push to world-class standards." That "big, big push" promptly got under way.

Advances on general quality measures and on detailed yardsticks, though, are the outcome of TQM, not its essence. The essence is human. "Quality definitely drives you to go for more and more empowerment," says Fournier, "to diminish the number of layers and increase the span of control." In 1993, fifteen people reported to him as CEO: when he was general manager in France, the number was only seven or eight. Self-managed work groups, he points out, by definition lead to fewer managers, and these groups have been spreading throughout the operating companies.

Xerox has been at pains to regroup the center and to reduce the omnipresence of what was once "a huge monster" that used to duplicate the functions at the operating units. "A lot of central time was spent managing the center, not the company." After division into various groups, and clarifying roles to eliminate "confusion between support and direction," headquarters became very small: for example, only some 150 people work at Rank Xerox's international HQ.

The improvements generated by Xerox's nine years of effort are plain. So is the reason for their necessity. Professor Kasra Ferdows of Washington University has distinguished a pattern which shows that, with quality as the base, a hierarchy of capabilities begins to form:

1. Quality, which leads to . . .
2. Dependability, which leads to . . .
3. Speed, and finally to . . .
4. Cost-efficiency

You must keep investing in the base to obtain wider and wider benefits from the other strata of this pyramid. In other words, the contribution of quality to the bottom line isn't simply direct, but works its full wonders through its impact on other non-financial measures—reliable performance and rapid response. Those in turn come through to the bottom line. The issue is whether you need the full program of PD to reach that destination.

The PD process begins with a vision of where the company is heading over the next five years. Next, you select your business priorities—what PA Consulting describes as "breakthrough improvement themes." Those priorities set the scene for the deployment of objectives, from which plans are deployed in turn. Implementation follows, with its results reviewed every month, leading up to the annual review, when the whole process begins all over again.

The real issue isn't the rights or wrongs of PD. It's whether you can manage a business—any business—while omitting any of those stages. In one form or another, they happen in any organization. The choice is between haphazard and controlled occurrence. Put that way, there is no choice. The label on the package doesn't matter. The contents do. And so does another essential: the package must be transparent. Everybody must be able to see what's inside.

What's inside the vision is crucial. The words of Rank Xerox's guiding-light statement, for example, are unexceptionable: this "is a Quality company. Quality is the basic principle for Rank Xerox. Quality means providing our external and internal customers with innovative products and services that fully satisfy their requirements. Quality improvement is the job of every employee." So far, so good: except that you could substitute any other company's name. It's the specifics which generate the results.

The whole exercise is founded on metrics ("the right measures to judge performance") and practices ("the best practices to support world-class performance"). Best practice may well be found outside Xerox: "When you go to a company," reports Fournier, "and say you appear to be the best, tell us what to do, we find very open people." With operating companies across the world, though, Xerox has ample opportunity for useful comparison across its own frontiers.

When managers see where their peers are excelling, the "buy-in" to change becomes much easier. For example, in customer retention, Austria had the best practice, developed after looking at Belgium. "They stole from Belgium and, in the spirit of continuous improvement, developed a much better one." The special importance of retention arises from straight business economics: the sale of a machine is the foundation for a continuing stream of service income. "If the customer replaces our machine after two or three years, we lose a lot."

Progress on all such measures is targeted by Quality Improvement Teams, often cross-functional and often drawn from several sites. "Continuous improvement in customer satisfaction"—including that of internal customers for internal services—is the unchanging target. Before the quality journey began, Rank Xerox had a "market-oriented reputation, but we weren't market-oriented enough, not market-driven." Going for major improvement in customer satisfaction was made a priority in 1986, with bonus payments linked to measures of satisfaction.

Measured in various ways across five markets in fifteen countries, 75 parameters are involved: as reported in the first chapter in this section, in 1989 the customers rated Rank Xerox first on only 9 of these: the next year it was 32, the year after that 45, and then in 1992 the score hit 60 out of 75—which "still gives us some way to go," says Fournier dryly. That is part of the essence of continuous improvement: the gap never goes away. Yet only 3 percent of customers are now dissatisfied. You can't get much better than that.

To have 97 percent satisfied employees, however, is a much more formidable task: probably, nobody gets near it. Dissatisfactions expressed by Xerox employees are the same across Europe *and* in the United States: pay, communication, organizational change, career opportunities, and job security—meaning fear of job loss. Many criteria are used, and Quality Improvement Teams are appointed when areas for improvement are highlighted. There's one QIT for management behavior: Fournier takes on that one himself.

His own behavior isn't sacrosanct, either. Twice a year, the

CEO's own reports rate him on twenty-seven criteria. After debriefing discussions with his team members, possible solutions are proposed. That's a basic principle: nobody's perfect. There's no sin in falling short of perfection, or even falling short of the competition. The sin lies in doing nothing about the performance gap thrown up by benchmarking, which assumes that, whatever the chosen activity, somebody, somewhere is doing better.

The first step is to analyze and cost your processes (which usually generates immediate ideas for improvement). Then you study other people to compare their costs and processes to establish which costs are lowest and processes best. Above all, you change methods and continue until your data match, or better, the best: even then, you don't stop. The cycle of plan, do, check, act circles continuously—or will do, if nobody throws a monkey wrench into the works.

In a financially driven group like Xerox, profit pressures have sometimes had that effect, making it "very difficult to protect quality investments." Squeezed operating managements find cutbacks in quality an easy short-term expedient. Defending the long-term interests of the business against short-term economies "is a permanent conflict," says Fournier. "A few companies" in Xerox, "stopped the quality drive, and the indicators went down," a result that was predictable, and unacceptable.

Aiming at constantly rising indicators and permanent improvement requires strenuous effort, which can look discouraging. In the right company, though, the effort only encourages more effort. In the wrong company, forget it. But there's one vital point to remember. *All* genuine Total Quality processes succeed. That's because they operate on the fundamental principle of identifying and correcting the causes of less-than-perfect performance. That isn't TQM: it's TQ*o*M—Total Quality *of* Management.

TQ*o*M takes in everything: product, process, organization, leadership, and commitment (what former U.S. Air Force general Bill Creech calls the Five Pillars of TQM). All five must be mobilized. More, they must interconnect in a way that permeates the whole out fit and influences all its members. That isn't achieved by exhortation, but by action. If that action cascades down the organization, binding together all levels, the name of the process doesn't matter. The result will be continuous reinvention.

The
Non-Managing
Managers

Like the ten companies mentioned in the first chapter in this section, the following four cases all have something in common. This time the answer isn't Total Quality Management—but this is also powerful medicine:

1. A plant in California became the most improved in Clorox's household products division after a woman manager asked the one hundred workers to reorganize the operations. Her role was solely to ask a few questions as "a team of hourly workers established training programs, set work rules for absenteeism, and reorganized the once traditional factory into five customer-focused business units."

2. A disposable diaper company has given five managing directors equal power. Each has a functional role, but they share responsibility for major decisions—which always depend on consensus. (I know a venture capital firm which likewise insists on unanim-

ity before making any investment.) Sales in 1992 grew by 24 percent.

3. When S. C. Johnson Wax moved towards self-managed teams, the human resources manager took a small staff down to the factory floor to teach management techniques like statistical analysis and "pay for skills." The time taken in switching a line from liquid floor wax to stain remover came down from three days to thirteen minutes—thanks to a worker team. The Racine plant overall moved to 37 middle managers instead of 140, and productivity rose 30 percent compared to eight years old.

4. The U.S. outpost of France's Thomson electronics giant has "a successful high-end line of TVs," called Pro-Scan. Each member of a cross-functional team (from design, marketing, engineering, and manufacturing) took turns as team leader, while continuing to perform in their normal jobs: "all the team members subsequently moved on to bigger and better things. Says [one], 'It made us all better generalists.' "

Such anecdotes should always be taken with a grain of salt, in the sense that somebody else's experience is never as valuable as your own. But the pattern of this new approach to management is clear enough. The task is to make people offers they can't refuse, because they want to accept; and where that acceptance will markedly improve the behavior of individuals and groups. That can't be done in isolation from the business realities. Indeed, such isolation will negate the improvements.

The four cases all appear in a *Fortune* article ("The New Non-Manager Managers") that starts thus: "Call them sponsors, facilitators—anything but the M word." What's happening is nothing less than reinvention of the management process. Managers are ceasing to function as part of an order-and-obey chain, and becoming instead links in a process that binds everybody together, from top to bottom of the company.

The magazine's distinction between the old and new manager notes that the latter "invites others to join in decision-making," while the former "makes most decision alone." The one hoards information, which the other shares. The passé manager is bound up (often almost literally) with the chains of command. The new style non-manager "deals with anyone necessary to get the job done." That means colleagues, people in other departments, and people in traditionally lower spheres: like the "workers."

As work gets more intelligent, so the distinction between the worker and the manager (who presumably is also a worker) becomes even harder to sustain. Workers have long been known as untapped sources of valuable knowledge—like the Milliken textile man whose new boss mentioned a costly, long-standing technical problem. The veteran suggested a solution, which worked out fine. When had the brainwave occurred? Long years before.

Tapping an operative's skill and experience makes indisputable sense, but "non-managers' go further. Like managers at BA Engineering, whose astonishing cost savings were mentioned earlier in Part Ten, they ask operatives what help they need to perform better. This isn't namby-pamby stuff: the targets for improvement are (and must be) pitched high and taken dead seriously. But the changed approach changes attitudes and takes the first step towards long-term and lasting betterment.

This isn't Utopia: rather, it's the hardheaded reality of some hard-nosed companies. The new concept can be approached from a different angle. Many companies are now proliferating team projects. Those can't be managed by order-and-obey methods: yet somebody has to keep the projects on track and on target. The management contribution is vital, but "facilitator" is the correct description of a role which is by definition temporary.

The "manager" job, in this and other ways, is becoming less stationary and more flexible, which is just as well in volatile times. But what if your company (like most companies) is light-years away from this new culture, and persists in the set organizational ways that can be summarized as "large-company disease"? That's what Honda's president has identified in his own business. His remedy is one that (alas) must also be used with managers who can't adjust to non-managing in a new-style company: "For those who are inflexible and refuse to do what they have to do, the only option is to fire them."

But what if the company as a whole is inflexible, and refuses to do what has to be done? In that case, the dread disease has a strong hold. The individual manager can try to fire it in the sense of ignition. If that doesn't work, the only option is to fire the company as an employer. Non-managers won't stay where they can't non-manage. But more and more, that's the way the world is being run—and soon there won't be any option. Non-manage, or else.

Reinventing the Manager

6

Everybody knows about the manager of the future. Every guru has been painting much the same portrait for years. Whether the path to the vision leads through Total Quality, or business process reengineering, or modern manufacturing, or the search for competitive advantage, or leadership, or anything else, the final picture remains the same: an unanswerable, undeniable formula for twenty-first-century success.

Manager 2000 will practice cooperation and collaboration with everybody, inside and outside the firm, from colleagues and subordinates to customers and suppliers. He/she will be a tolerant teamworker, tolerant of different and new ideas, forgiving of errors made in the cause of progress, putting the objects of the team above the ambitions of the person. The environment will encourage these behaviors by devolution of power and delegation of duties—right down to the empowered, self-managing worker near the top of the inverted pyramid.

The inversion of the traditional hierarchy places the top management at the base, and the customer at the summit. Thus, the whole management process will be geared to the non-stop search for competitive advantage, which in turn is dedicated to providing the customer (who always comes first) with the best in quality and service. That's the vision. It has a major drawback. It's everybody's ideal, and eminently practicable. But, as I wrote in *The Super Chiefs,* hardly anybody is doing it—yet.

My argument is that, as the next decade develops, managements will either adopt their own versions of this mode, or their organizations will drown in the competitive tide. There's a powerful analogy. In 1990 I published a book called *Culture Shock,* which pointed out that developments in information technology, especially those revolving around the networked personal computer, were going to change management processes radically.

Like the tools and techniques of the management reinvention described above, this IT revolution wasn't state-of-the-art: it was already off-the-shelf. I soon found that the reactionaries far outnumbered the revolutionaries. That may still be true: all the same, the networks are proliferating at an unstoppable pace. By early next century only the graybeards will have desks free from keyboards; briefcases lacking laptops, notebooks, or palmtops; and files littered with non-electronic communications. Much better information will be available much faster, and shared much more widely.

IT is the enabling mechanism of the management ideal. But plainly the doomed resistance, both to the computer and to the new management modes, has deep roots. Most managers have not yet come to terms with fundamental change in their worlds as the horizontal principle displaces the vertical, right across the board. The outcomes of business processes are becoming all-important, while procedures and rituals are receding into the past. Innovation, like quality, has moved from the realms of lip service into those of necessity.

That must have profound effects on the allocation of the power and the glory. Those have long been driving forces in management, as in politics. I once wrote that power, like hot air (and often accompanied by it), rises to the top. The general attitude of the powerful is to approve heartily: but that's lately been tempered by much talk of "empowerment" of those lower down. That only perpetuates the fallacy. As noted earlier in this book, empowered people aren't being "given" power that doesn't belong to them; they're simply having less taken away.

Every piece of research confirms that what is more properly called "enablement" produces much better results for the individual and the firm. The issue isn't giving people the ability to manage or work more effectively: it's about ceasing to thwart them. But management reinvention has to start at the top. The roles of the chairman, the chief executive (who shouldn't be one and the same by 2000), the board, the executive management—all these have to change before any other lasting changes are possible. And it's beginning to happen.

Previous chapters in Part Ten have described many ways in which management is being reinvented. For example, I related what's been happening at Rank Xerox. Managing director Bernard Fournier, who is no shrinking violet, submits to twice-yearly feedback from his own fifteen direct reports. The same goes for them. Like everybody else in the company, I noted, each of these top managers has a "Blue Book" which sets out the company goals, objectives, and strategy, and also lays down their "vital few actions."

Everybody knows specifically what's expected of them, their departments, and the whole company, and everybody is involved in deciding what they have to do. Whether you call this "policy deployment" or not, what's afoot is simply a different method of managing—mandated not by whim, but by the exigencies of competition. That's also why the non-executive chairman of Compaq, Ben Rosen, went behind the founding (and now ousted) CEO's back, aided and abetted by two juniors. He had to prove that a low-priced line of computers, vital to beat the clones, could be produced faster.

Competitive pressures also explain why youthfully led project teams in well-run car companies now have total responsibility for new models, from start to finish—and why even towering chief executive egos can't override them. Reinvented managers, at any level, are similarly concerned with unleashing potential all around them and all the way down. Leaders who don't hear the messages from below, which should come all the way up, won't be listened to themselves. And that will be fatal to their only real authority, which is their flexible ability to enable organizational success.

Old-style, fixed authority is a framework for establishing and keeping the rules. That framework must crumble in an age when progress depends on breaking the rules—if that's the way to optimize the outcomes (as it usually is). The top-up principle is demonstrated in Total Quality Management and similar approaches. The wisest and best TQM programs start, as noted, with analyzing and improving the work of the board, not with the common first step: encouraging front-line staff to smile at the customers.

Moreover, quality initiatives, customer service programs, and any other efforts at improvement (which are mandatory) will fail unless they are comprehensive. Time and again, as I've observed, marvelous gains in productivity or customer satisfaction are reported in parts of companies whose overall results bear no relation to these splendid achievements: the star players, so to speak, are locked into a team whose tactics and strategy drain away their skills.

Of course, the Augean Stables Syndrome is universal: no company is ever perfect in every respect. But unless the organization is seen as a system, in which every part relates to every other part, managers won't be able to manage effectively in the new century. One response to the syndrome is to cut down on the system's components, to farm out as much "non-core" activity as possible. This does produce simpler internal systems, and is, anyway, a trend enforced in many industries by the developing technology of both product and process.

The business system as a whole, of course, is unchanged in purpose by the subcontracting. But managers will be spending a lot more time working intimately with colleagues who are employees of other companies—or maybe not employees at all. In an era dominated by outcomes, those who can achieve results will be hired for that ability, not for their willingness to occupy the same desk in the same building every day. The consultancy mode and the manager mode are getting closer all the time and will eventually become interchangeable.

These developments should mean an end to one of the least attractive, least sensible management features of the 1990s: the major "restructurings" as crisis-torn corporations "reinvented" themselves. Often, the last state is worse than the first. The restructured business, shorn of key capacities and morale by the cost-cutting, goes on losing jobs without repairing the lost profits and stagnant growth that precipitated the crisis.

A kind of corporate *kaizen*—continuous management reinvention—is the only answer, and is evolving under various names. As this book has emphasized, they all mean broadly the same thing. In its fullest sense, "business process reengineering" means looking at customer requirements with totally fresh eyes, and reshaping the entire corporation, right back down the supply chain, in order to meet the redefined customer need. The "virtual corporation" lives by the same credo, seeking to meet those needs in the shortest possible time by continual adaptation.

As a virtual reengineer, the manager can't expect his/her own job to be static: rather, the business process will determine what's expected at any given time. Since horizontal business processes are all multifunctional and multidisciplinary, the manager is being led in similar directions. Cross-functional, synergistic, and interdepartmental working is unavoidable now: so are task-specific teams. That's all to the good, because the reduction of hierarchical layers (itself a result of the information technology revolution and improvement in management processes) is cutting the number of possible promotions.

Managers will have to advance in prestige and pay by moving from one successful assignment to the next, not by exchanging one title for another. This kind of career progression will be a great deal more enjoyable than playing corporate politics. The idea that work should be enjoyed (at all levels in the organization) is inseparable from psychological theories about people's behavior at work. Though old-established, these ideas are now coming into their own. They run like a bloodstream through all the developments discussed in this book.

Theory Y, with its basic belief that work is as natural as play, will dominate new-century management as organizations seek to tap people's own motivation by genuine involvement—by liberating their energies and rewarding their initiatives. These sound like "soft" values. The latter, like the idea of shared corporate values itself, are far more commonly aired these days than the "hard" disciplines. Management badly needs both, for the "hard" work of TQM or reengineering is the fastest route to "soft" improvements—and to excellent results.

At companies in technological or market-driven transition (which takes in nearly everybody), values do, however, provide a steady guide through upheaval. Here's a characteristic set from telecommunications: "[1.] We put our customer first [2.] We are professional [3.] We respect each other. [4.] We work as one team. [5.] We are committed to continuous improvement."

That comes from British Telecom. At AT&T, its increasingly close rival, the values reported in Part Four are not much different:

"respect for individuals, dedication to helping customers, adhering to the highest standards of integrity, innovation and teamwork." Managers in all businesses will have to come to terms with such value statements, and with "living the vision" by demonstrably acting in accordance with the fine phrases. But at both BT and AT&T, for example, that in no way lessens the demand for hard performance.

Nor can that demand dwindle anywhere else. On the contrary, new understandings of performance measures, financial and non-financial, are toughening the targets. Traditional bottom-line measures simply tell too little about past performance—and nothing whatever about the future. Many managers already have their bonus payments linked to a shopping basket of factors, which include items like customer satisfaction.

Without question, some of these baskets will include appraisal from below as well as above. That's perfectly logical. Ricardo Semler, the maverick boss of that small but revolutionary Brazilian engineering firm described earlier, has it right. His Semco managers who are rated below 70 percent are in danger of dismissal, not because their subordinates dislike them, but because they are losing the authority to manage. So they can't get things done. They can't achieve the necessary outcomes.

They can't, either, fulfill the new role foreseen by Jack Welch, the much-admired CEO at General Electric. Those words of his reverberate: "We've got to take out the boss element," because the twenty-first-century commercial wars are going to be won "on our ideas, not by whips and chains." The words are truly echoed by that Compaq worker who told his management that "you don't know what we can do." The task is to encourage effective, thinking self-management in people who mostly want precisely that.

It's no dream. Honeywell (U.K.) is only one of several companies where self-managed manufacturing cells have taken full responsibility for product lines under a completely changed style of supervision. This company is an affiliate of an American multinational: its initiatives are its own. Its best managers, though, are winning top responsibilities in the United States. Europeans or managers with high-level European experience now occupy the top positions in a considerable assortment of U.S. companies, from General Motors to Compaq, from Apple to Salomon.

Global markets mean global managers. Already, management teams in Europe, including American affiliates, are likely to include several nationalities, people to whom the boundaries between nations mean no more than those between departments. The boundaries between firms will also have much less meaning, not only because of the change in supplier relationships from adversary to ally, but because of the fast-growing number of other strategic alliances.

In an age when no company is an island, no manager can be insular. The key to the more open organization must be the more open manager—open to new ideas and markets, open to others, and open to instruction: because new processes demand new knowledge and know-how. The portrait of the reinvented manager is thus clear and complete. What's more obscure is how companies and individual managers close the gap familiar to strategists: between where they are now and where they want to and have to be.

An excellent start towards reinventing management is to involve all managers in contributing towards forming the strategies they will have to implement: not least because that forces companies to develop and communicate sound strategies in the first place. Many don't, which is one measure of the great distance management in general has still to travel. But you can feel the pulse of the forward movement in both strategy and tactics—and that beat is very powerful.

Those who resist the forward momentum will be swept aside, or overrun, along with their organizations. That's a doubly sad outcome, because the changes under way bring a new vibrancy to the age-old task of mobilizing collective human powers. That task has never offered more viable alternatives, more excitement, or more potential for brilliant success—for the organization and, above all, for the individual, liberated, invigorated, reinvented manager.

Bibliography

CHPOSKY, JAMES, AND LEONSIS, TED. *Blue Magic.* Books on Demand (University Microfilms).

A wonderful piece of reporting into the most significant episode—for both the computer industry and management practice—of the information technology revolution. A revelation in every sense.

CREECH, BILL. *The Five Pillars of TQM: How to Make Total Quality Management Work for You.* Truman Talley Books/Dutton, 1994.

The man who turned Tactical Air Command into a management success story doesn't write just about TQM: he expounds a comprehensive philosophy of the practical management that will achieve true excellence.

DE BONO, EDWARD. *Parallel Thinking: From Socratic Thinking to de Bono Thinking.* Penguin, 1994.

The inventor of lateral thinking has continued to develop new concepts to guide managers in using their most valuable tool—the human brain. In a discontinuous age, what he describes as parallel thinking is indispensable.

DAVIDOW, WILLIAM H., AND MALONE, MICHAEL S. *The Virtual Corporation: Structuring and Revitalizing the Corporation for the 21st Century.* HarperCollins, 1992.

Without question, "virtuality," as defined in this penetrating book, is going to form a major part of management life in the new century—and nobody will be immune.

DELAMARTER, RICHARD THOMAS. *Big Blue.* Dodd Mead, 1986.

A trust-buster's deeply frustrated account of the antitrust investigations into IBM that came to nothing when the Reagan Administration decided not to proceed with the case.

DRUCKER, PETER F. *The New Realities.* New York: HarperCollins, 1989. *Managing for the Future.* New York, Truman Talley Books/ Dutton, 1992. *Post-Capitalist Society.* HarperCollins, 1993.

The latest work by the master of management thought and writing builds on the two earlier works to create deeper understanding of the present and, through that, invaluable insights into the future.

GERSHMAN, MICHAEL. *Getting It Right the Second Time.* Addison-Wesley, 1990.

The subtitle tells the story: "how American ingenuity transformed forty-nine marketing failures into some of our most successful products." The lessons are many and rich.

GOOLD, MICHAEL, CAMPBELL, ANDREW, AND ALEXANDER, MARCUS. *Corporate-Level Strategy: Creating Value in the Multi-Business Company.* Wiley, 1994.

HAMMER, MICHAEL, AND CHAMPY, JAMES. *Reengineering the Corporation: A Manifesto for Business Revolution.* HarperCollins, 1993.

The authors have been the leaders in promoting business process engineering and in forcing managements to face up to its necessity—and to the reasons why too many reengineering efforts fail.

KANTER, ROSABETH MOSS. *When Giants Learn to Dance: Mastering the Challenges of Strategy, Management and Careers in the 1990's.* Simon & Schuster, 1989.

Wide-ranging, deeply humane, and highly informed, this book shows just why its author is the most popular exponent of the new management in all its aspects, from empowerment to strategic alliances.

MAGAZINER, IRA, AND PATINKIN, MARK. *The Silent War: Inside the Global Business Battles Shaping America's Future.* Vintage, 1990.

A well-researched and excellently argued description of how United States industry failed to meet the challenge from the East and of what was needed—and needs—to be done to achieve competitive success.

McKenna, Regis. *Relationship Marketing: Own the Market Through Strategic Customer Relationships.* Addison-Wesley, 1991.
One of Silicon Valley's key figures, as public relations guru, marketing leader and venture capitalists, expounds the modern theory of marketing built around customer satisfaction.

Nadler, David A., and Gerstein, Marc S. *Organizational Architecture: Designs for Changing Organizations.* Jossey-Bass, 1992.
The authors' metaphor of a building and its architecture, applied to corporations, offers a stimulating insight into the process and necessities of corporate change.

Ohmae, Kenichi. *The Borderless World: Power and Strategy in the Interlinked Economy.* HarperBusiness, 1991.
McKinsey's Tokyo head ranges far afield into the future of the interlinked world economy, but offers sharp insights into the business necessities.

Palfreman, Jon, and Swale, Doron. *The Dream Machine.* Parkwest-BBC Books, 1991.
A popular but enlightening account of the birth and growth of the computer and of the industry's transformation by the small personal computer and the even smaller microprocessor at its heart.

Pinchot, Gifford, III. *Intrapreneuring.* Harper & Row, 1985.
An entertaining journey that penetrates the corporate minefield which, alas, enterprising company innovators must negotiate in the effort ot turn their own decisions into action and get others to make any decisions at all.

Sekiya, Tetsuo. *Honda Motor: The Men, the Management, the Machines.* Kodonsha, 1982.
The story of Soichiro Honda, one of the most engaging Japanese tycoons, who came the hard way to leadership in motor-bike and auto technology—and also to enlightened management practice.

Semler, Ricardo. *Maverick! The Success Story Behind the World's Most Unusual Workplace.* Warner Books, 1993.

The author's small Brazilian engineering company has become a laboratory for some of the most fascinating experiments in management ever carried out—and carried out with great success.

SENGE, PETER M. *The Fifth Discipline.* Doubleday, 1990.
"However hard you push, the system pushes back harder" is only one of the insights which have compelled managers to think aloud the business system as a whole and the company as a learning organization.

SMITH, DOUGLAS K., AND ALEXANDER, ROBERT C. *Fumbling the Future: How Xerox Invented, Then Ignored, the First Personal Computer.* Morrow, 1988.
A case study of almost unexampled brilliance into the strange way in which a great R&D achievement became a total write-off for its owners.

WATSON, THOMAS, JR. *Father, Son, and Co.* Bantam, 1990.
One of the best business biographies ever written, this tells with great candor the inside story of the glory years of what was America's flagship corporation for two post-war decades.

Acknowledgments

This book could not have been contemplated, let alone completed, but for my good fortune in knowing so many of the thinkers who have charted, directed, and inspired the course of the real revolution that is overtaking the theory and practice of management. First and foremost (as all the other writers and speakers would agree) is Peter Drucker. Thanks to Management Center Europe, I have been privileged to chair seminars at which Peter has expounded his latest, luminous thinking. They have added profoundly to the years of education which I have derived from his friendship and his remarkable writings.

The Drucker seminars also introduced me to C. K. Prahalad of the University of Michigan, Peter Bonfield (chief executive of ICL), and the inimitable Mike Kami, among other brilliant minds. I owe each of them a great deal for their penetrating insights. I am also indebted to MCE and to the admirable Jenny Webb and Karen O'Donnell for my encounters with Rosabeth Moss Kanter of the Harvard Business School and Barry Stein: anybody who is concerned with the performance of large organizations must rely on their seminal work.

Equally, Peter M. Senge of MIT is the indispensable guide to the learning organization and mastery of the business system, while Manfred Perlitz of the University of Mannheim is a most penetrating analyst of global trends. I've also been fortunate to work with thinkers whose thoughts about thinking have influenced me greatly—in particular Mark Brown of Innovation Center Europe and, of course, Edward de Bono, my partner in the monthly *Letter to Thinking Managers,* which has been a major source for these pages. Michael Goold, Andrew Campbell, and Marcus Alexander showed me their work in progress on *Corporate-Level Strategy* and kindly allowed me to quote from it. David Benjamin sent me his very valuable notes on innovation.

References to the books on which I have gratefully drawn, by these and other authors, are in the bibliography. I owe a particular debt to the works by William H. Davidow and Michael S. Malone on the virtual corporation; Michael Hammer and James Champy on reengineering; Chposky and Leonsis on IBM's personal computer saga; George B. Stalk and Thomas Hout on time-based competition. My knowledge of Total Quality Management rests largely on my interviews for my book *The Quality Makers.* I'm extremely grateful to its progenitor, Sven-Erik Gunnervall of Norden Publishing, and to my interviewees—especially, for the current book, to Bernard Fournier and Dennis Kennedy, respectively the managing directors of Rank Xerox and Honeywell (U.K.), Claus Møller of TMI, and Jacques Horovitz of MSR.

The above by no means completes the list of invaluable sources, which includes Philip Sadler, formerly of Ashridge Management College, Bill Ramsay of Templeton College, and Constantinos Markides of the London Business School. Chloe Cox and Alan Mossman introduced me to their own work on organizations and that of Robert Fritz. David Wickens was my source on the human resources breakthroughs at Nissan UK. David Bundred of Lucas Industries let me use his brilliant paper on modern purchasing. Interviews with Ryazuburo Kaku, Sir Derek Birkin, and Ben Rosen, respectively chairmen of Canon, RTZ, and Compaq, Ricardo Semler, the driving spirit of Semco, and Ben Tregoe of the Kepner-Tregoe management consultancy produced invaluable insights and material.

In this field of contemporary history, I cannot praise too highly the work of the journalists, several credited in these pages, who have produced such excellent material for the leading publications: in the United States, *Fortune, Business Week,* the *Wall Street Journal, The New York Times,* and the *Chicago Tribune*; in Britain, the *Financial Times,* the *Times* and the *Independent on Sunday.* From the academic world, the *Harvard Business Review* has been as always a rich source of information and ideas: while in consultancy *The McKinsey Quarterly* is unique—its interviews with General Pagonis and Jay Forrester are outstanding contributions.

My close association with Kalchas, the British strategic consultancy, has produced a constant flow of ideas: I must thank Michael de Kare Silver in particular for asking me so many questions, and providing so many answers himself. Working for the editors of *Man-*

agement Today and *Business Solutions* has also been highly productive for me. The whole book arose out of a highly constructive dialogue with Truman Talley, my American publisher for many years. I'm grateful to him and my two agents, Ellen Levine and Derek Johns, for their patient midwifery. And I've been very lucky to have had the help of three excellent secretaries: Elli Petrohilos, Devon Scott, and Anne Mackenzie.

Index